GOD

End-time Updates

Ancient Alien History

Anthony A Eddy

Strategic Book Publishing and Rights Co.

Copyright and Publishing

Strategic Book Publishing and Rights Co., LLC

USA | Singapore
www.sbpra.net

For information about special discounts for bulk purchases, please contact Strategic Book Publishing and Rights Co. Special Sales, at bookorder@sbpra.net.

ISBN: 978-1-950015-63-4

www.thewebsiteofthelord.org.nz

	Pages	Total Words
10. "GOD End-time Updates Ancient Alien History"	310	86,461

Prepared on a 27in iMac™© with the use of Nisus®© Writer Pro. All trademarks™ and intellectual rights remain the property of their respective owners.

Dedication

To our fourteen grandchildren, and all they may accomplish in their lives.

Matthew & Ella;

  Phillipa & Jonathan;

    Jeremy, Ngaire & Trevor;

      Jake, Finn, Crystal & Caleb;

        Bjorn, Greta & Minka.

May our Lord God bless each one of you as you grow and develop,
as you strive and succeed,
as you mature and remember,
all that history has taught you,
in dwelling within the sky signs of—
the overarching rainbows of both Righteousness and Truth.

Acknowledgements

A very special thanks for a very special man and his lovely wife who dwell in a beautiful home on The Ponderosa within the foothills of The Sierras.

A man who knows what he has done,
who knows what he has been,
who knows what he has said,
who knows what he has suffered,
who knows what he has seen,
who knows what he has heard,
who knows what he has remembered,
who knows what he has both lost and gained.

A man who knows what he expects and how to satisfy his body, soul, and spirit,
in this season of the ungodly and the friction weavers in the end-time society:
where the marked of God,
with their entry missing from within The Lamb's Book of Life,
are being called unto account unless repentance quickly starts to reign;
in areas where God is still ignored,
and blasphemy with the lies rain down,
from the mouths of perjury onto the heads
of concepts from the loving and the kind.

For this is a man with a book deserving to be read: his struggles with his early life and how he left the worst behind.

For he is a man of languages and of journeying from his homeland.

For he is a son and father who has remembered,
who has long ago made a new beginning,
who has been attentive to the sowing,
who is now reaping the harvest of his lifetime fruits.

For entitled here is a book waiting to be read,
which is thoroughly recommended,
wherein
Kele D. Gabor wrote of

DECEPTION AND REALITY
LIVING THROUGH THE MISSING PAGES OF HISTORY

Without this very special man's direct knowledge and encouragement This Book of God you are now holding in your hands would be without existence.

It is truly amazing what our God can organise in the fulfilment of His Will.
For our God has had a major input to This Book on virtually every page with His Dictation. We both thank Him for it and accept such with much gratitude.

God End-time Updates

To His end-time call in His seeking of the hearts and minds of man,
Standing with The Spirit, in the pinnacle of historic revelation,
Where, as understanding comes, so does Wisdom follow:
As He now familiarises man with the ancient Truth.

Ancient Alien History

The Wisdom of God is a carrier of The Truth and won't disguise a lie.
Here, The Son comes forth to shed The Truth into the sunlight,
Bringing forth a full disclosure of the historical Truth;
To prepare man for receiving His introductions.

Anthony A Eddy

(Scribe)

Contents— Order Designated *(After Receipt)*

1 - 4 are the extant Tribes, while a, b, c etc are the sub-tribe Clans with their specific attributes,

Contents— Alphabetical

Prelude

I, The Lord Jesus

And I hear The Lord Jesus saying,
"I,

The Lord Jesus,
     speak to the inquisitive at large,
     speak to My People seeking answers in The Truth.

I,

The Lord Jesus,
     mobilize My People in a call to action,
          in a call to serving the needs of their fellow man,
          in a call to where My Word must reach in thoroughness,
               in completeness,
               in truthfulness,
               and in love.

I,

The Lord Jesus,
     do neither vacate The Father's Will nor The Father's Intent.

I,

The Lord Jesus,
     expend unremitting care upon the heads of those with unremitting commitment
                    to their Faith and Taskings.

I,

The Lord Jesus,
     open up world-wide discussion on the historical life of man,
          on the lied about life of man:
          by man within his power frame quest of rule and domination.

I,

The Lord Jesus,
     speak in This Book of the sequencing in the blending of man
          as mentioned* in My Word,
          as occurring in the escapades of life,
          as occurs within the fates of families.

I,

The Lord Jesus,
     reveal and expound on the actions of the past,
          that the past of man may be worthy for the exaltation scheduled for eternity,
          that the past will not be discarded in surprise and unbelief,
          that the past may be fully understood when Truth is firmly placed on

a pedestal emblazoned with The Light,
emblazoned with Righteousness,
emblazoned with the statements of occurrence with
the how,
the when,
the why.

I,

The Lord Jesus,
encourage all to read This Book in its totality,
so understanding with acceptance can bring these occurrences
into The Field of Grace,
and thus the mantle of forgiveness can be extended to The Repentant:
to be upheld so the generational impact can be modified through prayer:
in the binding termination of the curses imparted so very long ago.

I,

The Lord Jesus,
know the outward prayer fields of man;
know the inward prayer fields of God.

I,

The Lord Jesus,
have semblances of My Spirit at home among the incoming prayers of man,
at home among the outgoing counselling of God.

I,

The Lord Jesus,
bless the recipients of Grace with The Mantle of The Truth,
with access to the thoroughfares implicit in a journey.

I,

The Lord Jesus,
offer The Keys of The Kingdom open to be shared,
offer The Keys of The Kingdom deserving to be polished,
offer The Keys of The Kingdom as a gift awaiting acceptance:
so Faith may be deployed in opening the fountain to the fullness of life,
for supping from the overflowing streams of Living Water.

I,

The Lord Jesus,
bless and restore,
uplift and encourage,
affirm and heal,
all those awaiting at a turning point with generational concerns as to
the pathway forward.

I,

The Lord Jesus,
>will neither leave The Committed nor The Seeking astray in a lonely place,
>will not forsake My Disciples who may have missed a step,
>will not leave My Sheep in the middle of the night,
>will not fail to bring all with a concern as to The Way:
>>safely home into The Family of God."

Scribal Note: Refer to Settlers within My Garden *here in this section.*

My Content Study Aid

_____

_____

_____

_____

_____

_____

_____

_____

_____

_____

_____

_____

_____

_____

_____

_____

_____

_____

_____

_____

_____

_____

_____

_____

This Book

And I hear The Lord Jesus saying,
"This Book brings to the attention of the majority of man—
                    that of which he was previously unaware.

This Book breaks open the vaults of heaven,
          breaks open the mysteries of God,
          breaks open the relating of the guests.

This Book discloses a preparation deemed necessary for man within The End-time of
                              Faith with Grace,
          discloses an unevenness of knowledge,
          discloses a history suffering from ignorance by the many,
                    suffering from secrecy by the few.

This Book highlights the past into the here and now,
          highlights the hidden into The Light of day,
          highlights the secrecy of leadership:
                         with its content pages now to be opened wide in turning.

This Book comes forth to shed The Truth into the sunlight;
                    to shed The Truth to overcome the lies of man—
                         within the knowledge base as sworn to secrecy;
                    to shed The Truth upon a very dusty road:
                              whereon the winds of change love to linger and to play—
                    with swirls which mix the lies into a windstorm of misinformation.

This Book does not gather dust from its surroundings,
          does not confuse The Truth of God,
          does not contain the lies of man.

This Book asserts,
          declares,
          maintains,
          supports,
          verifies,
          enables,
     the knowledge base of man when in preparation for the reception of a milestone—
                         where the ramifications are as if spread upon an altar:
                         where the decision-making rests.

This Book is destined to travel across the lands and seas of both man and God,
          is destined to open eyes in both fear and wonder,
          is destined to announce and to proclaim.

This Book removes the stains of history,
          removes the throw-cloth from The Truth,
          removes the trespass notice from the field,

removes the content from the archived verbal vaults of man.

This Book whistles for attention,
  whistles with a message,
  whistles at a secret—
    judged due for disclosure.

This Book reaches to the heights of exultation**,
  reaches for an experience in exaltation***,
  reaches out to the stationary readied for a move.

This Book carries all before it;
  cannot be refuted—
  cannot be denied—
  cannot affirm the past—
    as recorded within the books of man:
      without an extension of a lie.

This Book sets the seal of God upon the words of God,
  sets The Truth in waiting to overwrite the lies born of deception,
  sets The Truth as a servant to vanquish the lies as birthed:
    by the selected specialists within each generation—
      as it still comes and goes.

This Book brings the future Truth from The Truth mostly buried in the past,
  brings the static into areas of movement,
  brings the compressed into expansion with fullness of expression.

This Book is like a hurricane at sea about to make a landfall,
      with a heavy load of Living Water;
  is like a tornado on the land about to raise a roof,
      so to release that which lies beneath;
  is like a volcano venting steam which dissipates as if The Truth—
      dressed in the purity of white:
    with all the colours gathered in and bubbling for release.

This Book wends its way from the beginning to the new beginning without end;
  wends its way from fear to bravery;
  wends its way from the lies of man unto The Truth of God.

This Book wends its way from invasion unto assimilation,
    from incursion unto a heritage,
    from charges unto an inheritance.

This Book leads to a discovery,
  leads to a confirmation,
  leads to the ongoing intent of God."

Scribal Note: **exultation: a feeling of triumphant elation or jubilation;*
  ****exaltation: 1. a feeling or state of extreme happiness, 2. the action of elevating*
  someone in rank or power, 3. the action of praising someone or something highly.

The Validation of This Book

And I hear The Lord Jesus saying,
"The validation of This Book is found in recent research,
is found in ancient records,
is found in the witnessing of My Spirit now at large upon
The Earth.

The validation of This Book can rest on its laurels on the findings,
on its laurels on the leafs of yesterday,
on its laurels on the extrapolations and supposition,
as voiced,
and as in a written record reposing on a shelf.

The validation of This Book rests upon the identities as found within the past,
as followed with much interest,
as composures of treatises from the
learned and the wise of man.

The validation of This Book has episodes of discovery,
has episodes involving bones,
has episodes involving the highest of technology presently
available to man.

The validation of This Book alights on the evaluation of the improved quality of DNA,
on the improved ability to determine age and to so
date accordingly,
on the improved interest and the enthusiasm of
hours so spent,
where returns can be quite meagre,
and the time spent hard to value.

The validation of This Book involves third party alliances,
involves the screening and the confirmations or denials;
the testing of hypotheses as postured,
and waiting for the agreement on the meaningfulness
of another's thoughts:
in drawing conclusions from the evidence displayed.

The validation of This Book lies within the channels of legitimate researching
of colleagues:
in attempting duplication,
or denial,
as results come in from a colleague's close inspection
with reports at hand.

The validation of This Book may well grow over time,
may grow when there are pointers to examine,

when there are indicators of survival of a species
long thought extinct,
when the ability to test The DNA is based on
solid linkages:
to both the present and the past.

The validation of This Book reaches the zenith of its apex:
when the original species of strangers are recognised
and introduced;
as the cross-breeders with the humans—
resulting in the producing of The Neandertals.

The validation of This Book determines the pilots of the incoming flying laboratories,
the leaders of the first migrations from the star of dominance with its planets,
the investigators enabling the eventual cross-breeding,
with the enlarging of the human brain cavity,
in further interbreeding of the day:
long readied to receive a leapfrog in capability of reasoning and of intellect;
which is yet to be achieved within the presented human race of man.

The validation of This Book drives the end-time hatching:
of the viability of man to wander through the universe,
to tap upon the shalls of God.

The validation of This Book will witness the releasing of the trigger,
which confounds the wise of man.

The validation of This Book will repose with the valued archives in the research libraries,
will repose within the active laboratories of DNA testing
and analyses,
will repose on the shelves of the researchers
and investigators,
as the intelligence of man outstrips the measuring capabilities,
as thought is applied to handling the concept of a
new beginning—
in dimensions sought and understood where life within the
spiritual is uncontaminated by the mortal,
with the sin as imprisoned in the sphere of time encirclement.

The validation of This Book is a headache for the non-believers,
is a headache brought on by its existence,
is a headache in its content and its relationship into the
distant past:
as categorized in this mortal inclusion within the scheduled
time of man.

The validation of This Book is based upon the past,
is based upon the knowledge of one who witnessed it

and knows,
is based upon the future of man by the designing hand
of God:
already in firm possession in waiting to unfold;
as man is about to witness My Spirit in the raising of
the veil on eternity;
as The Father so indicates in affirmation.

The validation of This Book is full and direct in the field of included revelation,
in the field of preparation for eternity with God,
in the field of assignment to the creative engineering of God,
in the field of introductions to the strangers and their offspring,
to their resonance with humans,
to their own development of a breeding
programme to inspire the stars,
to teach and to uphold the visions in eternity
with their sharing with new entrants,
with the capability of understanding
and directing:
both the development of technology,
in conjunction with the anticipated engineering.

The validation of This Book proclaims and ushers in,
settles the debates of ignorance,
enhances the understanding of the capable and the taught.

The validation of This Book ends the attempts to regurgitate the past:
in a semblance of understanding,
to spend the time on pondering,
to attempt to solve an algorithm as
proposed upon the performance
of the past,
when 80% still remains outside the written record,
to remain uncounted in equations based on only
partial feasibility,
and without the knowledge keys as borne by God."

My Content Study Aid

_____

_____

_____

_____

_____

The Crown of Thorns

And I hear The Lord Jesus saying,
"The crown of thorns was placed in mockery.

The crown of thorns was worn in submission.

The crown of thorns signified an awaiting kingdom.
                a kingdom held in promise,
                a kingdom birthed upon the coming cross.

The crown of thorns was there to mock a king where unbelief was rife,
                              where pain was intended and intense,
                              where blood was drawn by man,
                              where shouting released the guilty,
                                      consigned the innocent to death.

The crown of thorns is not for duplication,
            is a mock-up of a crown misused,
            is a mock-up of authority misapplied,
            is a mock-up misunderstood for the placating of a crowd—
                    of a crowd baying as if a pack of wolves attracted to the smell,
                                        of the flow of blood.

The crown of thorns was not intended as a crown of honour,
            was intended as a crown of ridicule.

The crown of thorns was not intended as a sign of victory,
            was intended as a marking of defeat.

The crown of thorns did not invite approach,
            signalled the keeping of a distance.

The crown of thorns invited the jeers of man without relief,
            did not expand the cheers expressed:
            in the achieving of a substitute destined for The Cross.

The crown of thorns was the headdress of The Lord,
            was the signpost leading unto the salvation of man,
            was the signifier of the coming triumph of The Lord,
            was the headgear as placed upon His head—
                                  in denial vested with disbelief.

The crown of thorns was accepted as an emblem of objection,
                            to the relevant but ignorant,
                            to the barrackers with the shouters,
                            to the mob as gathered to disrupt.

The crown of thorns was witness to the voice of many,

to the voice of many shouting in an orchestrated attack
upon the innocent.

The crown of thorns was seen to stumble through the streets of Jerusalem,
was seen to convert the status at Golgotha into an open mausoleum:
long remembered for its plotting and its death wish;
soon to bear witness of a death returned to life.

The crown of thorns fell unto The Earth and stayed there,
was trampled without discrimination,
was cast away as a discard no longer needed,
as a symbol of kingship and of suffering.

The crown of thorns had served its time upon the head of The Son of man.

The crown of thorns had served and heard the clap of thunder as the curtain tore in twain,
had served unto the end when life had bid farewell,
had survived only in the record of that which man had done that day.

The crown of thorns is a crown of sorrows,
is not a crown of honouring,
is a crown creating statements of desertion and of angst.

The crown of thorns is a measure of a nation turning its backs on their Messiah,
of waiting for another deserving of much honour
awarded to the priesthood,
of acknowledging the choice of others
where the miracles of God were wielded by
another who had gone before.

The crown of thorns did not bear the acknowledgement of the error in the absence
of recognition:
by those in The Levitical line of priestly authority who were
looking elsewhere than mingling in their midst,
in their expectations born of error in application,
to the already qualified and present.

The crown of thorns bore the present within mortality into a future within eternity.

The crown of thorns was carried for the sinful and the reticent,
for the followers of the law and the breakers of
The Peace,
for the wayward and the victims of oppression.

The crown of thorns met with,
was introduced to,
Grace upon The Cross;
saw the law fulfilled,
saw Grace arriving to be upheld as a gift from God,
saw the reconciliation of man with God:

XIX

with arms spread wide upon The Cross whereon Heaven and The Earth did meet,
in uniting eternity with mortality in a new covenant of Grace.

The crown of thorns had no significance beyond its time and space,
had no ascribed meaning except by noting the attitudes
within the time frame,
had no intent to honour—
was intended to detract,
had no intent to rise up for an occasion prior to the end result:
the presenting of an empty tomb yielding access to
a new way of life,
with understanding to the fore,
as The Spirit of The Lord made His first appearance at a gathering,
into the newly committed Temples of The Holy Spirit,
with the onset of Grace now replacing the subsiding of
the law.

The crown of thorns was present in witnessing in close proximity
the subsiding of the law with death,
the opening of the access way to eternity with
the resurrection's installing of Grace with
testimony into The Family of God.

The crown of thorns existed in a time of darkness most intense,
was not present when the light came flooding into the life of man—
in offering a new covenant complete with a fresh commitment to The Lord."

My Content Study Aid

_____

_____

_____

_____

_____

_____

_____

_____

_____

_____

_____

The Necessities of God

And I hear The Lord Jesus saying,
"The necessities of God are simple in their requirements,
    are upheld upon sincerity on the reading of a heart,
    are presented with approval,
         when non-compliance is not a factor,
    by My Spirit for a miracle on The Earth.

The necessities of God are the purity of the heart,
    are the full commitment of the heart,
    are the participation in communion in the fullness of understanding,
    are the complete absence of the use of lies of any colour,
    are the complete and cleared resolution of the embitterment
         of the soul:
      as brought about by unforgiveness,
   which quenches both the body and the spirit until the soul can overcome,
both as to the plumbing of the very depths as well as to the summiting of perfection;
as communion is consummated with Grace enabled to foreclose—
      on the sin residues so described,
      released and vanquished from the heart—
   within the parameters of responsibility for the actions of Freewill."

My Content Study Aid

_____

_____

_____

_____

_____

_____

_____

_____

_____

_____

_____

_____

_____

The Settlers within My Garden

And I hear The Lord Jesus saying,
"The settlers within My garden are from another time and space.

The settlers within My garden are external to the time sphere of man,
are beyond the beck and call of man,
are not within the knowledge base of man,
are mentioned in My Word° in passing—
which were not intended to be applied with certainty:
by every then current generation who brought opinions
to the fore.

The settlers within My garden are misinterpreted by man:
are claimed to be what they are not;
are claimed by man as being validated by future events as
timed within the past;
as bringing to present situations of the day—
that which could only thrive—
when standing in the shadow of Biblical authority*.

The settlers within My garden do not speak the tongues of man,
do speak the tongues of Heaven.

The settlers within My garden are also still having some with time within mortality;
are also transitioning with their bodies souls and spirits
into eternity with God.

The settlers within My garden have also had a place prepared:
where they too will feel at home in surroundings
of familiarity.

The settlers within My garden do not bring a clash of cultures,
are accepting of the changes,
are accepting of their rebirths from their graves,
are accepting of the need for thought transference and the
achieving of fluency of expression.

The settlers within My garden are not set in their ways with troublesome priorities,
know the same commandments,
have also tried life under the seasons
of covenantal law with Sacrifice;
of covenantal Faith with Grace;
and soon to become aware of governance of Truth in
Wisdom with Mercy pled at The Bema.

The settlers within My garden are jocular and friendly,
love the jokes and jests,

explore and understand,
seek and do not query,
are amused when struck by puzzlement,
are awestruck by a new idea,
have understanding serviced by the centuries—
as Truth gradually became the basic structure of societies.

The settlers within My garden are winsome and popular,
are respected and honoured,
are inviting and responsive.

The settlers within My garden are identified and recognized,
are welcomed and befriended,
are generous and likeable.

The settlers within My garden have stories of much interest:
have histories with generational accuracy;
have the scope and experience to enthral their new found
thought-recipients;
have the ability to listen to the concerts in
quadrophonic sound.

The settlers within My garden love to talk on their four feats;
rest with hems tucked tidily beneath:
can jump and run and leave a kangaroo behind;
can play and dart and check and run—
which leaves others standing still while watching
in amazement.

The settlers within My garden are there for the enjoyment of their achievements
of conviction:
of the souls they won
and welcomed;
of their sight lines of success
in applying their
telescopic "eyes".

The settlers within My garden have qualified as children of God,
for entry to eternity,
as overcomers of all which has been set
before them—
in a lifestyle of great hardship—
where the rewards are also great.

The settlers within My garden are welcomed by My People to eternity:
are welcomed by My People to My garden;
are welcomed by My People into The Family of God;
are welcomed by My People to their places as prepared;

are welcomed by My People as their fellow travellers in
My Gospel;
are welcomed by acclamation for all they have achieved
and done—
within the sight and tasking of God down through
their ages of existence."

Biblical authority* 1 Peter 3:18-20 (NKJV) Abridged ...
... [19] **by whom also He went and preached to the spirits in prison,** [20] **who formerly
were disobedient,** when once The Divine longsuffering waited in the days of Noah,
while the ark was being prepared, ...

Luke 23:50-53 (NKJV) *All verse references abridged for reasons of space.*
[52] This man went to Pilate and asked for the body of Jesus. [53] Then he took it down,
wrapped it in linen, and laid it in a tomb that was hewn out of the rock, ...

*Scribal Notes: The KJV and NKJV both say that Jesus "preached" to the spirits in
prison (verse 19). However, The Greek word used is not the usual New Testament word
for preaching the gospel. It simply means "to herald a message"; The NIV translates it
as "made proclamation." Jesus suffered and died on The Cross, His body being put to
death. But His spirit was made alive, and He yielded it to The Father (Luke 23:46).
According to Peter, sometime between Jesus' death and His resurrection (The Spirit of)
Jesus made a special proclamation to "the spirits in prison."*
Genesis 6:1-3 (NKJV) *Abridged ...*
... that **the sons of God saw the daughters of men, that they were beautiful; and they
took wives for themselves of all whom they chose.** And The Lord said, "My Spirit shall
not strive *(abide, in other Bible variants)* with man forever, for he *is* indeed flesh; yet his
days shall be one hundred and twenty years." ...

*These "sons of God" appear to be the "spirits in prison" who had earlier been
"disobedient".* **Emphasis is Scribal.**

The Settlers within My Garden is used by permission from Book 8 *GOD Speaks of
Loving His Creation*, which is Part 8 of *The End-time Psalms of God.*

My Content Study Aid

_____

_____

_____

_____

_____

_____

_____

Introduction

This is a most unexpected and surprising work of God with the placing of His scribe for putting pen to paper within the sphere of influence of a very special person, alive and well, on The Ponderosa in The Sierra Foothills.   *3.56am Saturday 14th July 2018*

These divine items mostly consist of Truth statements intermixed with counselling and are presented for serious contemplation as to their ramifications and how we approach them in the conclusions we may draw. For they are filled with great significance for these present times.

I testify here to one and all that these items are not of my writing nor instigation. These items do not stand alone but smoothly build on the preceding ones as if designed as an unfolding story with an establishing foundation. These items were initially encoded in their ordering for making little sense and needed two decodings (repositioning) at different times in their reception to bring forth the finished layout of The Lord. On the original individual documents the scribe has begun each divine call with the words: And I hear The Lord Jesus saying. This is the true stated origin of the content of This Book both by testimony and by claim of The Lord Jesus Himself.

The style of the book preserves the very few scribal comments in italics; while quotation marks denote and enclose text of a divine origin. British spelling is used for reasons of national culture. Layout simplifies ease of reading and personal study which allows usage of spare space within the book. A concordance or a thesaurus has not been used at any stage prior to, during, or after the receiving of these texts. A dictionary (Oxford Concise™) has sometimes been used to comprehend fully, the words of the divine voice used in expressing His intent. Because the items have been received via dictation spoken by the divine voice directly into the mind, the punctuation is subject to human interpretation. Occasionally however, when required for clarity or emphasis, the capitalisation of words, together with the paragraphing, have also been indicated by The Lord. Minor spelling typos are scribal and, if any, from a disobedient finger, annoy then it tenders its own apology herewith. Punctuation is usually scribal.. The item titles follow what is in the text.

Great care has been taken to ensure scribal accuracy in hearing and transcribing what are now these printed pages of divinely originated items. Every word is as received without later omissions, additions, substitutions or edits.

May The Holy Spirit so testify as such to every enquiring soul.

My Content Study Aid

Early Settlers Named

Scribal Note: Although unexpected, The Lord, on Friday 20th July 2018, identified these early settlers by name.

They were then referred to an Oxford Concise™ Dictionary for some background information:

Neanderthal / nɪˈandətɑːl / • n. 1 (also **Neanderthal man**) an extinct human that was widely distributed in ice age Europe between c.120,000 and 35,000 years ago, with a receding forehead and prominent brow ridges. 2 *informal* an uncivilized or uncouth man. - ORIGIN C19: from *Neanderthal*, a region in Germany where remains of Neanderthal man were found. **Unsubstantiated comment**: *The Neandertals were associated with The Mousterian flint industry of The Middle Palaeolithic which is the second subdivision of The Paleolithic or Old Stone Age as it is understood in Europe, Africa and Asia. The term Middle Stone Age is used as an equivalent or a synonym for The Middle Paleolithic in African archeology. Homo neandertalensis; now usually regarded as a separate species from H. sapiens and probably at the end of a different evolutionary line.*

In This Book, the 'h' is removed from Neanderthal as per current German location usage.

The Strangers in the early pages, have not been specifically named by The Lord other than as Strangers. They are the forerunners of the cross-breeding which produces The Neandertals - the early settlers with an inheritance "from another time and space."

Scribal Question:

'Where is this going to end, my Lord Jesus?'

"With a full disclosure of The Truth, Anthony."

Scribal Note:

Breaking News from The U.S.A.

'Just got new update that now they keep twenty-seven types of space travelers on the official list but they cannot tell which ones are genetically altered to be able to pilot these super fast crafts. Also, there is a universal language which is used among cooperative entities. (We should learn it.)'   *Received 9 January 2019*

My Content Study Aid

_____

_____

_____

_____

_____

_____

The Coming of The Strangers

And I hear The Lord Jesus saying,
"The coming of the strangers sets a test upon the character of man.

The coming of the strangers can introduce a mindset of dread,
                    can introduce a mindset of investigation,
                    can introduce a mindset of rejection,
                    can introduce a mindset of revelation,
                    can introduce a mindset of acceptance.

The coming of the strangers is aware of the residents,
                    know the incumbents and their positioning,
                    know their preferences and prejudices,
                    know their coming and their going,
                    know their work habits and their doings when in the time
                                      frame of relaxing.

The coming of the strangers verifies and typifies the rumours of the past,
              the lies within the past,
              the dishonesty of leadership in the quenching of the queries,
              the deceit in lying to the nations,
                    in lying to the witnesses,
                    in lying to the media—
            that which is mistaken and faced with being what it's not.

The coming of the strangers are vying for attention,
              are tired of living in the shadows,
              are ready to take their places in the outpouring of relief.

The coming of the strangers provides answers to the mysteries of centuries;
                        of ages within the writings of the ancients—
                            with the crossing of divides.

The coming of the strangers return the standing with the stares,
              return the proffered hand,
              are prepared to share their thoughts,
              are amateurish with speech,
              have sects within their clans which are dangerous
                                to approach—
            even with a smile of welcome or with an offered meal.

The coming of the strangers split into differing camps those with a friendly nature,
                        and those retreating into churlishness or worse.

The coming of the strangers out from behind their living quarters changes the reality:
                    of what is present and what is not,
                    of voyages completed within the distant past,

of motivations still in doubt,
of defences insecure,
of interrogations found unreliable and wanting
when in The Field of Truth.

The coming of the strangers has brought a different culture to The Earth,
has imparted a differing view of what is right and wrong,
has ventured here with a technology designed to operate as
a welcome to the stars.

The coming of the strangers set new standards of behaviour for both sides of the coin,
muddied up the before and now,
in exchange for tolerance in the present and hereafter:
where clashes can occur as common sense stays hidden in a cave.

The coming of the strangers brought about the violence as generated to overcome,
to relinquish and to vanquish the development of man,
to tear down and to violate the security of man,
as the weapons of tomorrow were brought to bear
on the weapons of the day.

The coming of the strangers brought capabilities unheard of by man,
possessed the equipment known for its miracles when
in action on The Earth,
fought the battles from the air with fire,
and vengeance for the lost;
fought the spears and clubs from outside the distance of
their reach;
fought the battle lines as drawn up upon a hill—
from where retreat was the only course left open
for acceptance.

The coming of the strangers did not bring The Seeking to annihilate the humans
as encountered,
did not bring the firepower to bear upon an open settlement,
did not try to eliminate man from his environment.

The coming of the strangers saw a dramatic change in circumstance,
saw the drawing on the rock face,
saw a new approach when drawing in a cave—
with the introduction of new designs:
for which words did not exist.

The coming of the strangers saw help available for positioning and lifting,
for fitting touching surfaces of stone to both merge and lock together,
for the dressing of the surfaces in consistency of style and finish.

The coming of the strangers introduce breakthroughs when sharing their technology,
enable the leaps and bounds of man as he forsook the past:

for knowledge in the present to address the future.

The coming of the strangers saw weapons far beyond the comprehension of man in
his naivety,
desperately wanted to possess them,
paid a very heavy price for the little
that was gained.

The coming of the strangers saw the sexism of man exploited in both genders,
saw the breeding technicalities exploited for adoption,
saw the laboratories within the flying vehicles in use both
day and night,
saw the achievement of a cross-breed with likenesses to
both the adapted strangers and the remodelled man.

The coming of the strangers have been here since the time of dinosaurs,
were the exterminators of the dinosaurs,
were the instigators of a certain way of life,
were the exponents of their technology when there was no-one
else bearing witness,
were the antagonists of civilisation long before it had a name,
were the founders of self-aware intelligence capable of
investing in the governance of The Earth,
were failures in this goal because of their extreme longevity—
still severely hindering the expansion of their numbers."

My Content Study Aid

_____
_____
_____
_____
_____
_____
_____
_____
_____
_____
_____
_____

Trysting with The Strangers

And I hear The Lord Jesus saying,
"Trysting with the strangers had very small beginnings,

could be numbered on one hand within the same numbered
centuries of years,
was disowned by the knowledgable,
was discouraged by the attentive,
was dishonoured by the controllers of activities at large.

Trysting with the strangers failed in the producing of any offspring,
failed in compatibility,
failed in the linking of the species one way or the other.

Trysting with the strangers was researched by the knowledge bearers,
was tried with the obvious,
was marked by ongoing failures.

Trysting with the strangers was eventually successful in creating monsters
without intelligence:
when experimentation moved into the splicing of The DNA
strands and sequences;
as selected for their relevancy to the creating of a halfbreed.

Trysting with the strangers was a long and drawn out process:
of repeated failures across many generations of the human strain,
was quick and fast for the strangers with their knowledge base:
in being achieved within a single generation.

Trysting with the strangers became an effort to forge acceptability of appearance
and of lifestyle:
as the threads and strands as gathered and incised in
place gradually were modified—
by such effort resulting in an acceptable conclusion.

Trysting with the strangers was then slowly moved in specific directions
of developments:
with the breeding out of 'faults' as perceived,
with the instilling of the traits seen as enhancing attractiveness—
increasingly approaching in similarity size and shape—
for the derivations of both the strains of the strangers and
those of the humans.

Trysting with the strangers slowly saw intelligence levels coming to overlap—
as they,
when seen to jump across the strains,
were selected for preservation.

Trysting with the strangers set very special difficulties for the dramatic differences
$$\text{in breeding,}$$
in the comparison of longevities of both strains as developing,
as resulting in taking such a length of time to reach evaluation:
of the one-sided progeny of the strangers—
in the time frame required for acquiring full maturity.

Trysting with the strangers was often far from voluntary,
was explored alone as specimens within isolation
and captivity,
with the end result often being death.

Trysting with the strangers,
as a programme under investigation by the strangers,
often had witnesses to a kidnapping—
where the victim appeared to vanish from the face of
The Earth—
not to be seen again.

Trysting with the strangers was a very rocky road with the appearance of humanity.

Trysting with the strangers was not the best way forward:
was not the confidence builder when based on investigations;
was not an outstanding success—
where trust was still amiss while queries filled
the atmosphere;
was not built on an openness of intent—
with a joint declaration of mutually shared objectives.

Trysting with the strangers was a somewhat one-sided long-term exploration of potential,
was a quest for a mutual improvement of the species,
was a window with a time frame for acceptance,
for an effort to splice and blend,
for an end-result of enhancement—
so to travel into the future of both man and stranger.

Trysting with the strangers led to a leap-frogging in development,
led to giant steps in understanding,
led to the practicality of the achievements of those as
previously seen as impossibilities.

Trysting with the strangers brought security to some,
brought fear to others,
founded callousness as a spreading acceptable way of life.

Trysting with the strangers did not lead to a moral improvement within the sight of God,
was not on the altar for acceptance,
was expressly forbidden as the practice grew in acceptability
between both male and female.

ANTHONY A EDDY (SCRIBE)

Trysting with the strangers became confusing and disjointed,
                    moved to being outside the concourse of acceptance,
                    ended up with frowns of disapproval,
                    saw the shutters drawn and fixed as the doors were also
                                        locked and set.

Trysting with the strangers has eventually set a breed apart,
                    has eventually set a breed capable of reproducing with
                                        continuing improvement,
                    has eventually set a breed of beings without a birthright
                                        of existence.

Trysting with the strangers has led,
                    down through the ages,
            to antagonism from the knowledgable who remain outside the breeding circle,
                    who are not physically linked in to the circle of deceit,
                    who are not the frequenters of a different way of life,
                    who are the instigators of the lies—
                            in order to protect the royalty of their life styles—
                            which their inheritance proclaims within the bounds
                                        of the utmost security:
                            intimately mixed with the flooding of the lies—
                            in full association with the bending of the analyses:
                            to reflect The Truth back upon itself,
                            to thereby also join the entries in the pit of lies.

Trysting with the strangers has led man to a sharing of The Earth,
            has led God to the acceptance of commitments with neither fear nor favour,
            has led God to prepare a place for all who profess a Freewill willingness:
                                        to participate within The Bride of Christ."

My Content Study Aid

_____

_____

_____

_____

_____

_____

_____

_____

_____

The Merging of The Strangers

And I hear The Lord Jesus saying,
"The merging of the strangers was far from an instant success,
    was not met with willingness to share,
    was not met with a welcome mat thrown out.

The merging of the strangers took centuries to initiate,
    took centuries to communicate successfully,
    took centuries to discover the understanding of objectives.

The merging of the strangers brought unheard of technology,
    which failed the test of man's understanding,
    which had no means of expression of ideas:
      not at home within a language.

The merging of the strangers was non-inclusive of their skills and craft,
    of their weapons with their physical abilities,
    of their concepts with their travelling far
      beyond the scope or the intent of man.

The merging of the strangers was a slow and painful experience for man,
    taught man to hide and shelter,
    taught man to guard and challenge,
    taught man to inhibit to prevent,
    taught man to watch and to wait,
    taught man to sneak up to observe,
    eventually taught man to introduce the concept of 'a friend'.

The merging of the strangers was very much one-sided,
    was very much within their favour,
    was very much dependent on how man was perceived,
  in conjunction with an evaluation of man's bargaining power,
  from within his knowledge base of the resources available in his environment.

The merging of the strangers saw the caves of man
    under attack for the ousting of possession,
    under attack when discovered,
    under attack where shelter food and access were
      prioritized just so,
    as the sea caves became much sought after:
      with food upon their thresholds;
      with firewood at their backs.

The merging of the strangers was not dramatic at the beginning,
    saw their interest set upon the threats from dinosaurs,
    saw their lasers in action as weapons loaded by the sun,
    saw the kill rate reach astonishing numbers

as the eggs were crushed and crumpled,
as the young and the parents were both killed from a distance,
as the flyers and the trampers were both brought down to thud
upon The Earth.

The merging of the strangers quickly saw,
in the matter of two score years,
the threat from dinosaurs extinguishing with
the stinking of the open spaces,
as well as at the retreats within the forests.

The merging of the strangers grew in confidence as dinosaurs declined—
both the carnivores and the herbivores—
as changes were wrought upon The Earth,
as The Earth became a nursery for man,
as The Earth became an early way station for the strangers,
who were now masters of The Earth,
who could walk or fly within their
transports or their scouts,
for whatever destinations they required.

The merging of the strangers saw them embroiled:
in locating the resources required by their technologies,
in their mining and their gathering,
in their picking and their choosing,
as they sought their ways through gathering
from the pristine larder of The Earth.

The merging of the strangers saw the investigating of all The Earth,
as a new home with much potential,
as a pleasant place to rendezvous on intergalactic travelling,
as a source available with all their needs sustained,
as temperatures stable within the bounds of life.

The merging of the strangers caused much surprise as they realized:
that they seemed to be the first to arrive,
that The Earth was quiet and undefiled,
that radio and video transmissions were unknown,
being neither received nor sent.

The merging of the strangers tried to keep their arrival as a secret,
minimized the traffic over many millennia,
eventually discovered the very small presence of man:
as he also became acquainted with his existence
within the security of his isolation.

The merging of the strangers became extremely interested,
in the species they had discovered,

watched it extremely carefully,
circumspectly uncovered the differences in their speed
of reproduction,
realized that they would be quickly left behind,
in the race for space in the colonisation of The Earth.

The merging of the strangers,
from the very beginning,
was obsessed with the power of man's rate of reproduction,
investigated it in detail,
decided on DNA transplants so both species could interbreed
with compatibility.

The merging of the strangers eventually was present:
as man splintered and subsumed as phases with new categories developed,
as they met with evaluation and were either hindered or advanced,
were either accepted or rejected,
as man trod a developmental pathway to latter-day success.

The merging of the strangers saw man in his maturity enabling his prime species:
to exercise control of their surroundings in terms of capabilities in the air,
on land,
and within the seas of man;
within the oversight of the strangers;
as man initiated an outreach to the planetary systems as observed and assigned,
to the gathering of information in confirmation
of the far reaching objectives:
as set by man for man through man;
as God was placed on the sidelines,
as He witnessed man's impositions on the creation field of God."

My Content Study Aid

_____

_____

_____

_____

_____

_____

_____

_____

The Culling of The Stock

And I hear The Lord Jesus saying,
"The culling of the stock encompassed all the dinosaurs.

The culling of the stock included the monsters of the seas,
                              the monsters of the lakes,
                              the monsters of the forests and the plains,
                              the monsters of the mountains with the valleys,
                              the monsters of the air.

The culling of the stock rid The Earth of its apex predators,
         signified an acceptance with a preparatory time frame making possible the showtime,
                    for the appearance of a new species capable of manipulating,
                                                  via their mantles,
                              the fresh DNA to be found upon The Earth.

The culling of the stock was complete for both the great and the small—
                              the monstrous and the hideous,
                              the small and the cute.

The culling of the stock silenced the majority of the vocalizations of The Earth;
                    as the roar of the dinosaurs no longer announced arrivals,
                                   or the challenges for dominance.

The culling of the stock saw the large and cumbersome become extinct,
                    together with their splinters of the smaller yet close relatives.

The culling of the stock had an immediate effect,
         as the smaller animals moved into the niche left vacant and unadorned,
         as food became abundant in supply for the carnivores and the herbivores:
                              all who restaked their claims to life.

The culling of the stock saw the small and the medium succeed in their survival quests,
         saw the food within the reach and speed of the pickers and the hunters,
         saw the resetting of the equilibrium of the surroundings for the adaptation of man.

The culling of the stock was a significant part in the preparing of The Earth,
         in the setting of the scenes for discovery and exploration,
         in the stocking of the seas as well as the moving land masses of The Earth.

The culling of the stock arranged for the toning of The Earth,
                    for the adjustments within the scope of climate changes,
                    within the access and the boundaries as to be allotted to man;
                    in his early years of establishment and investigation,
                    of his discovering of the solutions to his needs and wants,
                  as he took his stock to trade with the encountered and surprised,
                  as man's development advanced,
                              through the applying of his resourcefulness:

to the problems of the times.

The culling of the stock was not witnessed by man with understanding,
was not able to be compared with the before and after,
was not discernable nor verifiable to determine the prior causes
and effects.

The culling of the stock invigorated the development of man:
saw his speech and drawing skills start to spread with improvement,
saw his establishing of values for the power inherent in the accepting
of exchanges,
as trade burgeoned among the connections,
as growth appeared in the ability to reach out and to store,
as man settled on the valued as the standards for exchange.

The culling of the stock was well before the culling of the flood,
of the coming need for a boat with deployment as an ark,
of the skills of carpentry,
of the preparations for,
and the handling of,
the trees in large numbers in need of being gathered
for assembly of construction:
in readiness for the inhabitants to be brought and placed therein.

The culling of the stock was dramatic and terminal,
was necessitated by a 'Use-by' date falling due within a fulfilment of maturity,
where the inhabitants were able to prevent all future growth,
with the coming presence of man into the garden bequeathed by God:
implicit with man's ultimate pathway of return with his body soul and spirit,
implicit to the development of man as matched by the growth within his Faith:
in a future known to God.

The culling of the stock had its time of bloodletting:
as a sacrificial removal of a barricade to a future with intent.

The culling of the stock was final and complete:
has no need for repetition,
has no need to hunt for victims,
has no need to revisit,
to recreate,
or to reflect on that:
on which existence has expired within the oversight of God.

The culling of the stock enabled The Earth to become a friend of man,
to become a home for man,
to become the homing jewel of man,
to become the stable thruster into man's walk in space,
together with man's visiting of a long-term friendly satellite:

ANTHONY A EDDY (SCRIBE)

seen lighting up the night.

The culling of the stock opened up the future pathway to The Heavens,
opened up the rocky road to Hell;
opened up the selectivity of The Freewill of man,
as vested by His Loving God,
as the means enabling the opportunity awaiting confirmation:
of a willingness;
of a desire;
to return unto the surroundings of an eternal life,
within the authority of The Friendly Living God awaiting an adoption,
into a family with the filling of the existing place prepared.

The culling of the stock was a means unto an ending;
a means unto creating a new environment of progression,
a means of preparing for the installing of man in his garden home,
as prepared and readied for the new entities of existence,
and the living role of the strangers as known to God."

My Content Study Aid

_____
_____
_____
_____
_____
_____
_____
_____
_____
_____
_____
_____
_____
_____
_____
_____
_____
_____
_____

The Linking of The Sources

And I hear The Lord Jesus saying,
"The linking of the sources is the fate of trysting.

The linking of the sources is a timetabling of significance,
                is a timetabling set by readiness to advance,
                is a timetabling ascribed to experimentation of relationship
                                both in boldness and desire.

The linking of the sources reveals the will with the inclination,
                reveals the presence of the meeting of the minds,
                reveals the presence of a similarity of purpose with intent.

The linking of the sources brought adaptation to the life strains of The Earth,
                brought an interaction of two histories,
                brought a blending of objectives,
                brought the randomness of completion,
                brought the benefit of placement,
                brought the accounting of abilities,
                brought the intermingling as if of two searchlight beams into
                                one of strength and character,
        with developmental ability hidden in the potential for the future.

The linking of the sources instates and magnifies,
                improves and interprets,
                declares and justifies:
                        the existence of the two in one.

The linking of the sources advances and establishes,
                measures and resizes,
                accepts and moves ahead.

The linking of the sources sees a change in willpower,
                sees a change in assertion,
                sees a change within the reflection of empowerment:
                        with the outworking of fresh commitment to belief.

The linking of the sources bear on one another:
                integrate and solidify,
                rupture and regenerate,
                supervise and modify;
                select and review.

The linking of the sources creates a race apart,
                creates a race with similarities to the parents' stock,
                creates a race with the approval of participants,
                        with the eschewing of the negative traits:

perceived as both undesirable,
and as unappreciated.

The linking of the sources was difficult and time consuming,
was targeted upon inspection with the realisation of potential,
was set apart as objectives were slowly achieved within the
end result.

The linking of the sources has become standardized upon The Earth,
has become conditioned according to the expectations of the past,
has become a stable reference point for pointing to the future.

The linking of the sources saw a time of instability,
experienced a time of dramatic change,
was a time where war could have resulted:
with its pulling-down of the civilization long established in its
extended flourishing.

The linking of the sources was not widely known in its early days,
was not subjected to discussion and approval,
met with disobedience within a trysting pact;
within the bounds of authority;
resulted in imprisonment when it was too late for reparations,
as the cycle of regeneration had begun.

The linking of the sources is now delegated to the past,
is now delegated to the constituents of cause leading to the effects:
which testify today of the makeup of the ancestry of man.

The linking of the sources were explicit and determined,
were fragile and unstable:
until the medical teams moved in to bring understanding to
the end results,
where uniformity of being became the prime objective,
which was ultimately achieved.

The linking of the sources burst the bounds of social responsibility,
burst the repository of acceptable behaviour,
burst the purity of the participants,
burst the sacred for the secular,
burst the lifetime of obedience for the impulse of the tryst.

The linking of the sources posed many problems initially,
posed many problems without the comfort of solutions,
posed many problems associated with honour and of imposition,
posed many problems surfacing within maturity,
for later generations to either accept or remedy,
where the means often became extreme.

The linking of the sources were times of difficulty and disparagement,
               were times of sequestering and banishment,
               were times of heartbreak associated with judgement on deformities.

The linking of the sources has outgrown the big-head syndrome,
               has outgrown the aversion to hair,
               has outgrown the sensitivities to the breaks ín mental health:
                           where inheritance is true;
                           but The DNA is incomplete.

The linking of the sources was ultimately of much benefit to man,
             brought understanding on a scale never previously thought achievable,
             brought advancement to a goal still previously unknown,
             where targeting as a goal remained firmly outside the bounds of reason,
      while the moon continued on her way for centuries with extra weight imposed,
                           but without visible complaint.

The linking of the sources changes a lot of the assumptions still held by man as valid.

The linking of the sources should put to bed the theory of evolution
                      which destroyed The Faith of many.

The linking of the sources resulted in the faith-filled and the faithful
               growing in their God-given morality,
               growing in their relationship with God,
               growing as adoptees into His garden,
               growing as the qualifiers of Freewill choice,
               growing into an Eternity with God."

My Content Study Aid

_____

_____

_____

_____

_____

_____

_____

_____

_____

_____

_____

The Neandertals (1 Tribe, Attribute: Observers)

And I hear The Lord Jesus saying,
"The Neandertals (1) are a race apart,
>> are a race created for a sojourn,
>> are a race cognizant of the furthest reaches of technology,
>> are a race where morality is neither taught nor understood,
>> are a race dependant on the conclusions drawn from ethics,
>> are a race with hidden habitations,
>> are a race of tribes with differing capabilities,
>>>> with differing responsibilities,
>>>> with differing approaches to a problem,
>>>> with differing levels among their senses.

The Neandertals (1) hold The Majestic Twelve in the palms of their hands,
>> are negotiators which are not satisfied until their ways are met,
>> are the incubators of breakthroughs made available to man,
>> are the sitters and the watchers at the wars of man,
>> are the introducers of new weapons as modified for service within
>>>> the understanding of man,
>> are the leaders in constructive efforts which fill the eyes of man
>>>> with amazement,
>> are the experimenters with man as their guinea pigs of physiology
>>>> with particular interest in both the brain and
>>>> reproduction where strength is not the issue,
>> are the origin of unidentified flying objects where gravity and mass
>>>> do not control their flight patterns in the sky,
>> where consistency of flight is not necessarily true,
>> where consistency of flight can end in sudden termination,
>> where inconsistency of flight can embarrass The Majestic Twelve.

The Neandertals (1) can blend into shadows,
>> can blend into the appearances of man,
>> can blend into the heights of man depending solely on the
>>>> peculiarities of their tribe,
>> can refuse to blend at all and live separated from the general
>>>> knowledge base of man.

The Neandertals (1) are masters of disguise,
>> are masters in the practicing of camouflage upon The Earth
>>>> at large,
>> are masters in traversing great distances with senses and capabilities
>>>> still unknown to man.

The Neandertals (1) have a very long history upon The Earth far exceeding that
>>>> of pyramids,

have a history known to God,
have contracts with the leading nations on The Earth for
where a secret can be kept,
where a contract can be binding
to protect from random interference in
the life of man,
to protect from molestation of the women
where the probing and experimenting on
women is now contractually prohibited.

The Neandertals (1) have managed to prevent some tribes from becoming known to man
as seventeen is the tally known
to man within his contracts,
yet a further five tribes are in existence and
remain outside their count by man,
for they are small both in size and in numbers and use the octal
count for calculation in line with
the total digits on both hands,
the octal mathematical power of The Neandertals is blindingly
fast and surpasses the latest computers of man by
some four to seven times depending on the tribe.

The Neandertals (1) can be transparent on a summer's day,
can be visible in both day or night at will,
have many languages not understood by man,
comprehend and speak all languages of man,
sometimes do teach and instruct at the universities of man—
often use technology to circumvent the need for the presence of
a face.

The Neandertals (1) were present at the erection of all stone structures,
all stone monuments as discovered in the history of man,
know and shared the power of concrete when in its infancy
with its creating processes.

The Neandertals (1) understand the power struggles on The Earth,
understand how to maintain a Peace within an equilibrium,
understand the objectives of The United States of America,
understand the objectives of The Russian Federation,
understand the objectives of The Peoples Republic of China,
understand the objectives of The United Nations,
understand how to ensure the objectives of all the nuclear powers
as they are also kept in balance.

The Neandertals (1) are directed by an extremely long term strategy—
to gain the ability to govern the inhabitants encountered,
through proxies which are acceptable;

to gain the ability to govern all whom they encounter on
other tribal missions to the stars:
thereby to govern with the ultimate authority,
hidden and unrealised,
a planet's global entities which are led to believe
they have managed to possess and
own the power of which they seek.

On Earth The Neandertals (1) shelter behind The Majestic Twelve—
who think the power is theirs,
remaining unaware there are switches accessible only
for The Neandertals;
switches which can isolate an item from control,
in the belief of a temporary malfunction,
yet requiring a withdrawal from active service.

So the activity within the major powers to struggle for supremacy is controlled by the
release of new weapons,
of new techniques,
of new designs:
so enabling a jump into the lead for their days due in the sun,
prior to their orchestrated attempts at playing 'catch-up' to
their enemies' advances—
which are always beyond the current capabilities to match
like with like."

My Content Study Aid

_____
_____
_____
_____
_____
_____
_____
_____
_____
_____
_____
_____

The Neandertals— 'Who', 'Why', 'What', 'How'

And I hear The Lord Jesus saying,
"The 'who' and 'why' and 'what' and 'how' of The Neandertals arise in Truth:
        from the smokescreens of history as valid questions for this day.

The 'who' are The Neandertals,
        are not the bees hiding in a bonnet,
        are the intelligent beings resulting from a successful programme:
                of an eventual cross-breeding with the human sapients.

Their parentage was a species from very distant planets,
                who came in flights of saucer-shaped ships—
                both extremely large 'mother' ships staying at a distance,
                and much smaller scouting ships carrying between one and four.

Their parentage,
        for reproduction,
                required detailed examination of the humans:
                        with the eventual splicing of their DNA to attain compatibility;
                        between the genes involved for cross-breeds to eventually evolve,
                                as viable entities with their own existence.

The 'who' are now the result of many centuries with both cross-
                                and multigenerational inter-breeding,
                which have seen them flourish in numbers sufficient to replace the sapient:
                        unless such have been protected by extreme isolation with conditions
                                of complete internal self-reliability.

The 'who' are marked as the parentage precursors,
                                in conjunction with man as an early sapient;
                as derivations from the cross-breeding of this parentage of The Neandertals:
                        whose DNA is the resulting base sequence,
                as resulting from within the early interbreeding among the cross-breeds.

The 'why' was initially an intent to preserve a species from a longterm extinction;
        was modified by the longevity of a species seeking dominance,
                with a consensus to seek safety of the lineage,
                        within a programme achieving interbreeding,
                which could be supervised and steered by selection in the 'best' direction.

The 'why' was conditional on success,
        was conditional on longterm motivation,
        was conditional on an enhancing of the resultant genes.

The 'why' resulted in larger brain capacities:
        which were not completely matched by the increase in the intellect,
        which were not completely matched by an understanding of the engineering concepts,

which were not completely matched by the seesaw of instability,
                    with probability favouring either one side or the other,
        which were far from completely matched by a transfer of longevity,
        which were not completely matched by the fecundity as sought;
                    as fertility was lost at initially one third of a life span,
            later improved to the halfway point as medicines and food production
                extended the lifespans without an accompanying extension of fertility.

The 'what' tends to be a discussion of socio-economic behaviour:
                        of a grand alliance among the resultant life forms;
                        of an alliance among the clan derivatives of the
                                discernable tribes involved;
                        of a derivation favouring The Neandertal when
                                birthed with a superior intellect—
                        for piloting their vehicles and their weaponry,
                                as when in a quest to overcome.

The 'what' of composition dwelt among the extensibility of an enforced inheritance—
                within the age of dinosaurs which were selectively cancelled out;
                by weapons of destruction which were rechargeable from the sun.

The 'what' of performance quickly became dominant:
                        among an environment of giants and miniatures,
            where extermination was quite fast in terms of six or seven centuries,
            where the slaughter was extensive—
                        while the environment came to lose its sense of fear,
                        while battles were encountered against the skewers
                                and the staffs,
            as man started his development into the conquering of surroundings;
                        wherein a cave could be established as a refuge,
                            with the built in living quarters easily defended,
                            with firebrands from a fire set at the entrance,
                            with a deadfall trap within The Earth as
                                    camouflaged by the detritus—
            from the trees and vegetation set as the layering of dried branches,
                            which would not carry weight.

The 'how' of existence often swung upon the outcome of a conflict—
                where the weapons were one-sided and guaranteed a victory,
                where the vehicles had no understanding among the opposition races,
                            as the menfolk flung their spears,
                    to then scurry out of sight into the vegetation.

    Their efforts were a waste of time as machines took to the air:
                            for proceeding on a hunt and kill.

The 'how' of survival was not a challenge set for food,
                    was not a challenge set for water,

was not a challenge set by temperature:
unless it reflected a deliberate choice
where position was important,
or emptiness became attractive;
where fishing was easy on a shoreline,
or vegetation was discovered as edible—
were both seen in a surplus to requirements.

The 'how' of establishment dismays a 'Lone Wolf' where security could not function
in the presence of a non-existent tribe or clan;
suggested a huddling together;
suggested an improving of the weaponry;
suggested a moving to an area where conflict was unlikely,
where a family could be successful in both the wandering and the hiding,
together with the avoiding of the vulnerability when
sourcing or gathering the food."

My Content Study Aid

The Neandertals (1a Clan, Attribute: Leaders)

And I hear The Lord Jesus saying,
"The Neandertals (1a) is fifth greatest in human threatening,
                leader in intelligence,
                controller of all the others,
                operates on thought,
                        now has no direct need either to write or to read.

The Neandertals (1a) operate for the common good of both themselves,
                        as a clan within a tribe,
        for all their like and ilk with humans included yet acknowledged as a race apart.

The Neandertals (1a) physique is the seventh largest which does not affect their authority.

The Neandertals (1a) skin colour is a mid-point grey,
                which is variable in its shades,
                as muscle tenseness so decides.

    Beware when colour is tending to the black for activity of violence is not far away.

      Such should be avoided,
              be retreated from in Wisdom,
                    so threats are perceived as diminishing.

The Neandertals (1a) lives on Earth are long—
    usually in the range of between four hundred and twelve hundred earthly years and
                            tending to the latter.

      When dying they seek isolation.

      As gradually their bodies melt away from sight and presence,
                        with approaching death.

The Neandertals (1a) have a Godly awareness of The Humans' Loving Living God and
                do not infringe the rites of passage,
                    of destinies,
                  nor of belief among His People.

The Neandertals (1a) physical abilities far exceed those—
                in all the senses as known to and possessed by man.

The Neandertals (1a) have extra senses which give them their supremacy to be leaders:
                in their fields of survival and of knowledge.

    Some of which are:
      Languages—
          all of which they can speak and write at will;
    High speed travel—
          noted by their instant absence from a scene which may be mistaken as one

of invisibility—

especially so when they just as suddenly re-appear,
having travelled to,
and returned from,
a location which could only be referenced within the scope of many light years;
their knowledge base—
which far exceeds the libraries of the world,
to draw from where man has not yet gone;
their mastery of instigating cause and effect—
or its reversal of accurately evaluating effect and the resultant cause;
their ability to vary Time—
the effect,
speed,
direction and passage along a continuum within an enclosed and
operating sphere;
their ability to know—
and to understand all which impacts on their lives;
their ability to pilot—
the unidentified flying objects which so puzzle and confuse the sight,
and hence the memories of man.

Neandertals (1a) were the first to arrive,
possessing the assisted strength and the engineering principles to build and to align:
the stone structures as requested at the will of man.

Neandertals (1a) presence on the earth has witnessed the development of man—
from his time within the caves to the erectors of buildings:
now seen to pierce the skies.

This,
in the presence of man's assisted handiwork to destroy all he has struggled
to create—
as the hands and brains of man now rest beside their nuclear arsenals,
under the desire of seeking Peace—
in freedom from the realms of their combatants,
determined to rule through enslavement and command,
while spying on the able.

Neandertals (1a) have some of the facial characteristics of man,
some of which may be absent or slightly distorted.

Neandertals (1a) prefer Peace from war.

Neandertals (1a) breeding frequency,
which is mixed bisexual,
which is hermaphroditical,
is in line with their modal age—
determining the replenishment with the very slow expansion of their species."

ANTHONY A EDDY (SCRIBE)

The Neandertals (1b Clan Attribute: Explorers)

And I hear The Lord Jesus saying,
"The Neandertals (1b) have means of discovering where life exists:
what is its current level of development?

What is likely to be the potential structuring in reaching out in
the achieving of final considerations?

The Neandertals (1b) have no difficulty in flying their unidentified flying objects:
as lifting cranes within the sky,
when stones defy the reality of man to place as he would have them.

The Neandertals (1b) have thin bodies and appendages,
without the body fat of man,
but with amazing strength.

The Neandertals (1b) have large oval-shaped heads positioned on thin short necks.

The Neandertals (1b) have large black eyes which appear not to blink,
which dominate their facial expressions
much more than is the case within humanity.

Their fingers and their toes are bereft of nails,
ending in small sensory pads of super sensitivity,
so to be able to determine exactly what is underfoot,
enabling them to assess the compositions with great accuracy,
which also have hearing pits along their sides.

Their vision for the future is based on hundreds of years of experience
in gradual advancement:
know their way forward in a myriad of ways;
have a back drop of success;
expect it to continue;
seek domination over the smallest to the largest in a call for unity of effort,
of application,
of eventual conquest,
of freedom to roam throughout The Earth—
both of man and of God—
where impediments have all been overcome.

The Neandertals (1b) are docile in their approach to other inhabitants,
do not deviate from their long-term objectives,
outlive the memory banks of those seen to be
without integrity of purpose,
without the push to out-accelerate their opposition,
without The Wisdom to discern the need to fight their projected fate,
without the motivation to equip themselves for future encounters—
involving strategic planning—

so to outsmart the memory cells of the long-term intruders.

For negotiations are not the way of Wisdom.

For capture and immobilisation are not likely to succeed—
    against due strength and power,
    against superior technology and commitment,
    against a time frame difficult to imagine,
    against the first and last in fast coming to a head:
      where a decision will result in success or failure—
   for the struggle of humanity to retain their home among the stars.

Success,
  with the viable way forward,
   is to access the fire of God within the defence walls of the environment—
    which can be gradually expanded as boundaries at the front lines
      are empowered to cleanse,
        to move,
          to commit to the battle for survival—
    against an enemy now known but not fully understood.

For fire,
  where oxygen is plentiful,
   is only partially understood by the invaders of the past,
   is only partially related to the influence of water on the scene which they
           would prefer to avoid.

Flame throwers and carried flaming torches are the best lines of defence,
         are the effective forms of attack,
  where fire in all its many variations can overcome the lasers;
      can overcome the unidentified flying objects:
 when there are no pilots;
 when a firestorm prevails in invading a settlement for complete extermination;
     so freedom is conserved and policies are successful;
     in the applications as deserved and carried out.

The lasers are susceptible to a defense of reflective mirrors of protection,
       with the masking of one-way glass for visibility.

The inferno of the battle field heralds the shout of victory by man,
  in dealing with The Neandertals in their various attributes and skill sets,
     which would place man at a serious disadvantage.

Unless the fire,
  both of God and of man,
   is again brought to serve man,
    within the fields of companionship and might—
    where Authority Truth and Faith may all serve a grand alliance,
      for victory to be the assured result."

ANTHONY A EDDY (SCRIBE)

The Visiting of Neandertals

And I hear The Lord Jesus saying,
"The visiting of Neandertals follows recognition,
>> follows the asking of an informed question,
>> follows the confirmation of appearance and ability.

The visiting of Neandertals is not a common occurrence,
>> is in fact very very rare with the generalised belief:
>>> of extinction in the distant past.

The visiting of Neandertals will become a source of social interaction,
>> will become an interest without peer,
>> will become the access portals to the knowledge levels of
>>> the past,
>> with a practical reinstatement within the lifetimes of
>>> the present.

The visiting of Neandertals requires information on intimate locations,
>> acceptance of their fondness for security,
>> a sensitivity to the pressure when identity
>>> is threatened,
>>> and will not go away.

The visiting of Neandertals puts pressure on the timing,
>> puts pressure on conversations via the subject matter,
>>> and the intelligence levels as involved.

The visiting of Neandertals has location difficulties,
>> really needs a guide who can converse and lead,
>> really needs certainty of reference,
>>> which identifies the whereabouts with precision.

The visiting of Neandertals does not last for an extended time,
>> may have unfamiliar means of conversing,
>> may be brief and to the point.

The visiting of Neandertals see no reason for objection,
>> see no reason to be bothered,
>> see no reason to applaud either the standing or the seated.

The visiting of Neandertals leaves many questions unanswered,
>> leaves many looks avoided,
>> leaves contact alone and with a proffered hand still empty,
>> leaves others to detach to wander as they will.

The visiting of Neandertals are not worried about their secrets,
>> know the intellect to operate such is missing:
>>> from the pools of brainpower readily available.

The visiting of Neandertals is not for spending time in looking done a nose:
with an aura of superciliousness;
is not for navigating the social arenas,
where manners may be questioned,
and even so forgiven.

The visiting of Neandertals is not a time for picnicking,
is not a time for comparisons,
is not a time for examining the traits and peccadilloes
of the strangers:
previously unheard of and yet not so far from 'home'.

The visiting of Neandertals do not see doorways opened readily,
witness caution in effect with a minimal amount
of movement,
hear no questioning while the doors are closed.

The visiting of Neandertals employs a standing area before the door;
where attitude of a would-be guest can be examined;
prior to acknowledgment and entry through the
access way;
to an interior of alarm at what is on display.

The visiting of Neandertals are not alarmed very easily,
have a system of decorum where alarm is not seen,
as a practical reaction to activities,
where consent is required to enter.

The visiting of Neandertals sees the togetherness of the choice with the stubborn,
sees the exhausted lolling on the couches,
sees the subservient bowing to their princes,
sees the lifestyles mixing up their preferences,
prior to the singling out of individual selections.

The visiting of Neandertals will take a lot of getting used to:
in the areas of accommodation.

The visiting of Neandertals justifies the listing of the differences in behaviour,
the differences which highlight the day in passing,
which highlight the night approaching.

The visiting of Neandertals views neither disobedience nor punishment enacted.

The visiting of Neandertals is an exploration of our home—
by parentage still surviving,
to operate within the cockpits and control rooms of
their craft:
to all which has previously been denied,
by the strong and powerful,

ANTHONY A EDDY (SCRIBE)

by The Majestic Twelve,
only in their chosen name,
only in their selfishness and greed,
only in their lying to The World of man,
only in their seeking of advantage—
to maintain a secret which was never theirs to keep,
to commandeer,
to lie about:
so to evaluate the landfall of the visitors,
so to enhance their options as encountered.

The visiting of Neandertals has been going on for many centuries,
by the knowledgable and the confounding;
in holding hands with the importers 'par excellence':
who ferried information from afar—
so others could enrich an opportunity to tap a vein
of gold—
with access either denied or approved at the whim,
after the setting up,
of The Majestic Twelve.

The Majestic Twelve are the inheriting architects of deceit,
are the secret keepers of the developing progression of The Earth,
have confused the witnesses' sightings and declarations,
throughout the lifetimes of The Twelve,
as they have come and gone over the many thousands of centuries;
forming the accretion as they built and build continuously,
on the ages of succession.

The ways of man in hindsight are rarely seen as also being
the ways of The Eternal God."

My Content Study Aid

_____
_____
_____
_____
_____
_____
_____
_____

Discovering The Neandertals

And I hear The Lord Jesus saying,
"Discovering The Neandertals can be recognized in an instant,
      as they pass across the eye fields of man,
      as they pass to and fro on their well worn access paths,
      as they pass across the frontiers with subterfuge and disguises,
         on the scooters as used by man.

Discovering The Neandertals is the initial stage of an unmasking,
      is progressive in the process of identification,
      is meaningless in the rapid repetition of a chain of
         meaningless numbers—
      assembling in the head of man.

Discovering The Neandertals is not a rewarding thing to do,
   poses more questions than there are answers available which can be understood.

Discovering The Neandertals is usually just sufficient to know that they are there,
      is usually desirable to leave them to themselves as their
         preference of approval.

Discovering The Neandertals opens the portals of the doors
        to differing kingdoms of control,
        to differing cultures there encountered,
        to differing abilities and sensors,
        to differing strengths and separations,
      to differing body structures and styles of feeding
        which make no sense to man.

Discovering The Neandertals calls up questions on longevity,
      calls up questions on their origins,
      calls up questions to do with the 'why' and 'when',
       as unexpected silence reigns supreme,
       until the silence is again broken by man without
         a stylistic break,
         for the taking of a breath,
      calls up the potential myriads of questions where the
         answers don't make sense,
       within the experience of the relationships with man.

Discovering The Neandertals can be a benchmark in relationships where pauses
         are polite,
      where articulation is not a conversational facet used
         in depth,
      where the practice among themselves is one of the constant
      use of thought transference in either the singular or the plural:

ANTHONY A EDDY (SCRIBE)

when as set for within their groups—
either at home or abroad.

Discovering The Neandertals raises hopes with curiosity,
raises expectations with disappointment.

Discovering The Neandertals comes with technology as tremendously advanced,
as superior in every way imaginable and beyond the present reach of man—
unless buried alive in a technical institute under their instructional control,
where learning would be excessive and practice is essential,
over a non-defined period of successive years.

Discovering The Neandertals does not guarantee either access to nor instructions in,
their technology with the ability to apply in use successfully.

Discovering The Neandertals creates the difficulty of translation into English,
where word structures do not exist for the concepts needing to be
transferred as descriptors of the mechanics,
the mathematics,
the co-ordinates,
with the electronic circuitry as protected from interference,
with the utmost reliability,
when engaged in use.

Discovering The Neandertals should not be put off by quirkiness,
should not be gauged by any other experience,
should not be terminated unless in the presence of
the unfriendly—
who are an embittered strain of existence.

Discovering The Neandertals leaves many aspects worthy of exploration,
leaves many traits unrecorded as absent from discussions
or interpretations,
leaves many pipelines secured for objectives,
where enquiries can result in a feast of 'shows' and 'tells'.

Discovering The Neandertals should prepare for the warnings inherent in the
attributes affirmed,
should warn of caution when appropriate,
should warn of the likelihood of violence,
of attack,
when seen as a threat from a close approach,
when recognition fails and lasers are withdrawn,
when a history declares The Wisdom of a retreat into escape.

Discovering The Neandertals should record:
the location and the attributes,
an estimate of numbers within that in which they are involved,
a noting of their stability of location or whether they are setting

up to move,
which is quite rare when coupled with their longevity in place.

Discovering The Neandertals breaks a keeping of a secret known only by a few,
spreads it far and wide as belief remains uncertain,
as science steals a march,
as improvements in DNA analysis corrects the dating
of the past,
discloses the history of European man as built upon a Neandertal DNA base:
which rings the changes and the time schedules for man in his development;
as cross-breeding took effect on the later generations,
of the sapient at large.

Discovering The Neandertals with their imprint on the development of man;
is the secret of The Earth,
is the secret held within the kitchen-craft of nature,
is the secret beyond the noticing or the guesswork,
is the secret where God himself was silent until the secret
became too important,
as Faith declined with the lies of Evolutionary Theory
bursting to the shop fronts,
of science for display—
where the °fool declared there is no God,
where belief in God was seen to falter,
as The Truth demanded to be released;
from the sticky adherence to the falsity of
evolutionary theory,
now sliding down a very slippery slope:
to end up in the rubbish bin of science.

So the fools are gathered with their lies, their moral corruption, as exposed.

So God is returned unto the centre stage of life."

°Psalm 14:1 'The fool has said in his heart, "There is no God."'
New Spirit filled life Bible, NKJVersion, Used by permission.

My Content Study Aid

_____

_____

_____

_____

_____

The Neandertals (1c Clan Attribute: 'Superior')

And I hear The Lord Jesus saying,
"The Neandertals (1c) are the ones who do not like being touched by humans,
           do not like their body heat on contact,
           do not like the intensity of their smell which
           varies with the distance,
           do not like their handling of their food when
           seen from the viewpoint of active curiosity.

The Neandertals (1c) believe they are superior in every way imaginable,
       believe they can come and go without anyone to molest them,
       do not grant such freedom to others they regard with disdain,
         especially when coping with the seasons of The Earth with
         the recurring changes in the climate.

The tunes upon The Earth are not ones of Peace and reconciliation,
       are ones of contrast and of the struggle for ultimate superiority,
       are the end-time inaugurations of the settlement procedures,
   where the negotiators do not understand their opposition,
        do not understand the seriousness of each other's position,
        do not sympathise with what is being attempted to attain,
         with what the repercussions will be for a failure of intent,
         with what both sides will have to suffer:
           when hope and trust are both withdrawn,
     to stand upon the sidelines;
     to stand and to witness the preparation of the battlefields—
  where death and mayhem will celebrate the invidious loss of life.

The contact with The Neandertals are between a very select band of humans,
     a very small enclave numbered for their secrecy,
     a very difficult model to break out into the public arena,
     a very important aspect which needs to be addressed before it is too late—
  when conflict breaks out to surprise the world at large—
            who will not know what to do,
       except to scream and shout,
       to run around in circles—
with no thought patterning in mind which can resolve the issues amicably,
         which can resolve,
         with far reaching consequences,
      the concepts explicit in comprehending the need for symbiosis:
      prior to the effects where antibiosis could seal the fate of many;
   the need for a study of the full disclosure of a history,
   the need for open intelligent discussions as to the needs and wants of each—
  of how a consensus may be reached without plastering the walls with blood.

The anathema of one for the other is based upon ignorance on one hand
                                        and dominance on the other,
           of unwelcome news which is difficult to accept as Truth:
           which has been hidden by denials under the weight of many lies by man,
           which have not addressed the issues—
                      with any sense of knowledge or acceptance necessary—
                           for the settling on a feasible solution."

My Content Study Aid

_____

_____

_____

_____

_____

_____

_____

_____

_____

_____

_____

_____

_____

_____

_____

_____

_____

_____

_____

_____

The Neandertals (1d Clan Attribute: Destroyers)

And I hear The Lord Jesus saying,
"The Neandertals (1d) is a number not easily forgotten,
                           not easily befriended,
                           not easily met with a common purpose.

The Neandertals (1d) is set and structured for the destruction of humanity,
                           sees Earth as theirs by choice,
                           sees an inheritance being usurped by numbers,
                           sees a home installed long before the habitation of man had left
                                                      a footprint on The Earth.

The Neandertals (1d) have forsaken any interest in The God of The Earth,
                           have forsaken any desire for friendship with obscene invaders,
                           have forsaken any inclination to follow such a way of life:
                                        which is seen as ignorant and immoral;
                                        by the standards accruing from extreme long life.

The Neandertals (1d) are a synonym for violence,
                           are a synonym for attempted genocide,
                           are a synonym for destroying a competing way of life.

The Neandertals (1d) are not to be approached,
                           have stories told of untold savagery seen in action,
                                        of struggles for survival where they always
                                                      seem to be the victors,
                                        of the using and the destroying of resources for
                                                      which they have no need.

The Neandertals (1d) should be a name familiar to all the human race,
                                        to all who would survive,
                                        to all who would seek them out,
                                        to all who would attempt to square
                                                      the series of engagements.

   Foolish are they who would seek a power base without being clothed with
                                        the necessary aggressive power,
                           without the necessary flame throwers from a distance,
                           without the sense to turn and flee before the lasers
                                        come to bear with mirrors unaligned.

The Neandertals (1d) has the capability to release an electromagnetic pulse:
                                        a supra-cloud-burst—
                                        which would defile The Earth,
                                        which would revert The Earth backwards
                                                      through time,
                                        prior to the impact of technology,

prior to The Industrial revolution,
prior to the ability to monetize the
labouring of man.

This pulse awaits the ultimate stupidity of neighbours filled with jealousy,
of neighbours filled with hatred,
of neighbours filled with the capability
to injure all mankind,
to injure the load as carried by The Earth,
to injure the source and distribution of food,
of energy,
of the advancement of nations,
of the conceptual shallowness of the kings,
the despots,
the inciters of rebellions,
who would rule and reign without the authority of progression.

So the needs for acknowledgement on the morrow remain uncompiled—
evident within the empty fields of Love,
of Truth,
of Righteousness;
there waiting for the filling with the families holding the hopes for the future—
the growth,
the development,
the maturing,
of the children born of yesteryear:
still to seek their positioning within the timed and presented boundaries—
of the nations of The Earth."

My Content Study Aid

_____
_____
_____
_____
_____
_____
_____
_____
_____
_____

The Usurping of Leadership

And I hear The Lord Jesus saying,
"The usurping of leadership demonstrates the perception of the willingness of
inserting change.

The usurping of leadership speaks of dishonouring within the chain of command,
speaks of insubordination close to the leadership,
speaks of a waywardness in loyalty,
speaks of corruption which has trickled down,
speaks of an urgency to seize the reins of power,
speaks of enmity alive and well upon the boardwalks and
the cobbles:
now bent in closer jurisdiction,
now caked with the muddied prints of imposition,
now squeaking to a different tune from the basket of
the insurgency—
of the mediocre and indifferent.

The usurping of leadership declares a disregard for the standards of behaviour,
declares a determination to grab an opportunity to take
the learned with the legal,
declares the impressionists of disloyalty as alive and well,
declares an open opportunity when the leader is away
on business:
leaving the votes behind at home to be but swayed
and counted.

The usurping of leadership creates a vacancy of accountability,
creates a vacancy within the bounds of completion,
creates a vacancy in the allotment of provisioning.

The usurping of leadership encounters a surplus of confidence,
a surplus of independence,
a surplus of conviction on the rights and wrongs.

The usurping of leadership is oft treated as if a hayride through a meadow,
is oft treated with frivolity,
is oft treated as a cheap access to the guns,
is oft treated as a jump onto a bandwagon—
where loudspeakers are the norm.

The usurping of leadership is not often seen as a wakeup call,
is not often described as bringing an advantage to the led,
is not often described to the public,
without a lie involved,
in announcing an attempt at acceptability.

The usurping of leadership often leads to a raiding of the pot of gold,
     often is the objective of a thief seen in disguise,
     often results in the stealing of the liquid resources—
        so to be placed within a foreign jurisdiction.

The usurping of leadership is very rarely of any value to the people,
     is more likely just a changing of the guard,
     is more likely just a measure of the level of corruption,
     is more likely the intent to activate the transfers to
        a foreign shore.

The usurping of leadership is without concern to the betterment of lives,
      to the betterment of families,
      to the betterment of the work place,
      to the betterment of housing and
        of communications.

The usurping of leadership can simply be a change in greed,
      a change without a vision for The Multitudes at large,
      a change without concern for the welfare of the people.

The usurping of leadership speaks of change without authority,
     of change occurring in the darkness of the night,
     of change presented without any reference to responsibility,
     of change imposed without a planning for the future,
     of change achieved while a back is turned,
     of change manifested by a triumvirate of conspiracy,
     of change installed with dismissal of the caring and concerned.

The usurping of leadership destroys the means of credit management,
      creates chaos in the field of uncertainty,
      damages the records of understanding and indebtedness in
        the fields of finance.

The usurping of leadership has far-reaching connotations,
     can push back into the past,
     can raid the potential of the future,
     can establish cronyism with its difficulty of removal,
     can be the nightmare of disaster to the righteous and
        the truthful:
     as they find themselves surrounded by the dishonest
        and the puerile—
     with neither sense nor care for what the morrow brings—
     where is found the gathering of the storm clouds
        of dependency.

The usurping of leadership can derail development,
     can hearken to the ignorant,

can feast upon the pride,
can festoon and decorate the bubbles built on hope,
can subdue and overcome the angry and informed.

The usurping of leadership very rarely leads to a trail within the frost—
built on intelligence and concern,
rarely leads to savings protected and encouraged in
their growth,
rarely leads to benefits seen both as measurable and desirable.

The usurping of leadership places greyness on a day,
strengthens the darkness of the night,
weakens the lighting of the day.

The usurping of leadership signals its intent to destabilize the involvement of God,
is impervious to prayers and to the recompense attached
to reconciliation,
is blind and deaf and mute to any relationship with God.

The usurping of leadership inaugurates the dead zone of enlightenment,
the dead zone of Faith and Truth,
the dead zone of help and assistance,
the dead zone of selfishness where the 'I' of man
is seen as all important—
in governing the activities of man.

The usurping of leadership starts a chase for wealth,
initiates the schemes and plots,
feeds on the lies and deceit,
crafts the ingenuous to be qualified to become the con men
of attrition in the presence of the charities.

The usurping of leadership is not able to silence the call to God,
is not able to divert the care of God,
is not able to surpass the love of God,
is neither able to commandeer nor to silence the counselling
of God:
with an anticipated consignment to lost causes—
only seen as relevant when living in the past."

My Content Study Aid

_____

_____

_____

The Dead Hand of Man

And I hear The Lord Jesus saying,
"The dead hand of man accumulates and festers when thrust into the end-time works
of man.

The dead hand of man meets with head-on failure:
> cannot be resurrected,
> cannot be reconstituted,
> cannot be reactivated,
> cannot be made to operate the way it was designed to be.

The dead hand of man follows in the mimicking of the status of the brain,
> follows in the ineptitude of the response to thought,
> chases after what has long been exposed,
> ventures into the field of might-have-beens:
>> by attempting to restore someone else's discard,
>>> as found in the binnings of the past.

The dead hand of man fails with tests of movement,
> drops that needing to be lifted,
> breaks what should be stirred,
> watches while an overflow continues,
> is clumsy when accuracy is called for.

The dead hand of man cannot carry,
> cannot move to a higher plane,
> cannot be counted on to gauge the needs for security,
> cannot be assured of a testing for success.

The dead hand of man is best assigned to retirement:
> is useless in a laboratory,
> is senseless in the feeling of the forward way,
> is incapable of counting on the fingers,
> is not able to transmit orders to the brain with any degree
>> of reliability.

The dead hand of man cannot be trusted in a duplication,
> cannot describe the tasks requested in a day,
> cannot depend on guesswork,
> cannot buy a way forward,
> cannot be intrusive in a meaningful discussion,
> cannot be counted on for correctness of assumptions.

The dead hand of man is dangerous among machinery,
> is hesitant among the pulleys and the cogs,
>> among the wheels and the ratchets,
>> among the belts and teeth.

ANTHONY A EDDY (SCRIBE)

The dead hand of man arises and flops,
        retreats with a latent reflex,
        shoves and pushes without an acknowledgment of edges.

The dead hand of man is a mask waiting to be broken,
        is a mask mirrored on a face,
        is a mask where the muscles seem to be as outlaws called
                    to be enactors:
            of Freewill without control.

The dead hand of man can still impose a test of wills.
The dead hand of man can still arise and be counted.
The dead hand of man can still seize and run away.

The dead hand of man can still select and grab,
        can still approach and steal,
        can still rotate and mix the valuable and the precise,
              when left without a guardian,
        can still batter the useful into the useless without
              a moment's hesitation,
        can still break the eggs with a messed up mixing of the yolks
              and whites with shells.

The dead hand of man can be a common occurrence where life is no longer valued,
     where the objective is to introduce the presence of death,
     where the pastime is to magnify the resultant numbers,
     where the discarded shells are accepted with neither approval nor a questioning,
              with neither a listing nor a reporting,
              with neither an accounting nor
                  a checking.

The dead hand of man can affect the totals,
     can overlook the partial mistakes or errors born of judgment,
     can ignore the pained and the wounded in their attempts to find some help.

The dead hand of man can seek and find the sharpened tools of trade,
            with their ease of application,
            where a slash or stab will do to result in an increase
                in statistics:
              which do not honour cause.

The dead hand of man can injure and assert:
            when loaded with a weapon,
            when loaded with humiliation,
            when loaded with rejection as the cause of merriment.

The dead hand of man is an unsuspected instrument of death,
        is used with relish and revenge,

is used with speed and disappearance,
is used with planning and destruction.

The dead hand of man can motivate with fear,
can motivate with urgency,
can motivate with lies.

The dead hand of man can be motivated by the stupidity of control—
of drugs,
of alcohol,
of the selling of tests and trials
associated with the membership
of gangs;
can be motivated by blackmail in all its shames of darkness,
can be motivated by lies which build deception,
by jealousy bred of the viewing of 'success',
by stigmas born of rejection in the lowering
of self-worth.

The dead hand of man is difficult to recognise,
is difficult to discern the actioning of intent,
is difficult to overcome when stoked to a frenzy—
when hell is seen on view—
with the call for help unanswered by the wise and the selfish:
who understand both the season and the miming."

My Content Study Aid

_____

_____

_____

_____

_____

_____

_____

_____

_____

_____

_____

_____

_____

The Suspicions of Man

And I hear The Lord Jesus saying,
"The suspicions of man often are ill-founded.

The suspicions of man often are generated on an irrelevancy,
               often are based upon a supposition,
               often are developed on the origin of lies,
               often are treated as a fact which can be likened to the plough
                                before the horse.
The suspicions of man can be threaded and matured,
               can be examined and developed,
               can be seized on and reported,
               can be a source of mischief in the making,
               can be the basis of distrust with the ending of a friendship.

The suspicions of man can be enlarged upon and magnified,
               can be the sourcing of unbelief with character to the fore,
               can be the placing of a searchlight to examine the surroundings,
               can be,
                 and likely is,
                    the machinations of the entities which prefer the darkness.

The suspicions of man are difficult to clear,
               can stain and taint a relationship of Trust and Truth,
               can fracture and demolish the earliest relationships of youth:
                       the divisions among siblings;
                 the constraints which settle on the offspring and mingle
                            with the parents.

The suspicions of man can fluctuate with input,
               can fluctuate with susceptibility to gossip,
               can dethrone a king from his seat upon a throne,
               can impress the gullible to believe the very worst.

The suspicions of man can result in the relieving from responsibilities,
               can result in a re-arrest when out upon parole.

The suspicions of man can be fanned by the result from the output of a lie detector,
                     from the statements of the witness with an imagination,
                     from the brilliance of a lawyer who claims the night as
                            day and shows that it is so.

The suspicions of man rarely have the foundations of a rock,
               are more likely derived from footsteps on the seeping sand,
               are more likely to extend the likelihood of imprisonment:
                 rather than release into the delights of the freedom of Freewill.

The suspicions of man can be the subject of mirth in hindsight,
            can be the beggaring of a wastrel who cannot make his case,
            can be the basis of wealth transfer when published as The Truth,
            can be the cause of solicitation when reactions are misconstrued.

The suspicions of man can be easily aroused,
            can start an investigation,
            can destroy a reputation,
            can expose the hidden with a history,
            can declare a confirmation of a fact seen as supportive of the
                                   voice of reason.

The suspicions of man can separate relationships,
            can break the marriage vows,
            can infringe on privacy,
            can trigger recalls within a memory bank,
            can breed and fester in privacy in absence of a voice.

The suspicions of man can be the agent of a break-down of trust within a partnership,
                    of trust confounded by a holiday,
                    of trust split open by the record of malfeasance,
                    of trust spilt and unrecoverable by absorption
                              into the sands of time.

The suspicions of man can be widespread and auspicious,
      can arouse the unbelievable to be observed from the safety net of reason,
     can secure a place of safety for observation of either the secular or the spiritual,
                    either the foreign or the import,
                    either the invader or the traveller,
                    either the impostor or the heavy laden,
                    either the weapon carrier or the man of Peace.

The suspicions of man can dry up with the dust,
            can evaporate with the attention of the sun,
            can be blown away by the winds of change,
            can be absorbed by the holes without constraint,
            can be a relief upon a system showing the lack of a foundation,
                  where suspicion melts away within the sunlight,
                        as if the frost upon the windowpane
                        or resting on the early morning lawn.

The suspicions of man can lead into difficulty,
            can lead into discovery,
            can unearth a secret as kept for centuries under control,
            can verify the reality of that taken as impossible,
            can reinforce a growing suspicion as it becomes a certainty,
            can harness,
            can declare,

can bring to attention the presence of beings of existence—
previously unsuspected and as nullified by scepticism.

The suspicions of man are aroused by the modes of transport,
by the belief in presence meeting with denials by authority,
by the high level controllers of a nation's secrets who know,
who have seen and touched,
who have interviewed and witnessed,
who can describe and recount—
the attributes and markers of undocumented life.

The suspicions of man smear the probable into the certainty,
smear the possible into the viewable,
smear the exaggerations into the presentable,
smear the mystical of God into the reality of man."

My Content Study Aid

_____

_____

_____

_____

_____

_____

_____

_____

_____

_____

_____

_____

_____

_____

_____

_____

_____

_____

_____

_____

The Succumbing to Demand

And I hear The Lord Jesus saying,
"The succumbing to demand steals The Freewill of man.

The succumbing to demand in excess is the theft of choice in action,
                                    is the taking of more than is really needed,
                                    is the stowing of the surplus for a time
                                                        of unavailability.

The succumbing to demand speaks of a lack of sharing,
                        speaks of gathering in selfishness,
                        speaks of an eye set to keep a lookout in the avoidance of
                                                a neighbour.

The succumbing to demand speaks of a failure to find an alternative,
                        speaks of a failure to call-up a restocking of the shelves,
                        speaks of failure in the attempt to find a new supplier at a
                                                greater distance.

The succumbing to demand sets in place an international effort to fulfil the
                                                demand created,
                        sets in place the scouring of the fields of commerce across
                                        the adjacent areas of The Earth,
                        sets in action the upward bidding in a price war to purchase
                                                the commodity:
                                seen in such demand as it outstrips the capabilities,
                                where growth in demand is limited by the
                                                processing capacity available.

The succumbing to demand sets in place a growth cycle which is hard to slow—
                                        against the increase in demand.

The succumbing to demand calls for an ongoing increase
                in the mastering of the bottlenecks,
                in the mastering of resources as required,
                in the mastering of the needs as limited by a reading of the offtake graphs:
                        now seen as intent on going beyond the bounds of quite recent days.

The succumbing to demand means a rush for the supply of the components in production;
                                as needed in the supply chain of delivery.

The succumbing to demand means new estimates calculated and deployed for action,
                        means new totals calculated as accruing for deliveries
                                                going wild.

The succumbing to demand makes it difficult to determine the end-point of matching
                                                supply unto demand,
                        sees guesswork inscribed on white boards,

Anthony A Eddy (Scribe)

sees figures changing by the day,
enlarging by the week,
meets with erasure when the forecasts start to exceed
the bounds of common sense:
when being exceeded by the uproars
of unmodified dissent.

The succumbing to demand mixes up the salads:
in an effort to satisfy the tastebuds of the kings with their princes going wild.

The succumbing to demand sees the wildfire alive and flaring,
sees the call to stations occurring far too late,
sees the lack of water as inhibiting and serious,
sees and smells the smoke as it reaches for the skies,
within the wilderness of man,
within the new found wealth of man,
within the secrets and the outreaches as positioned by man,
where the fires are at their fiercest,
while the smoke is at its densest,
while man submits his levies on the services seen by all.

The succumbing to demand is a functioning of quality,
is a functioning of price,
is a functioning of the local population where the selective
cultures can be seen to queue.

The succumbing to demand has little likelihood of diminishing,
has little possibility of witnessing a decline in demand,
has little possibility of dismissal of the variants when
submitted for approval.

The succumbing to demand is seen to push demand even higher,
is seen to push demand past the ranging of medical relief,
is seen to crowd and push within the queues of those
awaiting service,
as prices soar without relief.

The succumbing to demand hurls insults at those seen limiting supply,
at those seen getting more than what is gauged
as a fair share,
at those in the front seen stuffing bags and
pockets with their purchases:
as they up and leave with their supplies deemed
sufficient for the next few days,
at those seen with inflated selling at the rear end
of a queue where scrabbling,
where scrambling,
attempts to share the transfer of interest in the given loads

now being held to ransom.

The succumbing to demand does not attempt to share,
        does not attempt equality in supply,
        does not attempt to match the production quality with the
                retail price.

The succumbing to demand is a hurdle not worth clearing in the race of life,
        is a hurdle where the height is immaterial,
        while the stride is only off-putting to the ones behind.

The succumbing to demand lies and waits in turn,
        lies and amplifies The Truth to a stage beyond
                due recognition,
        lies and eventuates in the spreading of the suffering
        with the nearsighted perceptions of the day.

The succumbing to demand has the measures of seed oil on back order,
        has the measure of the cannabis supplied,
        knows the variant for hemp,
        knows the variant for the daze of days.

The succumbing to demand measures the circling and the deciding,
        the invitations and the rejections,
        the pricing and the cost,
        the profit and the loss with the risking of a mania,
        with the loss of comprehension:
        for the ordering of the day.

The succumbing to demand is not an order being stated,
        is not an instruction shouted from a shelf on offer,
        is not on the approval list as a suitable companion for a walk
        with God.

Beware the seriousness of an overload with the hovering of death,
        neither of which originate from The Living Loving God."

My Content StudyAid

_____

_____

_____

_____

_____

_____

The Neandertals (1e Clan Attribute: Technologists)

And I hear The Lord Jesus saying,
"The Neandertals (1e) are the editors-in-chief.

The Neandertals (1e) are the protectors and the sharers of their technology,
    are the liberators and the limiters,
    are the releasors and the keepers,
    are the patent officers in charge,
    are the technicians with understanding,
    are the guardians of secrets discovered over centuries.

The Neandertals (1e) are the teachers of the leapfrog,
    are the signallers of advancement,
    are the improvers of stagnation,
    are The Settlers with the knowledge yet still seeking Wisdom,
    are the architects of ways and means leading into shedding light
          on the unknown,
    know the prototypes of construction which both work and fail.

The Neandertals (1e) bring engineering into the unknown,
    bring circumstances readied for improvement,
    are the instigators of change,
    are the masters of the practical concepts of discarding mass,
      of using gravity assistance from the universal waves
         where 'surfing' is a simile:
      of bending both into applications which defy the
         bounds of light,
        and the energy of rockets;
    can kick start progression into the post-nuclear age of man.

The Neandertals (1e) will share into an advantage,
    will assist when dealing with equality,
    will lead when introducing concepts met with an absence
         of understanding.

The Neandertals (1e) are instructive at heart,
    do not fear the past,
    do not fear the future,
    do not mess with the non-existent present,
    have preparations for when the fastest waves and strings become
      the vehicles on which to hitch the data for a ride.

The Neandertals (1e) have further cousins in existence,
    have further stops and stays,
    have specialists at large who can mimic and enhance,
    have maestros of discovery who can twist and bend,

have intellectual giants who can circumvent the accepted laws
of man,
who can fly and traverse where man has
yet to go,
who can investigate,
capture,
and cycle—
applications to what man has yet to imagine,
yet alone discover.

The Neandertals (1e) are the highlighters of success,
are the markers of the stepping stones of progress,
are the survivors and the overcomers of the trials and problems of
their past:
which still dwell without discovery in the future fields of man.

The Neandertals (1e) are the helping hands which lift from a past into a golden future:
where the gaze of man is affixed in wonder—
on all of which he has not yet even come to dream.

The Neandertals (1e) do not suffer fools,
do not deal with children,
do not enhance the obvious,
do not give credit for the copy,
do not enlist the obsequious or the clinger on.

The Neandertals (1e) are self-sufficient in all they say and do within the knowledge
bounds of their experience."

My Content Study Aid

_____
_____
_____
_____
_____
_____
_____
_____
_____
_____

Vying with The Robots

And I hear The Lord Jesus saying,
"Vying with the robots is not a viable option.

Vying with the robots cannot compete upon a level playing field,
      cannot complete the tasks satisfactorily without movement from a
           fixed position,
        without the anchoring of the feet.

Vying with the robots cannot match the strength,
      cannot match the speed with the precision,
      cannot match the reliability for the avoiding of mistakes.

Vying with the robots invites an endgame unlikely to succeed,
      invites an endgame between the flesh and bone and the mechanics
          and the oil,
      invites an endgame between the breaks for food and drink and the
         consistency of the electrics and pneumatics,
      invites comparison between the need for payrolls and the interest
         on the funding,
      invites comparison between the output as done by willing hands
        and as done by mindless repetition.

Vying with the robots demands attention be paid to the variance of both from the
        standard as requested,
       and the need to be retained.

Vying with the robots becomes even more difficult as numbers are increased,
       as facilities are expanded,
       as further supervision is resourced in
        unproductive eyes and hands.

Vying with the robots does not fare well in nearly every aspect excepting feelings
        and emotions,
     excepting analysis of coping with exceptions,
     excepting when called to supervise the brainless energetic:
    so bringing conviction of a lack of choice when involved
        with uniformity:
      in procuring speed of operation,
       as if a sleight of hand,
    to the newly fuelled and expanding courts of industry.

Vying with the robots is not a recipe for a sound night's sleep,
     is not a recipe for a successful return upon the expended effort,
     is not a recipe which the robot masters would employ.

Vying with the robots needs a change in attitude,

needs a change in perception,
needs a change in the modes of recompense,
needs a change in willingness to adjust to the rate of change.

Vying with the robots is silly in the extreme,
is an attempt to capture or to conquer:
that which can never be within the capacity of man.

Vying with the robots pits the physical of man against that now within the computing
power of giants.

Vying with the robots indicates a mindset not used to thinking to advantage,
not thinking to advance,
not thinking to manipulate the applications fit
for robots.

Vying with the robots shrinks the value of man,
shrinks his workloads to the past,
shrinks his knowledge of technology as it leaves him in the dust.

Vying with the robots closes eyes to opportunities,
closes eyes to prospecting for new developments,
closes eyes to securing a contract based on research with
future applications,
closes eyes from viewing the rejections of the here and now:
with the potential of the future—
as filled by and envisioned of what must surely be.

Vying with the robots does not develop opportunities to improve and to patent,
to refine and to increase the productivity,
to examine the current limits,
to think of a solution to the bottlenecks,
to think on the means of presentation to the processes—
so delays and stoppages are minimised to the benefit of all.

Vying with the robots can lead into a handgrip on the future,
can lead into an understanding of the needs of the robots,
can lead into a brainwave which gathers all in readiness:
for the new addition to the robot family.

Vying with the robots is still in its infancy,
should be encouraged to view the wider complexity of all which is
at stake,
should be turned to seize the training and the learning available
within the industries with applications,
should lead to a repositioning of the dated with the learned,
of the obsolete now fitted with a vision,
of the downcast and despairing now filled with
the discovered and The Wisdom:

ANTHONY A EDDY (SCRIBE)

as built on understanding.

Vying with the robots can lead to a thrilling and exciting ride—
by piggybacking on the efforts of the past,
by consolidating the achievements of the past,
to enhance designs where both the micro and the macro limits are firmly held in mind:
for readiness of the extension of the speed limits;
of the extensions of the size and reach;
of the extensions of the accuracy with refinement of the finishes.

Vying with the robots can lead to a golden future,
to a path fitted for the building of careers,
to a fortune there awaiting for the making,
to a retirement filled with the hallmarks of success,
to a family where finances are no longer the
consideration of the day.

Vying with the robots should see thought applied to the future of an inheritance,
a resolution of the goals in life,
the advantages which a partnership with God can forge and develop,
can change the ultimate destiny of man,
can build into the young and developing
their gratitude to God—
in bringing the bandaids of God into the needs as found within
their family—
as opportunities are gathered in and mated for success."

My Content Study Aid

_____

_____

_____

_____

_____

_____

_____

_____

_____

_____

_____

Small Endeavours

And I hear The Lord Jesus saying,
"Small endeavours have a birthplace especially selected.

Small endeavours have a nest especially constructed,
     especially provided,
     especially built for expansion in the world at large,

Small endeavours are dependent on a vision,
     are dependent on the foresight of establishment,
     are dependent on selection of those entrusted to its growth.

Small endeavours are designed for the advancement of man,
     are required to abide by the laws of man,
     are targeted both by the crocodiles and the giants,
     are assumed to be on the menu for the gobblers and imposers.

Small endeavours need to be held very tightly,
     to be protected from the perils surrounding the newly born,
     to be fed and watered with the nourishment they were designed to eat,
     to be watched and encouraged on their daily walks with man.

Small endeavours should have their sights set on a goal which is easily achieved,
     should know the stepping stones implicit in achievement,
     should celebrate success as a stomach is extended,
     should reward the protectors for their care and attention,
     should strive and struggle to shed the canopies of yesterday,
     should dress in fresh raiment which can grab the attention of
            a questioning enquiry.

Small endeavours can grow very quickly when fed the proper meals,
     are not brought to their choking points when vomit makes a mess,
     are not constrained and starved:
      because of bad hunting for a meal,
      because of bad taste when left within an opened mouth,
      because of a bad habit of robbing future growth by the removing of
            the linings as built on past success.

Small endeavours can only satisfy a waiting mouth with an intake sized to the digestion,
     sized to the capacity of the mouth when opened wide,
     sized to the capability of the teeth in crunching for the swallowing of
            the throat.

Small endeavours can be static and never permit a holiday,
     can become prisons checking and stalling the potential of both
            the day and night,
     of calling for hesitancy in the decision to accept a giant,

ANTHONY A EDDY (SCRIBE)

to manage to digest all there is on offer,
to jump and to surpass the objectives set for the day,
to invigorate and excite a baby's growth:
in an ability to satisfy all it is asked to do.

Small endeavours can sample and report,
can build a standing wave,
can establish an ebb and flow,
can fill a beach with sand,
can highlight the flecks of gold within the vista opened for inspection,
can enable the gathering of the gold of God for the purse of man.

Small endeavours can learn to accept the growth spurts brought by
learning to crunch the gravel,
learning to smash the rocks;
can leave the sand behind with its purpose well achieved.

Small endeavours are the starting points as sought by an inspection from the encircling
of the lip-lickers —
those who would capture,
fatten,
and prepare:
for an even greater reward as seen to be in the offing.

Small endeavours rarely reach their full potential within their expected timeframe
of existence;
can be the willing,
or the unwilling,
target of predation;
can be fully or partially consumed without a burp,
often brings a hiccup onto a scene of uncertainty,
can change gear and travel as a speedster,
in taking others for a ride,
in taking others to their intended destinations,
in taking others for dropping on the way.

Small endeavours can be as taxis dropping passengers at their selected destinations,
or as limousines held in readiness:
for the depositing with the collecting of the fares;
to then return in readiness for repeat performances.

Small endeavours can show their birthright to expansion,
can be enlarged by thought and action,
can be stuffed and fed as they relax within the sun:
to feed upon the desserts,
with wine according to their taste.

Small endeavours can testify as they build and grow,

as they develop and enlist,
as they search and find.

Small endeavours can be signed in answered prayer,
can be under the management of My Spirit,
can create a feast to which many are invited,
can create a surplus which can feed the hungry and neglected.

Small endeavours can be the influencers of nations,
the creators of the pathways which transfer the wealth,
the builders and the constructors of further opportunities as
associated with both God and man.

Small endeavours note the celebrations brought to their activities within
The Fields of Effort,
Righteousness and Truth."

My Content Study Aid

_____

_____

_____

_____

_____

_____

_____

_____

_____

_____

_____

_____

_____

_____

_____

_____

_____

_____

_____

_____

The Neandertals (2 Tribe Attribute: Friendly)

And I hear The Lord Jesus saying,
"The Neandertals (2) would like to be seen as friends of man,
would like to be made welcome on The Earth,
would like to come out of hiding from their cubbyholes,
would like to be accepted after centuries of misdirections linked
to denials—
for outright lies originate at the highest governmental
security levels of man.

The Neandertals (2) are not vagrants in the common sense,
are not subject to ageing as fast as is known by man,
are not unusual to have lives stretching past a millennium,
are not breathers with lungs as known to man but rather absorbers
via diffusion through the skin—
of carbon dioxide and nitrogen—
as carbohydrates and complex nitrates form the food of life.

The Neandertals (2) are more impervious to injuries causing death than their
human counterparts,
are more impervious to water immersion than the lung-filled;
are more indifferent to the rhythms of the body than
the oxygen dependant.

The Neandertals (2) have very few expenses requiring money,
are self-sufficient in nearly every aspect of their lives,
are quite tolerant of excessive heat and cold when judged by
the temperature zones of man.

The Neandertals (2) avoid the dust storms of The Earth,
avoid the predators of The Earth,
avoid the bright lighting of The Earth.

The Neandertals (2) have no need to sweat,
have no need for digestion,
have no need for waste disposal,
have no need for salt,
have no need to maintain a body fluid to a standard enabling activity.

The Neandertals (2) are fluent in all the tongues of man,
are fluent in all the tongues of Heaven.

The Neandertals (2) attain maturity very quickly,
grow very quickly,
have senses all capable of peak operation soon after birth.

The Neandertals (2) uphold their decision making,

do not stray down paths of unknown investigations,
do neither bribe nor corrupt,
do not have a sense of envy,
never kill just to eliminate,
would rather incapacitate where full recovery is quite viable.

The Neandertals (2) signify their intent by changing colour,
signify their loyalty by remaining silent,
signify their affirmation by clapping in a sequence
easily understood.

The Neandertals (2) do not often jump up and down,
do not often pat and stroke,
do not often cry or laugh.

The Neandertals (2) are serious in their considering,
do not tend to joke,
do not seem to take part in a greeting hand-shake.

The Neandertals (2) are often nervous and 'on edge',
are often stressed when changing colours quickly,
are often pretending to be asleep and unavailable for discussions.

The Neandertals (2) do not like to swing in trees,
do not like to climb to pick the fruit,
do not like to swim in water that is unduly deep.

The Neandertals (2) scatter when surprised,
gather for a forum,
sense the attitudes of the attendees.

The Neandertals (2) have exceptional memories for names,
have superlative facial recognition capabilities,
have spectacular language skills and understanding,
are very rarely seen taking notes to jog a memory.

The Neandertals (2) do not give rise to a friendly gathering,
are serious and inquisitorial by nature,
are withdrawn and difficult to engage in a conversation,
have a body language which is non-committal,
are not prone at all to lie,
tend to remain silent and aloof when faced with disagreement.

The Neandertals (2) can move very fast,
can outstrip a pursuit on foot,
can jump exceeding heights when deemed essential to their freedom,
can call up support very quickly when threatened by a weapon
as held by man.

The Neandertals (2) can evaluate and judge every situation where they may

feel threatened,
will invariably select the option to flee,
will nearly always make good their escape.

The Neandertals (2) cannot be tracked by dogs as they can vary their scent at will—
when dogs become confounded in going round in circles.

The Neandertals (2) have electronic assistance in nearly everything they do.

The Neandertals (2) are best left alone,
should neither be sought nor molested,
should neither be approached nor spoken to from a distance
seemed sufficient,
but in error.

The Neandertals (2) will not seek human assistance.

The Neandertals (2) have weapons of their own which are usually set to incapacitate
rather than to fatally wound even across
a distance deemed suitably safe."

My Content Study Aid

_____

_____

_____

_____

_____

_____

_____

_____

_____

_____

_____

_____

_____

_____

_____

_____

_____

The Neandertals (2a Clan Attribute: Trustworthy)

And I hear The Lord Jesus saying,
"The Neandertals (2a) are tenth rated in threatening behaviour towards man.

The Neandertals (2a) are willing to smoke the pipe of Peace in puffs without
                                        undue encouragement.

The Neandertals (2a) keep their word as if regarded sacred.

The Neandertals (2a) would not correct impressions if mistaken for the first arrivals—
            would be impressed as being thought worthy of the honour.

The Neandertals (2a) like to be standing in support where violence is not the issue,
                        is not the subject of debate;
            where content is not contentious in application,
                        is not malformed as an idea,
                        is not unjust within an out-reach,
                        is not the generator of discontent.

The Neandertals (2a) is the clan which seeks the contracts,
            is the clan who supplies the data which man now loves
                                        to copyright.

The Neandertals (2a) has a working relationship with The Greys:
                    who initially broke the bounds and rules of incursion;
                    on a scouting landing many multiple millennia ago,
                    when caves were not in use as man had not appeared,
                                        to so spread upon The Earth.

It was The Blues who received an inheritance:
        from The Greys who extinguished the life style of the dinosaurs,
                                both the flying and the walking,
                                with their lasers set to annihilation;
        from The Greys who enabled the bedding-in to a pristine environment
                                        filled with life:
                    where the dinosaurs,
                            as apex predators,
                    had been removed from contention,
                            in all their many shapes and sizes,
                with the preservation of their food chains as originally provided.

There is a birthmark on the inside of Neandertals (2a) right wrists:
                    symbolized as an uneven three pointed star,
                        somewhat indistinct and blurred and coloured blue,
                    in a lighter shade of blue than their skin tone.

The Neandertals (2a) prefer to keep this birthmark hidden—

to not reveal the image or the lineage.

This birthmark can be identified,
> when dealing with the blue tribe,
> during encounters for the meeting of their needs..

Now is the end-time of an age.

Now is the call unto a new beginning,
> unto the revelation long kept as a mystery of God,
>> long kept for the first cognizant beings on The Earth,
>>> as they manifested their belief to live and to let live,
>>>> without a threat to one another,
>>> as both travelled through time upon an aligned flagship
>>>> on a voyage of discovery,

>> long kept until man was readied to communicate,
>>> to understand,
>>> to not fear the unknown,
>>> to be honoured by knowing the populating
>>>> history of The Earth.

For through such did these humanoids attain their nationhood:
> as honoured by their standing.

For through such did they forge a relationship with God.

For through such have they protected man from the repercussions:
> arising from his lying failings and the greed within himself;
> while still struggling to overcome his warlike tendencies—
>> as dwelling within his machinations."

My Content Study Aid

_____

_____

_____

_____

_____

_____

_____

_____

_____

The Neandertals (2b Clan Attribute: Interlopers)

And I hear The Lord Jesus saying,
"The Neandertal longevity is also their main and very serious point of weakness,
for it cannot now develop fast reproduction.

The speed of reproduction of The Neandertals is a limiting capability on The Earth,
which so far has placed man in good stead.

Beware of a sign of any intended immigration from their source,
as an enhancing growth factor contributing to their presence.

'Seek and find' is not a simple quest upon The Earth,
demands the resolution of a solution plan as to what to do
when meeting with success,
of ready answers equating to the 'how' and 'why' and 'what' and 'when'
should be the method of approach:
of their encountering in the street,
of their accosting in the street,
of their appearance in the dusk,
in the night,

and in the fullness of the day,
of what is considered wise—
of the surveillance for confirmation wherever they are found;
whether they are teaching,
instructing,
or plotting for the future—
when they may be at work,
at studying,
at home,
or somewhere in between.

Close scrutiny is deserved when encountering the disguises of suspected interlopers
in the presently encountered,
whether dressed from head to foot in Arab feminine attire—
where concentration should be upon the eyes behind the veils,
or a Hoodie in the streets or on the public transport,
where separateness and seated solitude arouses much suspicion,
with the hiding of the facial features,
the wearing of gloves,
or hands as placed in pockets—
in the company of matching the use of narrow footwear—
to hide the sets of fours from the sets of fives:
as an arouser of suspicion.

Likewise is the motorcycle,
with helmet gloves and boots,

ANTHONY A EDDY (SCRIBE)

a favoured way of movement among the populace at large—
where their inherent features are no longer the drawers of undue attention
to that which either 'is' or 'is not'.

The Neandertal (2b) habitational grouping is a giveaway when located and observed as
a colony with activity in the strangest of environments.

The Neandertal (2b) habitational placements can be in the remoteness of ice caves on a
frozen continent,
or dwelling under the sea,
where nets and boats do not tangle in encounters,
with the underwater caves:
excavated for conversion to air pressurized cabins,
as comfit and seclusion are assured as are the transfers in and out.

So also is remoteness valued highly where viewing is nigh impossible,
as distance is measured within the scope of space,
of navigation,
of escape velocities,
puts their existing technology to use on the lady of the night
who now never shows her back,
while others circle to their heart's content.

The Neandertal (2b) combativeness varies with the heating of the seasons,
is at its most intensive in the cold where carbon dioxide is most
easily absorbed and muscles are expanded.

The Neandertal (2b) cold reaction time is much faster than within the warmth.

The Neandertal (2b) senses are at their most acute when within the coldness of
a climate where snow is both evident and permanent.

The Neandertal (2b) love and satisfaction with the cold puts their opponents at
a disadvantage,
where frostbite is a problem which will not go away.

The fracturing of ice poses no threat to their mobility,
have the speed essential to overcome entrapment,
to overcome potential instances of isolation,
to outrun an avalanche of snow,
to skate on ice as if the feet are flying—
with no hindrance existing to acceleration.

The interlopers are at their most dangerous when their ice possessions are
under attack,
when the weather is most threatening,
when earthly communications are at their worst:
in being subjected to interference with the intensive loss of understanding.

The battlefields of The Earth should be selected

both with Wisdom and with preparation,
both with foresight and with understanding,
both with knowledge and with an appreciation
of the enemy's capabilities and range."

My Content Study Aid

_____

_____

_____

_____

_____

_____

_____

_____

_____

_____

_____

_____

_____

_____

_____

_____

_____

_____

_____

_____

_____

_____

_____

_____

_____

The Neandertals (2c Clan Attribute: Compromisers)

And I hear The Lord Jesus saying,
"The Neandertals (2c) do not seek a confrontation which will inevitably reduce
their numbers,
would rather come to a compromise where openness prevails,
with an accommodation reached,
for each other's culture and existence.

So then would each be enabled to reach out together in Peace,
without an armed conflict hiding at the back of every mind.

So then in unity could one share with the other,
where the difference in physicality qualifies,
hinders,
or improves,
the knowledge base of both:
in opening the pathways to all decreed as possible—
with the advantages thereby befalling all upon The Earth.

The Neandertals (2c) are rather unremarkable in being without distinctive skin features
and in complying with their race,
in the lack of distinctive features on their face—
in the absence of a nose where breathing is unknown,
together with a mouth and tongue where absence of both lungs and
stomach contribute to the creation of a face.

Where the eyes could blink a message from the intellect to the 'Unthoughtful',
so communications could proceed among the species,
where the spoken word was,
and is still,
returned over many thousands of centuries from the few 'Unthoughtful',
with knowledge of Neandertal existence,
where the need for ears developed as receivers sensitized in pits upon the hands:
until the thought-lines developed with the capability of the brain,
and blinking became unfashionable unless in an emergency,
where such quickly became important.

The Neandertals (2c) come from an inheritance where there was,
and is,
no need for body hair to preserve the warmth—
either on the head or elsewhere,
no need for clothing other than for decorum in a gathering,
or to indicate a rank with standing,
or when dwelling in a remote ice and frosted enclave:
where temperatures are resolute as minimums are seen as minimums,
with no further leeway warranted nor expected."

The Neandertals (2d Clan Attribute: Morality)

And I hear The Lord Jesus saying,
"The Neandertals (2d) are the oldest of the old,
    have more generations in their history of life,
    are the wisest and most knowledgable,
    are the noble and the royal,
    are the understanders of the progression of life.

The Neandertals (2d) keep the shutters of eternity,
    hold the keys both to time and travel—
    between the star bases of the encircling planets.

The Neandertals (2d) are closely connected to The Will of God,
      to the outpourings of God,
      to acceptance by God,
      to the configuration of the heavens,
      to the sketches of position,
      to the attentiveness implicit in the thought
        processes conducive to eternity.

The Neandertals (2d) are the most robust and circumspect,
    are the honourers of life,
    are the detailers of consideration,
    are the holders of the confidence of God,
    are the protective surrounders of defences,
    are the architects gifted with the foresight of extrapolation.

The Neandertals (2d) are the grandfathers of the universe—
      either in the singular or in the plural,
      depending on the knowledge base—
    are the grandfathers charged with oversight of all given into
        their care,
    are the seekers and the distributors within the approved sight lines
        of God.

The Neandertals (2d) address and comprehend,
    modify and recreate,
    survey and classify,
    enumerate and quantify.

The Neandertals (2d) are the archetypes of heavenly assistance,
    are the assisters with the difficulties,
    are the gatherers of the prayers,
    are the sorters and the reporters,
    are the activators and the deliverers,
    are the inspectors and the verifiers,

are the keepers of the gates,
>> the portals,
>> and the doors.

The Neandertals (2d) are not the evangelists of The Earth,
>> are not destined as the curiosity of zoos,
>> are not intimidated by the evil and the cruel,
>> are not subjugated by the flesh of man.

The Neandertals (2d) are unique among The Neandertal clans,
>> are unique in their acceptance of morality,
>> are unique in their relationship with The Christian God of man,
>> are unique in their callings,
>> are unique in their application of their understanding of
>>> the scope of their Freewill.

The Neandertals (2d) are comfortable in attending and serving,
>> in assisting and visiting,
>> in immersing and cleansing.

The Neandertals (2d) direct the lost,
>> guide the seekers,
>> help the despairing.

The Neandertals (2d) are very rarely seen except by those who are both young at heart
>>> and in their early years—
>> while still unqualified for sitting at the feet of teachers.

The Neandertals (2d) numbering is not a part of progressive numbering steps,
>> are each secure and independent with freedom of expression,
>> are all endorsed by,
>> and familiar with,
>>> the clan and its range of interests and abilities,
>>> its intellectual powers,
>>> its compassion and its foresight—
>> as to the supply of needs where Faith upholds the prayers.

The Neandertals (2d) does a lot of harnessing and applying of resources,
>> of observing with attentiveness,
>> of meetings mixed with greetings.

The Neandertals (2d) has a widening circle of friends within the human race."

My Content Study Aid

_____

_____

The Conquering of Man

And I hear The Lord Jesus saying,
"The conquering of man is at an end.

The conquering of man was completed many centuries ago,
        was completed when Neandertals were thought,
           by current palaeontologists,
                to have gone extinct,
           who gave no thought to the interbreeding factor,
              which preserved most of their racial concepts and
                      intellectual abilities:
                with enlarged brain capacities,
                with their organs still intact,
                with the new progressive shedding of the hair
                      of man from his head.

The conquering of man was a way station of The Lord,
        was preserved in The Written Word,
        was not immediately lost to the knowledge base of the new breed
                      of man,
        was not lost to My People who recorded the factors of significance,
        was lost when the scripture references became confusing through
                      loss of understanding,
        as the priesthood of My People of the tribe of Levi was disbanded
                      in the scattering:
              to not be re-assembled before The Throne of God.

The conquering of man was not crippled by his past absorption:
                into a combined race of intellectual superiority;
                enabled and so qualified to adopt morality via
                      My commandments,
              to so graduate from the raw product to the new
                    potential state of intellectual prowess—
                as built on mental stability,
                  as demonstrated in the art of war,
           to thereby preserve and expand their then current functioning.

The conquering of man saw a sea change in his appearance,
        saw a sea change in his abilities,
        saw a sea change in his social order,
        saw a sea change in his belief structure,
        saw a sea change in his relationships built upon stability,
        saw a sea change in his relationship with God.

The conquering of man slowed down the growth of physical violence,
        removed the need for killing face to face,

took the quest of life to a new stage of honour and of integrity,
with the establishment of kingdoms supporting the
royal households.

The conquering of man saw the adoption of the necessity for Faith,
saw the adoption of the age of chivalry,
saw the challenge presenting through the corruption of the states,
saw the conversion of the agricultural smith into the hammer
of an industrial revolution.

The conquering of man saw him riding a seesaw of decisions as presented by society:
as in a separation of the tiers with firm markers of identity and standing,
as in a captive labour market whereby man learnt the value of exchange—
as his time started to impact on his purse,
whereby the dependency of a family saw their rations and their clothing,
determined through the means outside of their control.

The conquering of man saw him failing to attain his freedom,
saw him controlled by dependancy on the standards as sought
and set by society,
saw the onset of winter with its tests,
saw the coming of the spring with much relief,
saw the suffering at the onset of sickness and disease:
where medicines gave no closure of success,
where hardships brought no pity from the able and the self-contained,
where empty cupboards in the morn stayed the same throughout the day,
where both happiness and education were impossible to achieve
on the basis of relief,
on the basis of the progress of a family into the class above.

The conquering of man saw the water of the stand,
within the boundary declared by God,
as the water in the sand.

The conquering of man was weaned off his previous way of life,
was introduced to better ways of doing things,
to better ways of calculating,
to better ways of manipulating the world in
which he lived.

The conquering of man led to an improvement in his status,
in his thinking,
in his rate of progress in his daily labouring,
in his ability to shorten his workload by the
introduction of new tools and weaponry.

The conquering of man brought understanding:
of how the world at large operated and interacted with his life,

of how his physical rewards could be increased,
of how his social graces could uphold his efforts at relationships,
of how his accrual of wealth,
of animals,
of transport,
would all blend in to a harmonious whole.

The conquering of man grew in leaps and bounds with respect to his mental agility,
as his understanding grew,
as his thinking capability brought its own reward of
an improvement:
in his overall demeanour and his circumstances,
in his particular environment where adjustments
were required,
where the food was changed
and varied,
as the sources came and went throughout the year,
as hunting became more effective,
as fishing became more productive with larger offshore boats,
as fowl were captured for their eggs and meat,
as growth in knowledge and in practise became blended:
into an education from within the drawings on the walls,
to that which eventually merged into the written books of man.

The conquering of man left man with his identity of naming,
but removed him from his pagan viewpoint,
left him with his emotions,
with a new morality,
but enabled the substitution to lead him on an ultimate path
of victory to the moon,
the planets,
and the coming stars beyond.

The conquering of man brought God into the equation of life upon The Earth:
with all which man has achieved within the coaching,
the instructions,
the counselling,
through the history of his acceptance of a discipled walk
with The Living Loving God—
into God's sacrificial sharing and practicality—
in offering man a progressive merging of life within
mortality into life within an eternal destiny of choice.

The conquering of man knows The Freewill of man is alive and active—
either within his spirit or his soul."

The Mouthwash of Man

And I hear The Lord Jesus saying,
"The mouthwash of man often does not achieve its objective,
        often leaves the residues in place,
        often does not bring cleansing to the environment wherein
                it is placed.

The mouthwash of man is tasked for success,
        is not expected to fail,
         knows the expectations,
         knows the desired end result,
         knows where the emphasis is placed.

The mouthwash of man requires a spit to empty,
        requires a spit in the discharging of a mouthful,
        requires a spit in the reviewing of the effort when mixed with
                the result.

The mouthwash of man is designed to gather and eject,
         to remove and vanquish,
         to topple and consign,
         to master and to subjugate,
         to command and to vacate,
         to absorb and to discard,
         to rinse and to change,
         to measure and to destroy:
    the presence in the mouth,
    the presence in the throat,
    the presence of a sojourn which is neither desirable nor tolerated,
        that which is known to have outstayed its welcome,
        to be no longer suffered in its stay of occupation of a mouth.

The mouthwash of man signals the coming of the bath day of the mouth,
        where the scum and clingers-on are given their marching orders:
            for an orderly evacuation,
            for an orderly dispersal in the world at large,
            for an orderly dismissal of unsought attention.

The mouthwash of man removes the stuck and volatile from an interrupted journey:
                not to be completed.

The mouthwash of man searches like a tidal wave into the nooks and crannies,
        sweeps all away in the foam and froth,
        quits all the deposits which have not been appreciated,
           which did not seek permission for their stay,
           which are the interlopers present in a cavern,

which are the picnickers who have settled in
for a feast of choice.

The mouthwash of man misses specificity,
goes for the wash and swiping of the tongue,
goes for the extermination of the odours and the tastes,
goes for those found to be holidaying where they are not welcome,
goes for a replacement,
with a reassurance of a freshened situation,
with the freshening achieved.

The mouthwash of man services both the mouth and the throat,
both with a swish and with a gargle,
where cleansing is the motive for the move,
where cleansing is seen as the remover of the build-up,
where cleansing is foreshadowed by the effort in establishment.

The mouthwash of man gargles to achieve the cleansing of the throat,
gargles for the removal of the build-up of bacteria:
so set to prolong the mischief of disease beyond control,
gargles to restrict the opportunity for the incremental soreness
of the throat.

The mouthwash of man perseveres with repetition;
perseveres to overcome;
perseveres to bring relief;
perseveres to clear the throat;
perseveres to clear the vocal cords;
perseveres to release the vocal cords:
to enable the reaching of the pitch and keys among the notes of aspiration.

The mouthwash of man should not spit out blood,
should not mistreat either the mouth or the throat,
should not be the conveyor of concern,
should not be the overarching enemy handled with much caution,
should not be an inspection process carried to excess.

The mouthwash of man is not a linkage to identity,
is not a clue to self-service,
is not an indicator of an usurper seen at work,
is not the blanketing of an organ held in stress,
is not the pickaxe for a tooth,
is not the rake released upon the lining of the throat.

The mouthwash of man is an assistant used in style,
is an assistant used with experience,
is an assistant bringing measurable results.

The mouthwash of man serves both man at large and the servants as attached to God.

Anthony A Eddy (Scribe)

71

The mouthwash of man assists the personal speaker with a confidence,
assists the singer of the songs,
assists a sore throat calling for relief:
in overcoming an overload of the troubling kind.

The mouthwash of man is the hygiene friend of man when not carried to excess."

My Content Study Aid

_____

_____

_____

_____

_____

_____

_____

_____

_____

_____

_____

_____

_____

_____

_____

_____

_____

_____

_____

_____

_____

_____

_____

_____

_____

The Tempting of Man

And I hear The Lord Jesus saying,
"The tempting of man is alive and as vicious as ever.

The tempting of man is circuitous at best,
                    is round and round the idol worship leading to defeat.

The tempting of man leads a life of danger and of invitation,
                    leads a life where 'I' remains the most important,
                    leads a life where 'forgiveness' is long overdue,
                    leads a life where 'self' should be discarded on the chopping block
                                                                of change:
                                        being completely segregated,
                                        so to permit the inclinations to follow
                                            a life of generosity and love,
                                        within the overflowing will of God.

The tempting of man never polishes the soul of man,
                    never is concerned with the greater good,
                    never indicates the desirability of a change of heart
                            to the beautiful and true,
                            to the magnificent and The Godly,
                            to the hope-filled spread by the keenness of anticipation,
                            to The Committed who know The Love and Care of God:
                                where Faith enables a destiny among the stars of God.

The tempting of man is satisfied by achievement,
                    is satisfied,
                            by completing a circuit of the mountain,
                            by finishing a cycle ride of endurance,
                            by the completing of a jigsaw puzzle with an image cut
                                                        in thousands.

The tempting of man can be in many forms,
                    can be in many flights of fancy,
                    can be in repeating trials of pain and suffering.

The tempting of man can be of a sexual nature,
                    or of holidays abroad;
                    can be careering down a snow slope,
                            or in helming a boat at sea;
                    can be being upended in a drag car,
                            or landing in an emergency on a beach or road;
                    can be stuck on a big dipper,
                            or the extracting of a fish hook,
                                        from where it should not be.

ANTHONY A EDDY (SCRIBE)

The tempting of man can be based upon his wallet,
> when shopping with his eyes,
> when admiring from a distance the polish on a car,
> when at a field day and viewing the tractor of his dreams,
> when in a shop with small ones which are tugging at both hands.

The tempting of man can be affirmed by a spur of the moment decision,
> where pride and satisfaction only last until the morrow,
> where recrimination robs the joy and storage needs do steal the balance,
> > of a resurfaced memory from the youth-time of the past,
> > > as spent on a ride-on mower.

The tempting of man has an objective of ruination,
> has a hidden agenda of downloading trouble;
> has an accident in store where an arm is put at risk;
> has a distraction where the eyes do wander,
> > and the body goes submerged as if a submarine.

The tempting of man can bring some hard learnt lessons:
> can bring regret for the stupidity of the day;
> can bring a bout of laughter in the summer,
> > when memory has softened the icy winter road,
> > which reversed a car journey,
> > > with a 180 salute,
> > > > from when control was lost,
> > at the rebellion of the car.

The tempting of man can vary with the pitch and chase,
> with the bet and the horse ride of a lifetime,
> with the kick and all eyes on the ball,
> as it wandered on its way and skirted both the goal posts,
> > as the whistle blew full-time.

The tempting of man can occur in a restaurant,
> or before a meal at home,
> can occur before a pack of cards,
> or when standing in a jeweller's shop,
> can require a bouquet of flowers to mend a broken fence,
> > and a door which slammed.

The tempting of man,
> when succumbing,
> > is a folly and a fraud—
> > > in the robbing of restraint with the circling of the lure;
> > is a negative not easily forgiven,
> > > when memory is extended for a long bask in the sun,
> > > and drags the meatless bone for company,
> > > which does not assist in the settling of the anger,

as a voice reminds.

The tempting of man can see a slate fully loaded,
        with what should be erased.

The tempting of man can inscribe a time set for erasure,
     can ditch a broken slate,
     can have a new one,
       clean and tidy,
      so presented with a smile and curtsey,
      as the chalk remains within a pocket,
          for another day.

The tempting of man can violate a trust,
     can violate a vow,
     can violate past promises for a life within a future:
         based upon the desertion of the present.

The tempting of man is neither just nor fair,
     is neither honest nor rewarding,
     is neither worthy of significance nor of recompense,
       for past demeanours which arouse suspicion.

The tempting of man is not a function of wealth,
     is not a function of a dare,
     is not a function of a jet.

The tempting of man is a test of character,
     is a trial of strength,
     is a measure of resistance,
     is a testimony of loyalty,
     is an indicator of deep regard for a family and home.

The tempting of man can not survive within surroundings borne of God,
      within surroundings where love is cherished,
      where its neighbours of Truth and Righteousness—
        are valued and encouraged.

The tempting of man withdraws—
     when the love of God is at home;
     and His tasks are plentiful and opened as a flowering of My Spirit;
      where healing is released and active on both
        the prayerful and the prayers:
        with the answering of God."

Anthony A Eddy (Scribe)

The Neandertals (3 Tribe Attribute: Survivors)

And I hear The Lord Jesus saying,
"The Neandertals (3) are static in their development,
                are in a survival state,
                are not a threat to man,
                have knowledge from a great distance,
                are willing to drip-feed their knowledge base to man,
                are willing to assist in man's development,
                are willing to oversee man's technical advances,
                are willing to share according to man's scale of Wisdom,
                are not willing to share beyond man's commitment to control.

The Neandertals (3) are quite considerate and careful in their release of data,
                in their release of how to construct the circuitry,
                in their release of processes requiring intimate understanding.

The Neandertals (3) never are present at the starting of a war.

The Neandertals (3) are scarce to find upon a battlefield.

The Neandertals (3) prefer to operate by remote control.

The Neandertals (3) are careful to avoid—
                the high level spies,
                the dealers in the weaponry,
                the destroyers of the balances on the battlefields in time.

The Neandertals (3) brought with them the skillset to repair and to amend,
                to construct and to build,
                to secure and to sustain,
      the technologies which enable reaching into the star belts of the galaxies,
      the technologies which accompany travelling both through space and time,
      the technologies overcoming gravity and mass to no longer be a hindrance either
                to speed or to destination,
      the technologies which bring understanding to black holes with their counterparts,
                to string theory impacting on the
                bending waves of gravity—
          with the resolution of light so its speed no longer limits:
                as the star ways become open.

The Neandertals (3) have secrets never before dreamt of on The Earth,
                have used their knowledge in fairness and with Wisdom—
                to bring man's development forward in leaps and bounds.

The Neandertals (3) were sent on a oneway trip,
                are not desirous of ever returning home,
                know the way with the ability,
                but are missing the will to perform:

to carryout the preparations required to surpass the speed of light by
many powers,
to plot co-ordinates so to survive penetration of the light wave
colour boundaries on the journey home.

The Neandertals (3) are comfortable where they are,
have their needs confirmed with ready availability,
are content wherein they dwell.

The Neandertals (3) do not clash with angels,
know them very well,
meet and mingle with The Blessings of God,
as both groups of beings attend together to both the welfare and
the triumph of man as man becomes
eternal in the fellowship of God."

My Content Study Aid

_____
_____
_____
_____
_____
_____
_____
_____
_____
_____
_____
_____
_____
_____
_____
_____
_____
_____
_____
_____
_____
_____

The Dithering of Man

And I hear The Lord Jesus saying,
"The dithering of man wastes the end-time of man,
　　　　　　wastes the time to exercise the given Freewill of man,
　　　　　　wastes the time to check on the theory of evolution,
　　　　the theory without the support of science,
　　　　the theory now laid bare upon a bed without the sheets or blankets
　　　　　　　　　　or the willingness,
　　　　　to attempt to make the bed within which the theory must survive,
　　　　　　　　with the critical fragments which are missing,
　　　　　　　which common sense and inspection say do not exist,
　　　　　　　　　in failure to support reality,
　　　　as science turns again to gather in the support of creation as the
　　　　　　　　　　ultimate means,
　　　　of explanation for that which exists in nature when it shouldn't.

The dithering of man hesitates and avoids,
　　　　　　prolongs and hopes for the best,
　　　　　examines and shakes his head in disappointment of the
　　　　　　　　　　contrary evidence—
　　　　which now shouts aloud that which was previously rejected—
　　　　in awaiting confirmation of the assumptions and the presumed
　　　　　　　　　to all fall in place.

The dithering of man now sees before his very eyes the stupidity of his past acceptance,
　　　　　　　the stupidity of his guesswork,
　　　　　　the stupidity of bending difficulties
　　　　　　　　　into a network,
　　　　where relegations of non-compliance are posted to
　　　　　　　　　the 'Too-hard basket',
　　　　being left for others to resolve the details of the difficulties which,
　　　　　　　　　taken collectively,
　　　　were the breakers of the theorem into the many pieces arising from:
　　　　　　　　the compilers of the 'want-to-be's;
　　　　　　　　the deniers of the critical;
　　　　　　　　the affirmers of the ridiculous;
　　　　　　　　the shouters of the false beliefs;
　　　　　　　as both truthful and permanent in application.

The dithering of man now pours doubt upon a certainty assumed,
　　　　　　now corrects the papers exposed throughout the night,
　　　　　　now attempts to despatch the recalls where enthusiasm
　　　　　　　　　bred signatures,
　　　　　　upon the errors and the suppositions,
　　　　　that Truth was being overseen to be carried forth:

to have treatises returned from the peers who disagreed right
at the start,
now not hesitant to have smirks upon their faces,
with hands placed in the pockets,
as the 'told-you-so's' increased in numbers never seen before,
among the cacophony created by the shouters down in
ignorance now regretted,
as The Bible relevance was called into question along with the
existence of God.

The dithering of man brings no credit to assertions,
now seen as false,
brings no credit to the declarations and the oaths,
now seen as based on ignorance,
brings no credit to the followers and the hangers-on,
who believed what they were told—
to so readily join the throngs of claimants,
stating that they knew what they were being asked to affirm
as The Truth,
under the false premise that common sense was the guideline
for the testing:
when it failed the outflow of reliability.

The dithering of man is an excise in non-conformity,
is an exercise of false evaluations,
is an exercise of manipulation to maintain the logic inherent in
the errors running wild.

The dithering of man sears the hearts of man with apologies to God,
with repentance for the lies stretched to insinuate
The Truth,
with Grace requested to erase the stupidity of the
joiners of the herd with all it trampled under-foot.

The dithering of man now deserves the tears which should be upon his face—
the repelling of the stupid and untrue—
the rejecting as accompanied by the blasphemy
of God.

The dithering of man has marked a point in history,
has vilified the sacred and the holy,
has denied their very God who loved and died upon The Cross
of Sacrifice,
as The New Covenant of Grace was birthed especially for
the access:
to an eternity within the fellowship of God.

The dithering of man requires forgiveness for The Freewill which teachers misapplied,

for the downplaying of The Bible,
for the uplifting of the emphasis upon the cell of life
postured as the instigator being the sole cause of life:
happening solely by being rested within the mud,
without the spark of life,
where salt water was an agent of sterility—
free from the bacteria and the germs of much more recent date.

The dithering of man lacked agreement to set the stage for the conversion:
of a 'would-be' theorem into fact,
had a chorus crying out for confirmation,
while the thinkers stood aside in asking to be convinced—
that which was claimed to be born out by
the endeavours,
as the semblances inspected.

The dithering of man could not carry:
the conditions as imposed,
the conditions as prevailed,
the conditions raising eyebrows,
the conditions which silenced the tongues of man;
could not carry the fast reversal of the changes;
could not carry all the varied instances—
dependent on the resolving of the chicken or the egg;
which needed to be simultaneous in application so life could continue,
with the prepared and the working:
so interlinked details could keep to the critical timing;
within reciprocating actions remaining in step;
within the oversight;
within the planning;
arising solely from within The Will of God."

My Content Study Aid

_____

_____

_____

_____

_____

_____

_____

_____

The Veracity of Man

And I hear The Lord Jesus saying,
"The veracity of man is an aspect of his character,
     is an aspect of his system of belief,
    is an aspect closely associated with an evaluation of what is right or wrong.

The veracity of man is a view taken on his character,
     is a view which balances a life,
    is a view on which hangs a belief in showcasing a destiny within eternity.

The veracity of man is critical to his progression within mortality,
     is critical to clarify confusion,
     is critical for an accurate summation of the whole.

The veracity of man is hindered by doubt,
     is hindered by a bad example,
     is hindered by a poor decision by an umpire,
     is hindered by the flesh without access to the heart of man.

The veracity of man is promulgated on a 'say-so',
     is promoted as it stands or falls,
     is spoken with intent when ignorance is absent,
     is spoken with deceit when knowledge breeds a lie:
          which remains uncorrected.

The veracity of man is tested by the machines of man,
     is tested by the reactions of man,
     is tested by the 'recall' of man,
     is tested by the testimonies of man,
     is tested under oath which does not forswear the lie.

The veracity of man is obvious to The Spirit,
     is obvious to The Son,
     is obvious to The Father.

The veracity of man is essential to morality,
     is essential in the presence of commitment to The Lord of The Cross,
     is essential to adoption into The Family of God.

The veracity of man should be solidified by man as if in concrete:
       when checking on the fate assigned to Lucifer,
       when lying in The Throne Room of God.

The veracity of man should reach out in honesty,
     should not enhance the given,
     should not entice by the ropes of exaggeration.

The veracity of man is dependent on the absence of the lie,

ANTHONY A EDDY (SCRIBE)

is dependent on The Seeking for The Truth,
is dependent on the establishment of The Truth:
>as the precursor of Righteousness,
>as the precursor of Peace,
>as the precursor of a sought walk with God.

The veracity of man should be staunch and stand firm,
>should be active and accepted,
>should be verifiable and permanent.

The veracity of man should be able to be upheld,
>should be as a light within a beacon,
>should be as a foghorn hidden in the fog,
>should be as a safe harbour able to be found:
>>with an anchorage secure in the night.

The veracity of man impacts in many aspects on the life of man.

The veracity of man is tested in a war,
>is suspect in a war,
>is doubtful in a war,
>is likely to be the first casualty of war:
>>where The Truth is too expensive;
>>as it becomes the reason for an extending loss of life.

The veracity of man is harmed by the media,
>is harmed by a chain of linkage,
>is harmed by degeneration into the rumour of the day.

The veracity of man is scattered among the sheep and the goats,
>the thoughtful and the thoughtless,
>the eager and the bored.

The veracity of man partially separates the runners from the chasing and the fleeing,
>separates the audible from the silent,
>separates the calling from the jeering.

The veracity of man highlights the goals of man,
>highlights the progress of man,
>highlights the achievements of man.

The veracity of man discards the failures with the lies,
>discards the antagonistic who become the aggressors on the hunt,
discards the likelihood of failure when matching up the possibility of success:
>>which makes a life outstanding with a race well run.

The veracity of man knows The Truth when it is heard as encirclement completes,
>rings familiar bells within the head,
>turns on the lights of acquiescence to requests as received.

The veracity of man is checked as if a learner of a walk within The Field
of Righteousness.

The veracity of man is not requiring of the over-indulgence of man,
is nor requiring of the garnering of a surplus,
is not requiring of a meeting on a corner,
is not requiring of a single Truth stretched unto the breaking point.

The veracity of man is not a function of the temperature,
is not a function of feelings,
is not a function of what passes in an envelope,
or via a cacophony of wires and fibres of the day.

The veracity of man seeks and holds to The Truth,
takes pride and comfort in dealing with The Truth,
poses neither stupidity nor charm on recalling the backgrounding imagination:
to the imposing of a lie regardless of its colour of perception.

The veracity of man boldly seeks his becoming trustworthy,
leans on others for support,
relies on others for their witness of confirmation and agreement.

The veracity of man is as a ball rotating inside a head on its way to being polished,
determined to escape out through the mouth,
determined to be heard by other ears within proximity,
determined to say what was initially believed to be The Truth:
when Wisdom suggested otherwise,
as time supplied the evidence.

The veracity of man holds man to a club of veraciousness and hunger,
of seeking and searching,
of ultimate responsibility
for all that issues from the mouth;
for all that issues from the hands and fingers;
for the tainting and the colouring;
for the perspective
as mixed with the reality of The Truth,
as set free to pass through the lips of man,
as released to escape into the landscape,
and the living space of man."

My Content Study Aid

_____

_____

_____

The Pressure of Comparison

And I hear The Lord Jesus saying,
"The pressure of comparison can impart a load of dread—
> where hope and trust are both under stress.

The pressure of comparison can seize the cogs of meshing,
> can slip the belts on drive shafts,
> can still the movement due the motors as the switches
>> are thrown:
>> in the absence of control.

The pressure of comparison assesses like with like,
> assesses the mismatch with the forbidden,
> assesses the champion against the also-rans.

The pressure of comparison encloses the failure with the stalwart,
> places the prisoner in shared accommodation,
> sizes up the holidaymakers of the bungalows with the
>> sandhill loungers of the tents.

The pressure of comparison examines in some detail,
> tests and finds what's lacking,
> serves in discovery of the manners as brought to bear
>> with relevance,
> looks at the mess created where apologies are missing,
>> where the kernel is not cracked.

The pressure of comparison loads the nerves of justice and of fairness,
> discards the bringers of complaints,
> slices and spits out the embittered and pragmatic,
>> where theory is not committed to the stewpot of success.

The pressure of comparison touches those with deep concern,
> those with imagination running wild,
>> those where the script is smudged by haste and speed
>>> as made without a rest.

The pressure of comparison does not create the singular of opinions on a time frame
>> of the circular,
> does not fire up emotion where drudgery is long drawn out
>> without reprieve,
> does not lend a hand to the injured or the casual where
>> disaster is waiting just out of sight.

The pressure of comparison affects the accuracy supposedly present:
>> in the process of decision-making.

The pressure of comparison sometimes follows flights of fancy,

has lost touch with reality,
            is focussing on being carried by the lies.

The pressure of comparison is leading to dropped stitches in the knitting,
            is calling forth errors in computations,
            is nailing down the give and take as floorboards start
                                                to creak.

The pressure of comparison should be sustained by common sense,
                should be built upon the justified wherein Freewill does
                                apply in handling an application,
                should be researched in the time of preparation
                        where accidents are eliminated,
                        where clocks are not the surveyors of progress,
                        where the intelligent and the competent can
                                    reach for their tools of trade,
                        with the minimum of fuss and confrontation.

The pressure of comparison cannot square a corner,
                cannot create an arch,
                cannot erect a chair on which anyone wants to sit.

The pressure of comparison watches trust fall by the wayside,
                watches measurements confused by continual checking,
                watches the saw marks failing in their consistency
                                        of approach.

The pressure of comparison achieves very little except the wasting of time and the
                                    doubtful finish on the job.

The pressure of comparison strikes a pose of unfortunate disdain,
                strikes a pose where uncertainty is evident,
                strikes a pose where satisfaction with the finished effort
                                    appears to be in doubt.

The pressure of comparison is not a seeking process of the best,
                is not a seeking process of the worst,
                is a seeking process based on relativity,
                        where the average and the mean both outstrip supply.

The pressure of comparison jumps in leaps and bounds,
                assumes and leaves behind,
                whistles and is heading for the lead.

The pressure of comparison sets the headings for the naïve and the wondering,
                    for the friend of the architect and the banishing of favours,
                    for the cyclone of activity and the wastrel in the chair,
                                    where sleep has overcome.

The pressure of comparison compares the bakers of the cakes,

the brewers of the beers,
the shapers of the midriffs,
the furnishers of the homes,
the leaders of opinion within the daily news.

The pressure of comparison sets dancers in a row,
sets singers in a chorus,
sets drummers in their seats.

The pressure of comparison sees the numbering of results,
the listing of the standings,
the growth within a market,
the trips upon the ships,
the visiting of locations favoured by the chains,
the hopping of the islands where competition draws
the feet to action,
the bodies to investigate,
while the mouths are busy tasting,
as the brains long to sleep.

The pressure of comparison is often on the wallet,
is often on the deal,
is often on the specials which fly both to and fro.

The pressure of comparison has very little feedback,
has very little integrity of purpose,
has low sensitivity to the results of downright lies—
where honesty goes to the last in line,
where Truth exists nowhere in the lineup,
where price cuts as encountered today only partially offset,
the price increases imposed yesterday,
at the close of business.

The pressure of comparison is not within The Will of God,
is widespread among the flesh of man,
is presented with the bargains of deductions,
as publicised ad nauseam on The TV channels seen in homes,
where bickering with similarity are the signposts of collusion,
as the prices change in unison,
for the benefit of the vendors to the transport fleets
of commerce,
to the individual with a car where fill-ups are very rare,
as the wallet and the purse are examined carefully to discover
the litres to be ordered in the struggle to make ends meet:
as the robber barons dodge their customers on the forecourts,
with pricing always ending in a nine as they take the last razoo."

The Heating of The Ice

And I hear The Lord Jesus saying,
"The heating of the ice depends upon its speed and its intensity,
                depends upon its volume and its temperature,
                depends upon the insulation,
                depends upon the installation,
                depends upon the hesitation.

The heating of the ice listens for the cracking,
                pays attention to the calving,
                stays a distance from the wave.

The heating of the ice destroys a footprint in the snow,
                destroys the foundation of the frosting,
                destroys the walk of penquins to and from the sea.

The heating of the ice is a welcome to the killer whales,
                is a signature attracting the dolphins,
                    the walruses,
                    and seals.

The heating of the ice puts the penquins' life at risk when fishing out at sea,
                          when returning to their young.

The heating of the ice melts and reduces the ice cap on the lands,
                melts and reduces the ice cap on the seas.

The heating of the ice does not seek the help of a volcano nor a thermal vent,
                rather seeks the basking in the sun,
                mixed with the shedding of the weight.

The heating of the ice drains the slush down to the lowest point,
                drains the slush to form a stream,
                    a river:
                    a barrier worth evading;
              until the tumbling of the ice becomes transfixed in silence;
              as the death wish of the ice is pawned off unto the sliding,
              with the splashing and the dumping to the sea.

The heating of the ice encounters an effective multiplier:
                when bordering the sea,
                when dealing with the warming currents,
               when dealing with the energy in a turgid wave,
               when attacked in depth by the warmth within the wind—
                          from the seaward side.

The heating of the ice occurs quite readily with the creation of an iceberg:
                which is freed to sail away,

to where the climes are warmer,
with the limiting of its life,
by the violence of the ocean.

The heating of the ice surrenders for a melting moment to the pressure,
reseals to re-adhere as soon as the pressure is relaxed.

The heating of the ice brings contraction to the fore,
brings puddles pooling on the surface,
brings drainage conquering a path to freedom:
with the final blending in an amalgamation.

The heating of the ice absorbs all the heat on offer,
absorbs the radiance of the sun and the good tidings of the lady
of the night.

The heating of the ice is not carried to an excess,
knows the benefits to be found within stability,
knows the disasters where glaciers collapse,
to shatter the orderliness of the watershed:
with an attack of saturated ice flowing at a downhill speed.

The heating of the ice can assist a body needing cooling,
can give rise to a tinkle in a glass pending disappearance,
can result in melting on demand when flavoured,
and posted to the mouth:
to so rest upon the tongue.

The heating of the ice is the farewell to a wintry morn:
where temperatures have no safety limit;
are treated to a night-time freeze of dew;
where the sensitive foliage of life has its cells all ruptured;
to be beyond the possibility of repair—
as offered by the rising sun.

The heating of the ice farewells the rims around the puddles,
the sheets across the puddles,
the solidness which can only be shattered with a
childhood stomp:
which sounds as if a breaking pane of glass.

The heating of the ice enables ball games to commence,
prevents the slips and slides,
stops the skates and slithers,
where the ice was still too thin:
for safety from a fall.

The heating of the ice is frowned on by the fisherman returning from the sea,
where ice sustains the present presentation of the catch:

on the journey to the shore.

The heating of the ice can frustrate a refrigerator:

when switched to a mode enforcing a defrost,
can be a disaster as an unexpected interruption,
to the power supply—
turns the ice into meltwater,
and the food into the rubbish tin.

The heating of the ice can be an adventure going sour:
a ski trip falling flat as the wind delivers heat to the threatened icicles and snow.

The heating of the ice can keep the curlers watching anxiously,
for the conditions to improve:
where the curling may not be able to continue,
where the curling may need to wait for a final team resolution:
in another winter's time,
where the ice is sufficient to stand the tests—
of both the curling and the skating.

The heating of the ice brings acceptance of the warmth of spring,
bids farewell to the winter's clear starlit nights,
of frosts with ice and freezing temperatures:
which can damage the tender and the beautiful,
the tended and ignored,
the frost prone and the frost bitten,
which presents a frosted stem with its blackened leaves.

The heating of the ice exposes the death of the bringers of disease,
unto the plants susceptible,
the kills of the grubs and worms who were still exposed:
either under leaves or remained too shallow in the soil of God.

The heating of the ice recalls the seasoning of God:
of how He fulfils His purposes for His creations:
to so fulfil and participate in the cycles of life:
within the very time frames as set and known by God."

My Content Study Aid

_____

_____

_____

_____

_____

The Neandertals (3a Clan Attribute: U.V., Shyness)

And I hear The Lord Jesus saying,
"The Neandertals (3a) is eighth rated in threatening behaviour towards man.

The Neandertals (3a) are reluctant to approach man in the daylight,
have better eyesight in the dark.

The Neandertals (3a) would rather have matters of interest to them sorted out by others.

The Neandertals (3a) are ready to co-operate with man when there is a
joint understanding of what is both desired and planned.

The Neandertals (3a) scream and cavort at unexpected times:
when lacks of understanding act as seizures within their motivational forces,
as they try 'to simplify' such difficulties.

This does not sign of impending violence,
does not violate a time frame ruled by peacefulness,
does not threaten the external,
only signs the internal dissipation over a short passing of time
of 10-20 seconds,
before there is a visible recovery of control.

The constancy of differing contacts,
is fraught with the unknown,
as coming face to face,
makes The Neandertal humanoid just as anxious as The Human.

It is most unwise to carry weapons when meeting with these Neandertals:
as any portable weaponry of man is of very little use,
when entering into a confrontation,
where loss of face is at stake on both sides of the weapon.

This can unnecessarily be seen to raise the tensions already presenting as
an impasse:
which always proves difficult to resolve.

All Neandertals can be identified by submitting them to Ultraviolet radiation:
when regardless of their physical abilities and properties,
will have their exposed skin surfaces fluoresce;
in the colour of a greenish hue,
which cannot be mistaken.

Beware and watch your step.

They are all antagonistic and self-conscious when in the presence of the
wavelengths of Ultraviolet light.

The chemistry within their body frames—

is both highly complex and mature;
neither follows a cycle of oxygen dependency,
nor of 'scrubbing' in oxygen regeneration processes;
is dependent on the presence of Carbon Dioxide and Nitrogen;
in a skin cellular diffusion process,
which is more porous than the human envelope with hairs.

Carbon Dioxide dependency is a sign of the presence both of the components,
and the presence of either fire or/and life,
on the distant sites where their survival and development—
were appropriate to the environment,
where such a culture could first be possible—
to so later flourish.

When The Neandertals are seen mining,
it is nearly always for magnesium carbonate as Magnesite or
calcium carbonate such as Limestone,
so carbon dioxide can be captured—
to later be released in quantity,
or placed in storage for enrichment of The Earthly Air.

A body is operational when their multiple body temperature sensors,
as located in each body,
collectively re-adjust to meld,
to equate,
with their surroundings—
which will be no longer be out of balance,
so diffusion may proceed at a stable steady rate."

My Content Study Aid

_____
_____
_____
_____
_____
_____
_____
_____
_____
_____
_____

The Neandertals (3b Clan Attribute: Dwindling)

And I hear The Lord Jesus saying,
"The Neandertal lines are still not particularly numerous,
              are developing in numbers quite slowly,
              are mostly a threat unto themselves,
                      as the clan generations are seen to fight within themselves,
                              for supremacy within a local area—
                              much as the mobs in Chicago in the1930's.

The Neandertal lines are varied in their makeup from the top of their flight
                              to the lowest of the menial,
                      charged with the mechanics of maintenance and circulations.

The Neandertals (3b) colour,
              mottled in browns and greys,
                      is despised by the others,
                              those still in contact,
                      who regard this as a sign of impurity within a makeup,
                              no longer attributed as a uniform worth wearing.

      For mottling has become of great importance as an issue,
                              within the terms of evaluation,
                      in driving down their popularity among those,
                              within The Neandertal clans,
                              with whom they still have contact.

The Neandertals (3b) quest in life is one of insurgency against the leadership instated,
      has resulted in dwindling numbers not being replaced,
                      for they have now dropped below one hundred,
                      from a start of several thousand many centuries ago.

      For numbers have been slashed by others,
                              as attrition,
                              with rebellion,
              has drained and exposed their weaknesses from which they will not,
                                      are not,
                              either willing or able to reject or change."

My Content Study Aid

_____

_____

_____

_____

The Neandertals (3c Clan Attribute: Generous)

And I hear The Lord Jesus saying,
"The Neandertals (3c) are friendly with man,
           are friendly and helpful,
           are friendly and thoughtful,
           are friendly and the teachers of their up-to-date technology,
                      which is active and deployed.

The Neandertals (3c) is not afraid of man;
           has a belief in The God of man;
           has assemblies known to praise and worship;
           has motivations based on Godly morals;
           applies the sanctity of God unto a life with a birthright to survive,
              to be cared for until maturity,
                to be taught and supported with the needs of life,
                  while immature and still dependent on assistance:
                  backed with caring and explanations,
    as to 'why' and 'when' and 'what' and 'where' and 'who' and 'whom' and 'how',
              are met along the way—
              where 'yes' and 'no' are not meaningful replies.

The Neandertals (3c) mixes freely with man,
           treats him as an equal,
           treats him as if he is yet to reach maturity,
           treats him as a tongue speaker:
   where thought reading is still only in development in installations of great rarity;
   where the installer is mostly still unknown or ignored even when 'lead-ins' are
                              on offer.

The Neandertals (3c) shares and shares alike,
           is not a hoarder of the desirable,
           is not a seeker of a fragment,
           is not an absconder with a 'treasure',
           is not party to a theft,
           is not a beggar of a favour,
           is not a sitter on a fence.

The Neandertals (3c) would explain the intricacies inherent in their technology,
           have great difficulty to explain the background to a concept:
              when the words of relevance are still waiting to be birthed;
           seek to explain the physical by relying:
              on the reality of a 'show and do',
              on the 'demonstrate and practise',
              on the experiencing of results and how they are obtained.

ANTHONY A EDDY (SCRIBE)

The Neandertals (3c) has the tools to make and mend,
                    has the ability to manufacture,
                    has completion detailing The Seeking of the required resources,
                    has the knowledge base which leads unto success,
                    has the force which melts and melds,
                    has the light beams which do not waver,
                                        which can annihilate,
                                        which can target,
                                        which can win an argument,
                                        which can win a war:
                    when opposition is at its strongest and discussions do find
                                        the best ways of assault.

The Neandertals(3c) scope and scan their surroundings,
                    peruse the thoughtful and the planned,
                    calibrate and calculate equipment under their control,
                    beckon and encourage the participation of man:
                                        in all this clan seeks to do and visit.

The Neandertals (3c) does not kill unless trapped in defence,
                    unless exposed to an ambush,
                    unless threatened by technology under other
                                        clans' control,
                    unless in a situation where death is being
                                witnessed and a ceasefire is not possible.

The Neandertals (3c) is generous when taking stock,
                    is generous when needs are great,
                    is generous when surpluses are present,
                    is generous when questioned,
                    is generous when demonstrating,
                    is generous when handing out their knowledge with
                                reference to weapons."

My Content Study Aid

_____

_____

_____

_____

_____

_____

_____

The Neandertal of Choice

And I hear The Lord Jesus saying,
"The Neandertal of choice does not go round in circles,
            does not secrete and hide,
            does not withdraw into surroundings born of mystery and of lies.

The Neandertal of choice stays within a meaningful displaying of the attributes,
            stays within the boundaries of the enclave,
            stays within the area as allocated for existence,
            stays and grows and dies within the calling of the clan.

The Neandertal of choice has similar values to those as held by man,
            has similar concepts where The Truth is valued,
            has similar beliefs accepted as have been taught attentively
                           and with understanding.

The Neandertal of choice is not a bully boy,
            is not a signatory to the practising of deceit,
            is not a castaway yearning to go home.

The Neandertal of choice is happy wherein a dwelling place has been found,
                  to be established over centuries.

The Neandertal of choice has much to say for ears to hear when meeting
                    as acquaintances.

The Neandertal of choice summarises and expands upon request:
              of which is condensed and deserving of much thought.

The Neandertal of choice can be selected from a choice,
            can be refined from a sublist of particularity.

The Neandertal of choice can be a friend for life,
            can be a friend which grieves at each loss as it happens,
            can be a friend which will guard and care for an inheritance;
                  from the birthright of a will,
            can be a friend in depth as a trustee of a trust:
              where integrity is just as important as Honesty and Truth;
              when required within the bounds of RRighteousness.

The Neandertal of choice can be a friend for life,
            can be the guide on a lifeboat to the stars,
            can be at home with a few circles round The Earth.

The Neandertal of choice will visit and relate,
            will host and be polite,
            will greet and welcome strangers into a home of talent,
                  and an ability with saucers.

ANTHONY A EDDY (SCRIBE)

95

The Neandertal of choice needs a general update on a public image:
a general update on the concepts of those considered to be among
the weird and the extinct,
for the last forty thousand years according to
the estimates of man;
a general update on the presentability of the considerate and the kind,
the voyagers and discoverers;
a general update on the outposts of intelligence across the universe,
which was braved by the pioneers of discovery and of settlement;
where the darkness was chaperoned by the light accompanied
by warmth:
with the fitments sheltering the life forms of success.

The Neandertal of choice has encountered and enthused with:
the wanderers as searching for the sanctuaries;
the wanderers at large within the seas;
the wanderers within the atmospheres of planets
with their suns.

The Neandertal of choice can enliven a winter's night beside a fire,
with the retelling of adventures built on voyaging through life,
and all which was encountered.

The Neandertal of choice has a myriad of tales to recount,
has a life style cloaked in mystery,
has a reticence to come into the fullness of the day.

The Neandertal of choice signals to the trusting,
signals to the trustworthy,
signals to the trusted and the true.

The Neandertal of choice knows The Faith installed and active,
knows The Faith accruing and as charted,
knows The Faith expanding and enhancing the viewing of The Earth.

The Neandertal of choice sees and understands the changes initiated by man,
the changes brought about by sole consideration of man's own Freewill,
the changes as wrought without due consideration of the damage,
as brought about by the footprints of man.

The Neandertal of choice sees the footprints of man upon the waters of The Earth,
sees the footprints of man from the valleys to the mountaintops,
sees the footprints of man stretching from shore to shore across
the landscapes of The Earth.

The Neandertal of choice sees the trail of damage,
sees the trail of rape and plunder,
sees the trail of selfishness and greed:
arising from the footprints of man.

The Neandertal of choice sees man squeeze his body into wherever it will fit upon
or in The Earth.

The Neandertal of choice should take the hand of man,
should instruct with The Wisdom born of ages,
should lead and develop so the footprint remains invisible,
so the footprint does no harm,
so the footprint does not cause a bursting at the seams,
so the footprint leaves yesterday today and tomorrow
without the need to change.

The Neandertal of choice can bring forth a revolution in the attitudes of man,
to the way he rushes in,
to the way he departs and forsakes,
to the way vested with very little thought,
with very little attention to the details,
with very little concern for the problems
about to fall upon the heads of man.

The Neandertal of choice can be a key performer,
can be a key instructor,
can be a key insulator from the brazen or the frenzied:
with their attacks upon The Earth.

The Neandertal of choice can arise and make a difference:
of benefit to all life upon The Earth.

My Content Study Aid

_____

_____

_____

_____

_____

_____

_____

_____

_____

_____

_____

_____

The Neandertals (3d Clan Attribute: Rescuers)

And I hear The Lord Jesus saying,
"The Neandertals (3d) have false noses,
                 pencilled in eyebrows,
                 with false eyelashes.

The Neandertals (3d) have a foreign sounding way of speaking English,
                 which they find difficult to maintain—
                 when long sentences appear within a conversation.

     Conversations usually are limited to the key points,
                 sounding a little like the rattle of a machine gun,
                 in their forceful emitting of their missives—
                 which can stop and restart in the middle of the sentences.

The Neandertals (3d) mouths are oval and toothless,
                 carry very foreshortened lips which only seal around the edges:
                 where a mouth's only use is for the production of 'a voice'—
                 which is found tiring to maintain for an extended conversation.

The Neandertals (3d)'s variably coloured eyes are fitted with compensating
                             contact lenses—
     which meet the human standards of 'normality' when speaking face to face.

The Neandertals (3d) are often consistently seen wearing headgear to disguise their lack
                             of hair,
         are at home in a variety of hats,
         feel comfortable in turbans,
                 scarves,
         or hats based and shaped on felt.

     Straw hats are common in the summer,
                 with a chin strap to keep them in position,
                       when the wind becomes an enemy:
                       by attempting an unmasking.

The Neandertals (3d) only very rarely are seen publicly in clusters at a distance.

     Nearly always are seen as solitary figures leaning forward,
                       with a slight stoop,
         which hides their facial features in the evening—
         where the lighting is not seen as intrusive and disclosing of a being:
                 giving a somewhat unusual impression,
                     with the arousing of curiosity,
                     as occasioned by a stare.
     Young children are unembarrassed by such,
     sometimes approaching Neandertals (3d) for a better closeup look.

The Neandertals (3d) have no negatives of attitude,
    are positive and conservative,
    are happy and content,
    are joyous and in beat with the jubilation of the dance.

The Neandertals (3d) witness the crashing and the surging of a wave upon
    the defences of the shore front,
       of the breakwater confident of success,
       of the piers protruding far offshore with
         instructions to so tame the sea,
       of the mole which wraps its arms around the sea
        and quietens all to calmness and serenity
         within the harbour in its charge.
The Neandertals (3d) reach out and rescues,
    stops in answer to a call for help,
    search back and forth until eyes alight upon the lost or floundering.

The Neandertals (3d) testify of lives lived within The Fields of Truth and Righteousness,
    of lives sustained by integrity of purpose,
    of lives surmounting obstacles as they review The Field
        of Peace.

The Neandertals (3d) shine within the lighting umbrella of God in action:
    of calling out to man—
    with an offer of eternity—
    with an offer of adoption into a very special family—
    with an offer of inheritance which impacts on a life,
        to so be glorified by God."

My Content Study Aid

_____

_____

_____

_____

_____

_____

_____

_____

_____

_____

The Neandertals (4 Tribe Attribute: Dimensioners)

And I hear The Lord Jesus saying,
"The Neandertals (4) have no respect for elders,
        have no respect for mishaps,
        have no respect for breakages;
           sympathy is neither a trait they know nor would admire in others.

The Neandertals (4) only trust in their own self-dependency,
        are not enthusiastic in discussing others' home-grown technology,
        do not accept The Neandertals (4) can be dislodged from the highest
           mountain top whereon such as their technology is
                seen to dwell as the most deserving case.

The Neandertals (4) seek to furnish their own comfort,
        do not like cracks in their facades,
        seek to bind into an homogenous whole:
                where holes are not permitted;
                where water is not admitted—
                    to a structure with interiors.

The Neandertals (4) know the solutions arising from many earthly problems,
        know the answers to all of man's diseases,
        know their understanding of their surroundings,
                in the widest sense,
              is of great interest to man,
        know their capability to fly from here to there upon demand;
           to transport across distances as measured by man in light years:
           yet remaining unavailable;
           for man to paw what is within his reach—
        as if a child investigating something remaining close at hand.

The Neandertals (4) are not yet the masters of the universe—
                taken as a complex whole—
        yet are climbing up the ladder for that within their
                knowledge levels.

The Neandertals (4) know travel within dimensions way beyond the four registered
                  with man:
        where each dimension encloses its own universe:
        which is not easily escaped while retaining the
           methodology enabling a journey of reversal.

The Neandertals (4) hold the keys to time,
        can manipulate it freely,
        can freeze or hold it stationery while travel can occur.

      The passage of time can be speeded up,

can jump and suspend,
can vibrate and release,
can be unhitched from mass,
can be used to move the data to extremely distant destinations
where the location parameters with their co-ordinates are set and known;
as reconstruction of the data is assured without error.

The Neandertals (4) verify their lifestyles of discovery,
rarely depart before knowledge is complete and anchored
as understood,
rarely offer more than they gain,
tend to share their knowledge which they regard as out of time for
the local recipients;
and now of little value to the future needs of The Neandertals (4).

The Neandertals (4) can read the thought patterns of man directly from their brains,
can impose thought patterns on the brains of man of which he has
yet to learn control.

The Neandertals (4) converse at a level much higher than known by man within
his mortality.

The Neandertals (4) deal with thought transference as if an every day event.

There is very little need to write what is obvious to all when with the ability
to be a relay station—
to all who can tune into the patterning where mass does not exist:
as data rules both the day and the night of those who think,
who can transfer,
who can receive:
the data beyond the speeds imaginable by man;
as he still struggles with the speed of light.

The Neandertals (4) seek a destiny where knowledge has no bounds,
where sifting and sorting is instantly available,
where creating and advancing
is not limited to libraries,
is not carried by the readers and the writers,
but rather by the relay centres—
who report on all they do within their gloves,
on their journey through the mortal barriers of man,
into the homelands of their God."

My Content Study Aid

The Cruising of Control

And I hear The Lord Jesus saying,
"The cruising of control speaks of very few adjustments required on a flight,
                speaks of an automated navigation with accurate destination
                        co-ordinates at the base loadings of a journey,
              speaks of a system of checks and balances without a need for
                    tweaking the resolution of a landing site,
                        once established near the target zone,
              speaks of the tweak imposed on the downdraft regulator as the
                    flight goes into land with accuracy and aplomb.

The cruising of control does not require manual supervision,
              has warning systems galore calling for attention which include
                    situations previously experienced:
         of the shielding from the star dust,
         of shielding from the spatial radiation,
         of the hesitation of a sensor in the switching to alternatives,
         of movement unexplained,
         of disturbances encountered in the flight path,
         of circumstances where an astral body approaches in an
                  exposure creating risk—
        as the flight vacuum approaches the release of 'the jump',
        as prepared and held in readiness,
        as any threats to either life or to security are left and
                 cannot follow,
        as progression far outstrips all entities still in ignorance
              of the ultimate technology,
        enabling travel 'jumps' within the galaxies unhindered by
              the speed of light.

The cruising of control travels the pathways to the stars,
        where their satellites in orbit may radiate the signposts
              of distant life,
       which may still be in their outreach mode,
       awaiting to be read from a destiny not yet plotted,
       nor allocated an identifier within the spatial travel system.

The cruising of control is difficult to picture to destinations
            for which there are no flight plans,
            for which the flight plans were destroyed,
            for which no return flights were required upon
               the radar screens of crews.

The cruising of control was vested in the nearby localities suitable for bases,
        if replenishment is needed or replacement is required.

The bases out of the reach of man,
  out of the sight of man:
  are located on the rear side of the tidal mistress of The Earth,
                where mischief is afoot as man,
                    as short term visitors,
        established the woman of the skies is equipped with an echo
            which she should not have,
            which speaks of hollowness where there should not be,
            which speaks of construction on a scale of grandeur,
            which speaks of habitation in an environment of
                        planned invisibility;
  are located on the satellite of the sun man has named for war,
                where underground burrowing is endemic,
      with the entrance sites disguised both by depth and by the shadowing,
      with entry on the near vertical faces of the chasms and the craters,
      where a war was fought with those who attempted to follow on behind,
      with the intent to overtake and to establish dominance;
  are located on The Earth buried in the southernmost land of ice
                        and snow,
      where sea-serviced life abounds,
      where visitors are rare,
      where visitors carry their insulation with them,
      where aggregation in small colonies of discovery and cross-security
                    of tenure under time:
              with the emphasis on day and night—
          satisfies the survival instinct with the calls to bases,
                    on the foreign shores,
          from where accumulates the freight as timed
                        for despatch;
  are located under water where the caves are created within the
                    positioning of solitude,
          where the coming and the going is covered by
                        the night,
          where they are complete within their air bubbles
                as drawing from the water,
                    kept at a distance,
            yet treated as a friend of protection.

The cruising of control is automated and stands alone,
          is silent and extremely swift,
          puts the sea crafts and the aircrafts of man to the shame of
              centuries in the development of noise with size.

The cruising of control has gravity assist,
          rides the waves of gravity in open space,
                as if the surfboards on the sea waves of The Earth,

rides the waves of gravity as the data waves of transformation,
the data waves of reformation,
the data waves of reconfiguration,
the data waves as conjoined to be
carried in the absence of mass,
the data waves as the conveyancers
of energy,
across and through and over the gravity waves as the feeders of
the universe,
in compliance within the gravity fields of God.

The cruising of control is not a tiger seen roaming in a cage,
is not an elephant straining for release,
is not a mole burrowing in need.

The cruising of control is the apex of the mode for intergalactic travel,
turns the many multiple light year distances as calculated by man,
into the seconds of release where co-ordinates are a pre-requisite,
as an accurate reference among the star belts of eternity—
in the universes filled with wonder,
with the right to travel as a visitor with God.

The cruising of control on the grand scale of epochs is not available:
within the mindset or the ability of the mortality of man,
is not in line with man's physical design of mass,
is not in line with the body of man to withstand galactic acceleration,
is not in line with The Will of God."

My Content Study Aid

_____

_____

_____

_____

_____

_____

_____

_____

_____

_____

_____

The Cloaking of Man

And I hear The Lord Jesus saying,
"The cloaking of man is progression through the twilight zone,
               is progression through a zone of violence and attack,
               is progression through the hammers and the swords,
               is progression through the robberies and thefts,
               is progression through the bobbies on their bikes,
               is progression through the industrial chaos,
                    where far from everyone was better off,
                    where a revolution stuffed the pockets of the factory owners,
                         but not the ones upon the floors.

The cloaking of man is involved in making people invisible within their needs,
               when a shout only instals an echo,
               when a cry for help only reaches the unsympathetic,
                    who quickly cross to the other side,
                    or pretend they did not hear.

The cloaking of man masks the individuality of man,
               masks the colours of his birth,
               masks the colours of his preference,
               masks the colours of his feelings amid the trials of the day and night.

The cloaking of man is designed to serve up anonymity,
               is designed to remove the conspicuous and the outlandish,
                    the careless and the carefree,
                    the bloated and the extended.

The cloaking of man whispers in restraint,
               rejoices in conformity,
               apologises for a look-alike,
               disturbs the gay and the rejoicing.

The cloaking of man verges on the bold,
               retracts into a safety shell of black,
               shatters the coverings which scream a call to be noticed,
       clutches at the straws which can overcome within the field of prowess,
                   which can withstand the criticism of failure to comply,
                   which can suffer in silence the breaking of a heart.

The cloaking of man shrivels the spirit of man striving for access to The Light,
               enlarges a soul within the bounds of secrecy as a master of rebellion.

The cloaking of man simulates the drab and dreary,
               simulates approval of the second-hand materials,
               simulates the passer-by who neither nods nor sees a smile directed
                        at his face.

The cloaking of man speaks of subservience enforced,
        speaks of hope dismissed as irrelevant,
                as incapable of fulfilment,
                as no longer on the table for selection
                        as an attractive choice.

The cloaking of man compels the tunnels to become deeper,
        the light to be made dimmer,
        the voices to be hushed,
        the eyes to be partially closed:
            so offence is neither given nor noticed from wherein
                the corner in which he rests.

The cloaking of man holds the secrets close to his heart,
        does not share to manipulate,
        is not a whistler of a tune,
        is not a participant in joyousness nor the jollity of the laugh.

The cloaking of man fits well the cloak he wears,
        fits well into the drabness of his dress,
        fits well into the attributes associated with a saturnine outlook
                and display.

The cloaking of man yields very little in the way of pleasure,
        yields very little with appeal to others,
        yields very little by way of greetings,
            of openness,
            or of a welcoming invitation to visit,
                to partake,
            to share a meal to be set upon a table.

The cloaking of man speaks of a lone wolf trudging,
        speaks of a lone wolf alone and set in his ways,
        speaks of a lone wolf without an admitted need for companionship,
                for conversation,
        or for sitting before a fire well stoked and supplying all the warmth,
                as due on a wet and wintry night:
            where the rain attacks the glass assisted by the wind.

The cloaking of man is the hider of desires,
        is the denier of acknowledgements,
        is the segregator of the injuries from the platitudes at large.

The cloaking of man does not bother with the mirrors,
        has no use for reflections,
        has no desire to see what he has become—
      except for an odd reflective glimpse from a shop window in defiance:
      as he turns from the minuscule distraction and lurches on his way.

The cloaking of man speaks of secrecy in restraint,
> speaks of secrecy unyielding,
> speaks of secrecy defended,
> speaks of secrecy unencumbered,
> speaks of secrecy desired,
> speaks of secrecy achieved.

The cloaking of man seeks yet does not find,
> searches yet does not complete the link,
> hunts yet does not capture that for which he sought.

The cloaking of man surrounds himself in darkness where light is very scarce,
> surrounds himself with entities best suited to the darkness,
> surrounds himself with memories encompassing the darkness.

The cloaking of man mistrusts the light as an antagonist of the darkness,
> mistrusts the light based on the evidence of the darkness,
> mistrusts the light for hastening the removal of the darkness.

The cloaking of man is comfortable within the darkness,
> is accepting of what it offers,
> is following a progression into the depths of darkness,
> is not eager to retrace his steps back into the twilight.

The cloaking of man is like walking a railway line to Hell,
> where the branch lines are very rare and far apart,
> where the indicators on the track are always green,
> with the forward motion unimpeded:
> while reverse is nigh impossible.

The cloaking of man is a study in indigestion,
> is a study of intelligence misapplied,
> is a study of a lost cause seeking:
> yet unwilling to correct the leading of his Freewill into
> the caverns of despair."

My Content Study Aid

_____

_____

_____

_____

_____

_____

The Senses of Man

And I hear The Lord Jesus saying,
"The senses of man need to be enlarged for a home within eternity.

The senses of man need a wider field of application,
                need a wider field of operation,
                need a wider field where 'Thought' overcomes the deficit in
                        the communication gap.

The senses of man determine his interaction with his surroundings,
                his interaction with other living entities,
                his interaction with the mortals of the past,
                    the present and the future—
                        within the clocks as set by man.

The senses of man impart knowledge to react with Wisdom,
              impart the ability to measure and adjust,
              impart the concepts of space and height,
              impart the ability to negotiate the dimensions of familiarity.

The senses of man can grow in effectiveness,
              can sort the differences as limited,
              can inspect all the eye can see until curvature presents the horizon
                        scale to man.

The senses of man need to be sharpened and extended,
              need to be focused and conveying,
              need to be assimilating and exploring,
              need to be accommodating and perceiving,
              need to be prepared and applied—
                for the future servicing of man within his newly found Freedom.

The senses of man can be improved and refined,
              can be magnified and resolving,
              can be sustaining and discovering.

The senses of man have many fields where the gates are swinging open for man
                        to gambol:
                in the fields of joy and happiness,
                in the fields of interest and refinement,
                in the fields of rest and relaxation,
                in the fields of thought and communication.

The senses of man have yet to seek and find all which The Loving God has set:
              as an introductory menu nor previously encountered.

The senses of man will vibrate with the fresh pulses of conceptual advances.
The senses of man will shake in acceptance as fresh inputs are received and absorbed.

The senses of man will thrust and parry with the incoming loading of the patterns
yet to become familiar.

The senses of man need to learn:
to sift and sort,
to store and recall,
to apply and circulate,
on much grander scales.

The senses of man are to be refined and scoped,
are to be sensitized and fitted with the bins of allocation,
are to be nurtured in extensions and fitted-out with modelling,
are to be set upon the steps leading to advancement and authority,
are to be placed within the courts of judgment and of resolving justice.

The senses of man are being sourced for updates,
are being qualified to think outside the square,
are being prepared to think where others have not gone:
in seeking their solutions for the voices in the clamouring.

The senses of man can square the accounts outstanding;
with all aspects of the lives to be encountered—
across the whole gamut of injustice as weighted with emotion.

The senses of man can view and form opinions which are both valid and correcting.

The senses of man can circumscribe and delete the obvious,
can carry to so discard the obnoxious,
can investigate with queries until answers fit the facts,
can identify the lies where deceit is weighed and balanced,
can circumvent the voluble with a concentration on the record
of relevancy.

The senses of man are valuable to God,
are comforting to man;
are seated by God,
are positioned for man;
are heard in action by God,
are evaluating man;
are adding to the records of God,
are resolving the injustices incurred by man.

The senses of man operate in the presence of My Spirit,
operate in the subservience to demons;
operate in the welfare of man within The Will of God,
operate within the captivity of Satan—
where the downward path steepens over time;
operate with a flowering of his spirit in companionship with God,
operate with the onset of darkness—

as constraint is strengthened on the approaching of the gates of hell.

The senses of man govern his selection as measured by commitment.

The senses of man function either within the approval heights of God,
or within the satisfactory depths of Satan.

The senses of man should be sensitive to the fragrance of My Spirit in covering,
in bringing together,
all aspects of His deeds of favour,
with His operating calls for the flow of miracles and wonders:
before the prayer needs as held in association with,
the expectant faces of man.

The senses of man are set to accommodate the needs of man,
when invited for adoption into The Family of God:
there to dwell in The Garden of Superlatives—
where both choice and grandeur prevail;
beyond the boundaries of both time and space."

My Content Study Aid

_____

_____

_____

_____

_____

_____

_____

_____

_____

_____

_____

_____

_____

_____

_____

_____

_____

_____

_____

The Sniffing of A Dog

And I hear The Lord Jesus saying,
"The sniffing of a dog varies with the location of the dog.

The sniffing of a dog varies with the inbound scent,
>   varies with the outbound scent.

The sniffing of a dog identifies and assesses,
>   stores and remembers,
>   locks-in and reacts,
>   lays the groundwork for the tableau of his surroundings.

The sniffing of a dog knows and follows,
>   tracks in holding to a similarity,
>   frequents and acknowledges where the freshest scent is found.

The sniffing of a dog shows and tells,
>   uncovers and discloses,
>   acts and recovers.

The sniffing of a dog follows the highway of the scent to the destination as built
>   over time.

The sniffing of a dog is a guide unto an escape route,
>   is a guide unto a hidden package,
>   is a guide unto the separation of the scented when mingling in
>   a crowd.

The sniffing of a dog is at ease beside the leader,
>   is at ease when in a time of rest or partaking of a meal,
>   is at ease when tethered to a kennel,
>   is active when restricted on a leash and presented with an
>   interesting source.

The sniffing of a dog is observed very carefully,
>   is not retarded from moving in the desired direction,
>   is not checked and held unless the scent has led to a recovery
>   requiring care and caution.

The sniffing of a dog is a telltale of interest to the dog,
>   is the prior encouragement of a rabbit crossing over from a park,
>   or a cat on the night watch prowl going up and down a street.

The sniffing of a dog can lose the stale and tired,
>   can lose the encircling and the misinterpreted,
>   can lose the track,
>   when placed within the water course which washes all away,
>   when leading through a rain storm which gradually destroys.

ANTHONY A EDDY (SCRIBE)

111

The sniffing of a dog can find a home where he is valued,
                                        taught and trained,
                        where he has earnt the honouring for his capabilities—
                                        in servicing the needs of man.

The sniffing of a dog can do what man cannot,
                        can place a scent upon a nose and follow where it goes,
                        can establish which is which;
                                        with the highlighting of a choice,
                        can select a kennel full of scents carried in his base load:
                          to locate one hiding in a selection where it should not be,
                          to locate a scent at rest as it waits for the due use of the contents.

The sniffing of a dog can be meaningful or meaningless,
                        can be productive or a waste of time,
                        can produce the goods or end up empty handed when encountering
                                        a blank.

The sniffing of a dog learns the scents required to be found as a pathway to reward.

The sniffing of a dog does not turn up its nose,
                        recognises the potential of every single sniff.

The sniffing of a dog is related to its partnership with man,
                        is an assistant in the maintaining of the law,
                        is an acknowledged expert in the signalling of 'a find'.

The sniffing of a dog is not a noisy operation,
                        does not involve a bark,
                        just comes with a wagging of a tail and the taking of a seat.

The sniffing of a dog is accurate in identifying 'the drop' of yesterday—
                        when hidden among the crowd of the unobservant and uncaring.

The sniffing of a dog enables justice to prevail,
                        enables motives to be confiscated,
                        enables the sought to be apprehended—
                                        without undue delay.

The sniffing of a dog enjoys the victory of the hunt,
                                        doesn't want to stop,
                        enjoys all aspects of the chase,
                                        awaits for the reward.

The sniffing of a dog does not mind 'the call to arms',
                        does not mind the lack of uniform,
                        does not mind the flourishing of guns or knives.

The sniffing of a dog loves companionship to go and do,
                        loves the catching of a snare before it traps and hurts—

those with interests in the drugdoms of both the day and
night at large.

The sniffing of a dog is not the onset of a cold,
is rather a confirmation of his love for his selected job,
of his love for where he's asked to go,
of his fondness for his handler,
of his contentment in sniffing out success
with the affirmation—
of a pat upon the back and an eagerness
for more."

My Content Study Aid

_____
_____
_____
_____
_____
_____
_____
_____
_____
_____
_____
_____
_____
_____
_____
_____
_____
_____
_____
_____
_____
_____
_____

The Secreting of Actions

And I hear The Lord Jesus saying,
"The secreting of actions impacts on a nation,
                puts security under test,
                puts fear of discovery allied to the lies,
                puts The Truth into the trash can,
                puts misinformation to the fore,
                puts intelligence at risk.

The secreting of actions creates political correctness in the speech,
                of many deemed to have authority to lie,
                to use the excuse in promoting 'misinformation':
                will not call it what it is,
                the lying to a nation.

The secreting of actions build one lie upon another,
                creates a chain in waiting,
                with fear of being toppled by a 'whistle blower',
                in readiness for an eventual exposure of The Truth.

The secreting of actions attempts to hide the illegitimate,
                the questionable together with the outright acts of warfare,
                in the crossing of frontiers,
                with the infringing of the sovereignties of nations,
                whether by land by sea or by air.

The secreting of actions can be initiated by a 'mole',
                can be prolonged by resistance,
                can be ignored by the media,
                can be forbidden by the law of the land,
                can be approved by the selective schedules of authority:
                associated with the nation's military and/or the secret services.

The secreting of actions may have a short or a long term effect,
                may deprive families of family members,
                may shatter hopes and expectations,
                may change regimes in toppling despots with the threats,
             in toppling the shouting heads of states busy with the building:
                of their favoured weapons viewed as undesirable possessions,
                with prevention as the cure.

The secreting of actions magnifies deception,
                hollows out the trustworthiness,
                stores up the reaction of recrimination,
                spreads the disease of dissatisfaction among the status quo.

The secreting of actions requires the secrets to be named,

requires the secrets to be identified,
requires the secrets to be established as definitively out of reach.

The secreting of actions sets up the targets for discovery,
sets up the targets worth the money,
sets up the targets for the spies,
the bribers and the hackers,
the thieves and the traitors,
sets up the targets for the cameras,
the set pieces for the copiers—
when supervision leaves its post and opportunity exists.

The secreting of actions create denials not believed,
create statements with their doubts,
create mysteries awaiting resolution for the
unanswered questions:
with the technologies and the microphones enhancing the methods of detection,
and the transporting of the details.

The secreting of actions is not limited to nations perceived as 'enemies of the state',
are also applied to 'friends',
independent of a classification,
when secrets are known to be withheld.

The secreting of actions can see a roundabout in action:
a friend of an enemy may not bother with protection,
may have it there bundled up and casually presented:
in perceived readiness for uplifting or downloading—
as a presented golden opportunity which cannot be passed up.

The secreting of actions often fall from honeyed lips,
often fall when wallets are opened,
often fall when a camera is present,
often fall when a microphone is live,
often meet with disclosure at the turning of an agent.

The secreting of actions has been a spy game through the ages—
since secrets were first kept and deemed to be valuable:
when others tried to wrest them from their resting place
in safes.

The secreting of actions are more easily discovered in the middle of disturbance.

The secreting of actions yield to duplication and to resignation,
yield to alcohol and drugs,
yield to pain and suffering,
yield to blackmail and to hostages,
yield to pillow talk and bribery,
yield to force of arms with a known location.

ANTHONY A EDDY (SCRIBE)

The secreting of actions can have discovery despatched and submitted,
   can have discovery processed and communicated,
   can have discovery deliberately accessible:
    where misinformation carries the weight of deceit,
    where clues are made available so suspicions are confirmed.

The secreting of actions can be the subject of social faux pas,
      when the tongue becomes voluble,
       as a party gathers strength,
      when a tongue is heard to slip.

The secreting of actions can have an army of protectors,
   can have an army held at bay,
   can have an army with the scent of blood which opens up
        the night.

The secreting of actions can cause an injection in an arm,
   can cause the opening of the field of torture,
   can cause the sound of a running tap.

The secreting of actions can cause a sleepless night or two or three or four,
     in the presence of the spotlight,
     in the presence of much sound.

The secreting of actions are sometimes not worth the effort of the secreting,
   are mostly already known and so pretense at secreting
      does nothing—
    but prolong the space and time of guardianship.

The secreting of actions,
   from the viewpoint of God,
     is seen as nothing but a joke,
    where smoke and mirrors are employed and silence
      is the norm."

My Content Study Aid

_____

_____

_____

_____

_____

_____

_____

The Neandertals (4a Clan Attribute: Terrorists)

And I hear The Lord Jesus saying,
"The Neandertals (4a) are first rated in their terror tactics against man.

The Neandertals (4a) sign The Muslim originated Pacts with the condition they
be hidden,
so their terror reign on the world may continue unabated,
may continue without undue interruption,
may continue with effectiveness,
may satisfy their thirst for violence without the risk of exposure,
may be concealed in camouflage as suited to their tastes,
as they secrete themselves abroad in daylight and at dusk,
within The Muslim burkas as such plot and plan,
with their identities unconfirmed,
while placing the emphasis on their female characteristics.

The Neandertals (4a) are concerned with setting the stage of life with being
the sole survivors:
so inheriting the efforts of the others.

No other Neandertal Variants will object,
if this variant species is destroyed by man,
as everyone is threatened,
regardless of relationship.

The Neandertals (4a) have a brownish hued skin,
with splotches of light green—
which appears somewhat as if a chameleon at rest.

The Neandertals (4a) camouflage well within the visual landscapes of The Earth until
movement is detected.
Lumps and bumps,
just under the surface of their skin,
are where the diffusion centres convert the energy sources:
from gases into the saturating of the adjoining tissues,
on which muscles are dependent—
when flexibility is geared to specific tasks.

The Neandertals (4a) do not like static electricity to arc through their bodies:
when it seeks to earth,
do not like warm water as it requires delay while seeking
heat compatibility,
do not like to bathe in heated water,
do not like to share all which they hold in ownership—
which is dubious at best,
do not like to go too long without a kill;

like to see the blood pumping before the hearts are stilled,
like to be expectant of success when pursuing a
wounded animal,
slowly succumbing to its loss of blood.

For these Neandertals (4a) Variants have no furnishing of a respected morality,
are solely driven by their ethics,
in guiding their motivations,
within their equivalent concepts of 'I' and 'me' and 'mine'.

Beware of their high intensity laser capability,
for it is light and mobile,
being easily carried and recharged,
to be deadly in effect at quite amazing distances,
which outdistance a rifle with its ammunition,
in both sighting and accuracy,
prior to taking down a target with excellent straight-line visibility.

There is no sign of cannibalism.

There is no sign of harvesting.

There is no sign of storing their kills.

There is no sign of moving their kills once dead,
but just leaving them wherever they may fall—
for the eventual discovery by a meat-eating feeder on the carrion.

The Neandertals (4a) social life is still centred on their attitudes to 'I' and 'me'
and 'mine',
as evidenced by their solo separation for amusements or games,
where each is the only participant,
to sit alone within a nest of comfort—
where study is the norm.

Arguments between them are basically unknown,
for knowledge,
blended with their Wisdom,
ensures everyone is on the same page with counselling,
when alternatives although obvious as to a likely course of action,
are easily selected when open to discussion.

The Neandertals (4a) do not like:
to be forced to move according to the temperature of the seasons,
to be centred in the heat within the tropics,
to be placed in a rainy season,
to be subjected to weather patterns where the wind force off
the sea can dismantle and destroy.

The Neandertals (4a) do not mind the temperate,

would much prefer the cold.

The Neandertals (4a) do not bother with a lineage of relatives,
> as they act as both the alpha and omega in their lines of descent.

The Neandertals (4a) Variants have neither sense of happiness nor of rest and Peace.

The Neandertals (4a) are only concerned with not being the last,
> so queuing is unknown,
> as is the sense of an appointment in the longevity of a lifetime,
> and sex is not an issue in any shape or form for the birthright
> of a hermaphrodite."

My Content Study Aid

_____

_____

_____

_____

_____

_____

_____

_____

_____

_____

_____

_____

_____

_____

_____

_____

_____

_____

_____

_____

_____

The Minefields of Man

And I hear The Lord Jesus saying,
"The minefields of man leave little to the imagination.

The minefields of man are the trademarks of the devil,
       are the residues of war,
       are the dropouts from recovery,
       are the leftovers without a home,
       are the maulers of discovery,
       are the shatterers of hopes,
       are the removers of the limbs,
       are the disfigurers of man,
       are the cripplers of a walk,
       are the handicappers of humanity,
       are the killers of the dreams,
       are the residues of war still fighting battles long after the referee
         has blown his whistle as the linesmen calmly walk away,
           without a backwards glance,
      to leave the minefield still to operate in war mode—
      in a takedown of the foolish and the intrepid,
        the young and the ignorant,
        the caring and the concerned:
      with the orphans still at play with a rolling ball.

The minefields of man are not limited to the leftovers of military ordnance,
       are not limited to what has been and gone,
        to what has come and stayed,
        to what was set in waiting as if rat traps sent
           on missions—
        to capture either as the wounded or the dead.

The minefields of man do not need an explosion to verify their presence,
       do not need the sign of blood to bring such to attention,
       do not need to damage the physicality of life when the mental
          with the spiritual also lie at risk.

The minefields of man can develop or diminish within the life of man,
       can be set upon a hill where the reach is very great,
       can be set within a valley where danger still exists as enshrouded
           in the fog.

The minefields of man require the attention of man where an explosion is internal:
         does no damage to the shell.

The minefields of man can arise from an argument of ignorance:
        with conflict brought of gender.

The minefields of man can arise from the complexity of finance:
>> where understanding is incomplete.

The minefields of man can arise from the lack of time:
>> where shortage clips the wings.

The minefields of man can arise from an obstruction:
>> which grows and multiplies the difficulties
>> in reaching a conclusion.

The minefields of man can arise from thought patterns:
>> as if stranded in a maze—
>> where the way forward is far from certain.

The minefields of man can be embroiled in commerce:
>> from which it is difficult to escape once the superannuation comes
>> into play—
>> with multiplying contributions designed as offers of entrapment.

The minefields of man vary with the seasons,
>> vary with the climate,
>> vary with the environment:
>> where calls and shouts are seekers of attention,
>> as conflicts gather their latent heads of steam.

The minefields of man are densest in the centre,
>> can be skated around with ease,
>> can open up and share,
>> can foreclose and deprive.

The minefields of man can change their colour and their influence,
>> their loyalty and their makeup,
>> their consistency and their variability.

The minefields of man can shove and push,
>> can trip and stumble,
>> can restrict and limit:
>> the end-time aspirations of man.

The minefields of man can stink and draw recriminations:
>> from the imperious and the thoughtless;
>> can harbour and not release:
>> the possibilities due for exploration;
>> can deepen and absorb:
>> the usefulness of toys both in their
>> application and enjoyment;
>> can delay and whither the finances of man:
>> while his attention is distracted;
>> can threaten to destroy the love life of man:

when attention becomes misplaced;
can harness and frustrate:
the efforts thought to bring success;
can hide and decline the opportunities:
which approach out of the fog and then retreat back into the mist,
where all are out of reach.

The minefields of man test and redistribute:
the residues of the wealth of man;
evaluate and balance the activities arising from Freewill:
which impact on a destiny;
mixup and confuse a memory still with a structured set:
waiting to be called into the action of the day.

The minefields of man surround the wayward and the recalcitrant:
drag them down into the mire,
where there is a struggle to break free,
as impacts shear off slices from the whole.

The minefields of man are not of God,
are not of His intent,
are neither of His gifting nor His counselling,
are not emanating from the university of God,
are neither carrying nor imparting to man The Wisdom of his God.

The minefields of man are bred in the dwelling place of despair,
are floated to the surface,
are inserted to cause strife.

The minefields of man materialise as the nets sent forth for the entrapment of man—
to hinder and to misdirect,
to retard and to drift,
to confuse and to delay:
in order to restrict assimilation of 'Righteousness' and 'Truth'
into residence within the character of man.

The minefields of man can be discarded and thrown out
before they have become a matter of concern,
before they have become embedded in a soul,
before they have become determinants of actions
affecting a longterm destiny of choice.

The minefields of man do neither bring happiness nor certainty to man,
do neither expand the cherished nor the loved within a protocol
of hate,
do not advance a Freewill commitment to God:
when the minefields of man are permitted to run amok—
in both thought and deed."

Neandertals (4b Clan Attribute: Lasers)

And I hear The Lord Jesus saying,
"The Neandertals,
     as a collective whole,
    have not previously encountered the effect of mirrors on a Laser weapon
           of commandment.

The Neandertals (4b) laser as a ranging weapon well outflanks the mobile weaponry
          of man,
    makes it nigh impossible for man to approach within the ranging ability,
         of his guns or fire hoses,
        so they can be brought to bear.

The defence of man,
    the attacks of man,
    is to clad his weaponry in mirrors so such can approach
        The Neandertals (4b) positions,
      without being threatened by prior destruction.

The tanks of man,
    with all encompassing mirrors,
    and fire emitters at the ready set for firing,
       over,
       or to the side,
      from behind protective mirrors,
    will create a travelling monster they have not encountered before,
      except as unclothed on the battlefields of man—
   where such were not a threat envisioned to be encountered,
     when to be clothed and readied for attack or defence,
       against The Neandertals's Laser mastery.

The mirrors become empowered:
    when such are driven through the mountings and their settings,
     so the laser beams can be refracted back,
     along the close proximity to the initial path as travelled,
   to so constrain The Neandertals (4b) sense of mobility and advancement:
      in an ordered array as used by them for centuries.

The international threat to man is the attack capabilities of
      the unidentified flying objects:
      which have both death beams—
 as per the lasers at a much higher intensity than those as personal mobiles,
 and attraction beams which lift into the air when gravity is neutralised by
     super high frequency magnetic forces—
      which blankets the ground.

So to await the whirlpool of wind which lifts objects in the focussed centre
straight into an open sliding trapdoor,
with a vent above,
with the trapdoor closing swiftly upon an entry of mass which then breaks,
and then permits the restoration of a beam:
enclosing that which has been received as tribute to
The Neandertals (4b) technology;
when operating that which is still a mystery to man."

My Content Study Aid

_____

_____

_____

_____

_____

_____

_____

_____

_____

_____

_____

_____

_____

_____

_____

_____

_____

_____

_____

_____

_____

_____

_____

_____

Neandertals (4c Clan Attribute: Individualists)

And I hear The Lord Jesus saying,
"The Neandertals (4c) as a clan is lacking in organisation,
        is a clan where the socially fragmented accumulate,
           where the independent and self-aggrandisement
                thinkers venture to interpolate,
           where the emphasis is solely on the individual,
           where modesty and honour are not subjects
                of importance,
           where cleanliness and presentation are ignored for
              scores of years without undue reflection,
           where fastidiousness is unknown,
           where the wayward and the self-elected govern the
              stance of centuries,
           where the larger size is a hindrance to their movements,
           where brush and bush and jungle form a habitat
              of random occupation,
           where the cold and the medium are preferences of
              choice when dwelling in a city.

The Neandertals (4c) are not permitted to pilot their discs of oversight,
        sometimes accompany others when extra muscle is required,
        sometimes help in searches for what is deemed desirable,
        sometimes mine and excavate when resources of much interest
              are discovered—
           so to be then laid bare in preparation.

The Neandertals (4c) do not have fitness routines,
        do not have excessive appetites,
        do not settle for the greatest comfort,
        do not unnecessarily eject and then takeover as an acquisition,
        do not manifest an appetite for drugs,
        do not become addicted to the addictions as widespread in man.

The Neandertals (4c) are slow in waking up—
        have sleeping periods of resting for days or weeks or months,
        leave sentries on watch at the nesting place,
        place armed guards on duty if there is a threat seen likely to develop:
           lifestyles with shortened expectations.

The Neandertals (4c) chase intruders away with generators of lights and sounds,
        rarely resort to violence,
        even more rarely permit discovery or intrusion of a habitative area:
           when leading to reports which will require an evacuation.

The Neandertals (4c) do not welcome strangers in as 'friends',

do neither offer 'food' nor lodgings to a lost or exploring traveller,
do not make such welcome in an interview to determine risk.

The Neandertals (4c) will investigate and manipulate,
will antagonize for reactions,
will assess motives and behaviour,
will ensure their habitat is not the subject of a random discovery,
is not often left open to the sky,
is not often 'stumbled upon' by the hitchhikers
or the trampers—
from a sight perspective as seen from a walk along a trail.

The Neandertals (4c) are a law unto themselves,
are a law aimed below that of their compatriots,
are a law where gratitude is extremely rare,
where healings are extremely slow,
where unforgiveness is alive and well—
does not dwell in an unknown morality.

The Neandertals (4c) is a place where lawyers gather,
is a place where arguments are loved,
where conflict is encouraged,
where hurts can be inflicted,
where hunger can be generated deliberately as rations
are made 'scarce'.

The Neandertals (4c) have little capacity for mercy,
have little interest in Grace,
will not behave in practice as did 'The Good Samaritan'."

My Content Study Aid

_____

_____

_____

_____

_____

_____

_____

_____

_____

_____

The Roundabouts of Man

And I hear The Lord Jesus saying,
"The roundabouts of man sees him passing 'Go' many many times,
    when within a lifetime lived in casualness with carelessness.

The roundabouts of man carry him without complaint,
    carry him in completions of encirclement,
    carry him where no effort is required so life replays repeatedly:
    without a single sign of progress in the scaling of the heights,
        known as achievable by man.

The roundabouts of man glide very smoothly to always come to a halt
        at the same position.

The roundabouts of man wait for a fresh attempt to board,
    start to move until boredom enters on the scene,
    and man is deposited exactly back where he began.

The roundabouts of man take and give no tickets,
    take-up the time of man,
    do not teach the outcome.

The roundabouts of man run at speeds slower than the speeds of incapacity,
    slower than the speed of walking,
    slower than the effort identified as sauntering.

The roundabouts of man are not going anywhere of importance,
    are neither promoting nor denying,
    are simply sitting in the sun and rain and moving within
        a stable need.

The roundabouts of man should be promoted and demoted:
    should be promoted as a means of progress;
    should be demoted from the travesty of time running in a circle.

The roundabouts of man should be realigned to operate for the benefit of man,
    should be realigned to carry and to empty,
    should be realigned to be the carriers fitted with objectives,
      as projects are evaluated unto completion of directives.

The roundabouts of man are similar in counselling to man's walk around a mountain,
    seeks the same defining moment of continual restoration:
      without completion of a screening;
  from the setting and the melting of the frost upon a static archived endeavour,
    which never proceeds any further than an unjustified tick,
    within a box upon a paper which is neither filed nor read:
      in the glory of the sunlight.

ANTHONY A EDDY (SCRIBE)

The roundabouts of man neither ease nor serve,
                neither construct nor complete,
                neither elicit nor condone.

The roundabouts of man are an utter waste of time,
                are not a plan in action,
                are not a grand design,
                are not a reward befitting for retirement,
                are not to be a dusty accumulation in a rest home.

The roundabouts of man deserve to be turned upside down,
                    to be inverted and reset,
                    to be issued with controls,
                    to be supervised and purged,
                    to be empowered and greeted with the rising sun,
      to be matured and implemented as a desirable ways and means awaiting servicing,
                        with the installing of technology:
                  which circumvents the drowsiness and napping on a journey—
                          on a roundabout at large.

The roundabouts of man can be encountered at an intersecting meeting of deliverance,
                can be encountered as the moving footstools of amusement:
                      in the arena fitted out for the young at heart;
                can be encountered in a fun park going nowhere:
                      without a ticket and stomach suited to upheaval.

The roundabouts of man are difficult to revitalize,
                are difficult to energize,
                are difficult to supervise.

The roundabouts of man are at the beck and call of no one,
                are neither challenged nor invigorated,
                are neither centred nor driven.

The roundabouts of man are victims of significance,
                are victims of a paucity of concern,
                are victims of a lack of maintenance and the loss of shine,
                are victims of the motiveless together with the impact of
                        the lackadaisical:
                as witnessed within the bounds of careless freedom.

The roundabouts of man neither preserve value nor of wealth,
                    sees both dissipate as they trickle through the fingers,
                    sees them pour out as if from a hole within a purse.

The roundabouts of man are friends of the penury of man,
                are friends of scarcity and hunger,
                are friends of begging touched with theft,
                are friends with a near empty larder:

as measured by the table,
or the upturned box.

The roundabouts of man succumb to trials and tests,
succumb to needs and wants,
succumb to lotteries with dependency on chance,
succumb to items seen as wasteful,
without cognizance of circumstance,
as overlaid by the clamour of the voices at a random meal.

The roundabouts of man lower expectations as the circuits are completed,
destroy the residues of hope,
impact on the spirit,
soul,
and body,
compete critically with the shortfall of the family on the staples
known to be essential:
in supporting life with both health and growth.

The roundabouts of man sees revisiting as essential to survival,
sees the places regularly,
where a helping hand does beckon,
to preserve a door from a wolf attack,
to meet the needs of life within a family
so survival may continue.

The roundabouts of man should be discarded for destruction if to be left alone,
should not be able to become the focus of the day,
should not circle continuously with the shell of life.

The roundabouts of man should not be there to weary man,
should not be there to author loss of hope,
should not be there to fragment and to nullify the prospects
of recovery.

The roundabouts of man should have its riders vanquish such,
to seek the understanding of a commitment to The Provisioning of God."

My Content Study Aid

_____

_____

_____

_____

_____

The Switching of Design

And I hear The Lord Jesus saying,
"The switching of design is neither practical nor realistic.

The switching of design does not serve the sole purpose of dissatisfaction,
        does not bring success marching through the door,
        does not eliminate the matters of concern,
        does not satisfy the points waiting to be fixed,
              calling for attention,
              seeking a fresh solution.

The switching of design is not a decision rating as a master stroke,
        may lead to an an end result ranking as stupidity,
        may cause financial suffering and loss,
            ineffectiveness and dismay,
        may prolong the finality of intent applicable to completion.

The switching of design is more likely to be the choice of the inexperienced,
            of those still waiting for inspiration,
            of those selecting by looking at The Earth,
        by stopping for a drink which heightens all the nerves,
        by stumbling in the dark:
            where the results are exactly what would be expected.

The switching of design is the considering of an anachronism out of time,
        is a blending of ideas not suited to one another,
        is a mismatch of integrity,
        is the building on a fault,
        is the grasping at a solution not fitted to the problem,
        is the grasping at a straw unrelated to the task at hand,
        is the grasping at a guess just based upon a hope.

The switching of design delays to introduce a compromise,
        guarantees a failure in the future,
        guarantees the need for further modifications,
        guarantees the patchwork of design.

The switching of design introduces 'wondering' to the mindset—
            which forsakes the reasoning of experience—
              in the absence of knowledge,
            for the introduction of the onset of disaster.

The switching of design is not,
        in itself,
        a recipe for success;
      is not,
        in itself,

a carrier of solutions;
is not,
in itself,
the be all and the end all when insight has deserted with the
intellect at rest.

The switching of design sometimes,
when all else fails,
resorts to trial and error,
resorts to reading books,
resorts to asking others unfamiliar with the difficulties yet
desperately in need of resolution.

The switching of design by man is an admission of defeat;
is an admission of misunderstandings of the needs to be
built into the sequences;
is the admission,
shown clearly by the evidence,
of the failure of the mindset to complete the
fit-out of construction—
which would produce a working model.

The switching of design by God is not a way station within existence as known by God,
is not deemed to be a satisfactory path to explore:
when the end result is know to generate—
more problems than it solves.

The switching of design by God would speak of a shortage of objectives without
the overlaps;
would speak of a design still incomplete—
of a design still being a work in progress;
would speak of too much compression applied to
the concept,
without the freedom of movement acting
as an accessory.

The switching of design is not a consideration in the workshop of God,
is not conducive to a backtrack,
is not conducive to a revamp,
is not conducive for introspection to bring forth an ending
suitable for commitment—
where progress is assured.

The switching of design is not a stepping stone of God,
would be a call to failure,
would not succeed in attaining the objective,
would be a mess upon a platform,
would not be the work of God.

ANTHONY A EDDY (SCRIBE)

131

The switching of design is not a pathway to creating life,
  is not the source which instils or instates,
  is not the method by which life results,
  is not the means whereby life multiplies in the gifting of self-creation,
  is not the conceptual means determining the certainty of success.

The switching of design is not present in the laboratory of God,
  is neither needed nor expected,
  is neither sought nor considered as an alternative pathway
                                        to completion.

The switching of design is not seen in the layouts of God,
  is not seen in all the variations of life established to proliferate,
  is not available for consideration as a workaround,
  is not the reason for success as developed by God,
  is not the leader to success for the striving of man—
          to reproduce life with his cut and splice,
          to have access to the building blocks of God,
          to have the foresight intended for creation,
          to have the key to the platform—
        where life is introduced into an environment prepared
                                        in readiness:
        where food with shelter is made available so life extends
                        itself on the receipt of energy—
                with reproduction installed and working in
                                minimised complexity—
                                for life within a cell.

The switching of design is not an option ever used by God,
  is not a means by which God has chosen to operate,
  is not the end-time solution to the quests of man—
                in his laboratory trying to emulate his God,
  is not released unto the knowledge base of man—
      where Trust is insufficient to be sure it will not be misapplied,
      in ignorance of exploration of all that man researches—
      on his chosen pathway to his intended fame and fortune."

My Content Study Aid

_____

_____

_____

_____

_____

Neandertals (4d Clan Attribute: Miners)

And I hear The Lord Jesus saying,
"The Neandertals (4d) hide from prying eyes,
                believe they themselves look ridiculous among the life forms of
                        The Earth,
                seek privacy carried to the most extreme lengths imaginable,
                listen hard for footsteps which may be following.

The Neandertals (4d) are the miners 'par excellence',
                spend most of their time in the mines
                        which rarely attract attention,
                        which rarely are close to centres of population:
                through distancing themselves,
                within their settlements,
                from the outreaching of the inquisitive and the searching.

The Neandertals (4d) would rather hide than defend,
                do not support lines of defence as being worthwhile,
                would rather go and start another mine elsewhere.

The Neandertals (4d) do not acknowledge one another with any form of greeting that
                        is discernible:
        restrict such to the thought patterning regardless of where the eyes are focussed,
        structure superiority with authority neither with acknowledgement nor by sign.

The Neandertals (4d) are mobile and athletic,
                are strong and versatile,
                are variable in height and in application of their skills.

The Neandertals (4d) are not 'rushed off their feet',
                are plodders with consistency,
                are achievers of consistency,
                are the producers of consistency,
                are the appliers of consistency to all they mine and do,
                are consistent in how they handle and encounter problems and
                        difficulties as soon as they arise.

The Neandertals (4d) have a proud history on The Earth:
                    of independence from involvement with the other clans;
                    except when the mining has generated a surplus
                        to be shared,
                    with carbonates available for dispersal.

The Neandertals (4d),
                and all in general,
                have no use for money,
                have long since turned away from its false attraction as a store of wealth,

prefer to touch and feel the results of their abilities and skills:
in caring for the needs of their particular lifestyles and requirements—
where suitability and commitment to the tasks have long been borne:
by their longevity and experience,
in the successful preparation of all for which they seek.

The Neandertals (4d) do not bother with appointments,
have found them unnecessary when time is not at a premium,
when 'tomorrow' does not have the urgency as associated
with humanity.

The Neandertals (4d) are not impressed by a call for urgency,
do nothing with alacrity,
are not the followers of timetables,
although knowing the schedules off by heart—
in being built upon past practise.

The Neandertals (4d) do not have a sense of sympathy,
are practical and forthright,
are synonymous with expediency in the completion of their tasks.

The Neandertals (4d) is the calling card of veterans,
have practised what they teach,
have practised their beliefs,
have practised their approach to life,
have practised their approach to death.

The Neandertals (4d) do not live a life of hypocrisy,
do not live a life of lies,
do not live a life based upon the immateriality of The Truth.

The Neandertals (4d) have freedom within their clan to come and go at leisure;
will not have their absence noted;
will not have their presence either sought or requested;
will not be penalised by being absent;
even when their presence would assist the functioning of the clan.

The Neandertals (4d) have transparency of occupations—
where all are able to perform the tasks of others,
where all can stand-in for another with neither fuss nor bother;
where undue effort,
stress,
or tension,
does not build into an individual's explosion of exasperation.

The Neandertals (4d) are impervious to time-based matters,
which bring about frustrations in the equivalent human work force.

The Neandertals (4d) each have an internal Peace:

which oils the framework of the whole of their communities,
where bickering and arguments,
with jostling and violence,
are unknown for their occurrence,
and so never break the sense of Peace and order implicit in their communes—
both of the day and of the night."

My Content Study Aid

_____
_____
_____
_____
_____
_____
_____
_____
_____
_____
_____
_____
_____
_____
_____
_____
_____
_____
_____
_____
_____
_____
_____
_____

The Incumbencies of God and Man

And I hear The Lord Jesus saying,
"The incumbency of God is a position of great trust within the sight and reach
of man.

The incumbency of God is recognition of His existence,
of His being and authority,
of His presence and His love,
of His concern and caring for the whole
of His creation.

The incumbency of God arises,
and is sustained,
from man's seeking of his God during his journey through mortality,
from man's acceptance of a Sacrifice of Reconciliation on The Cross,
from man's commitment to the instatement of his Living God of Love,
from man's appreciation of a new covenant within The Inheritance of God,
from man's invited participation within The Bride of Christ,
from man's Faith in the validity of The Promises of God—
in the resurrection into eternal life,
in the balancing of the scales of justice—
in weighing the end effects of The Freewill of man,
in mortality and in the future prospects of eternity in a garden—
where the incumbency of man can meet with,
and relate to,
the incumbency of God.

The incumbency of God encircles man in life with his second birth of baptism,
encircles man in death with his crown established,
encircles man in his third rebirth from the grave into
eternal life—
to then participate within all the scenes which
the preparation of God has laid out for man.

The incumbency of God invites the sequencing of man:
the stepping stones of man;
the qualifying of man;
the progression of man;
the destiny of choice there awaiting the completion of
man's journey home back into The Family of God.

The incumbency of God accepts all the responsibilities,
all the devotions of the hearts,
all the praise and worship,
all the aspects borne of an intermingling of relationships,
all The Promises to man as kept securely within The Faith of man,

all the miracles and favours reserved for the prayers of man,
all the healings and the pain relief as Satan is retired from his
interference in the mortal life of man.

The incumbency of man is established by his Freewill.

The incumbency of man welcomes God into his life of Freedom:
answers to the flood tide of fulfilment,
the flood tide which overcomes objections,
the flood tide which introduces Peace,
the flood tide which presents the choice of destiny,
the flood tide which acknowledges The Presence and Reality of God,
the flood tide of Grace which knows the repentant heart on the incoming flow;
which cleanses would-be Temples of their carried sin
when on the outgoing ebb.

The incumbency of man is identified with God,
is impressed in readiness for eternity with the changes wrought,
modifies behaviour in conformity with The Standards for The Bride,
is prepared for the return of Christ coming to fruition:
in fulfilment of His promise given many centuries ago.

The incumbency of man honours The God of Nations,
has a Holy Fear for The Altar of The Lord,
is circumspect with his tongue's activity:
as speech is opened to control,
as silence reigns in participation in Communion,
as memory addresses and respects the soul's reaction
to all abhorrent sin—
overlooked with permitted tainted freedom—
so to be active within The Very Temple of The Living God.

The incumbency of man deplores the attacks upon the spirit,
soul,
and body by the vile and evil—
where the dominion is outlined,
where the dominion is to be curbed,
where the conflict is committed to be vanquished:
with Time and Faith and Grace;
with the onset of a Kingdom's rule;
with the coming of A New Day which ushers in
a change of governance.

The incumbency of man separates the faith-filled:
from the intransigent,
separates the new-covenant keepers:
from the ignorant of purpose,

separates the reconciled with God:
from the sinners arising from their
behaviour in the garden.

The incumbency of man is accurate with arrows collected on a horse ride with
a bow—
as destined for their due release with a message for each heart—
still seen to be at risk.

The incumbency of man follows the taskings as set by God,
follows up the divine appointments,
heals and blesses under proxy ministry with The Authority
of Instruction:
as made known by God.

The incumbency of man is a player within The Will of God,
is the servant within the servanthood as spelt out by God,
is an overcomer who has persevered,
who has qualified for an entitlement to be
seated at a table:
a table for The Honoured and The Free."

My Content Study Aid

_____

_____

_____

_____

_____

_____

_____

_____

_____

_____

_____

_____

_____

_____

_____

_____

The Tongues of God

And I hear The Lord Jesus saying,
"The tongues of God confirm the highway to the stars.

The tongues of God assist the counselling of God,
                    assist conversations with God,
                    assist the transfer of entries in The Lamb's Book of Life.

The tongues of God achieve their objectives of two-way communications:
                                    via a relay station as installed.

The tongues of God express the heart of man in a language dear to the heart of God.
The tongues of God express The Wisdom as a part of the downloads from God.

The tongues of God are secure and free from hacking,
                    are intense and condensed with built-in compression,
                    are vibrant and yielding to requested interpretation,
                    are meaningful and thought-filled when subjected to interpretation,
                    are uplifting and encouraging when interpretation speaks to
                                  the many and informed:
                        with understanding and confirmation of the erstwhile
                              outpourings and counselling of God.

The tongues of God separate and conquer the reticence displayed,
                    open and adjust the airways of God for homing on the spirit and
                                  the soul,
                    introduce with wonder at the complexity involved:
                        with the clarity of reception and transmission.

The tongues of God festoon the airways of God,
                    the airways of the heavens,
                    the airways protected for the use of man in contact.

The tongues of God are issued and directed,
                    are allocated and combined,
                  are introduced and seated in:
                  as unfamiliarity is first encountered prior to the formality of usage.

The tongues of God proclaim the activities of heaven,
                  receive and record the activities of man as furnished with
                                his tongue:
                  which enjoys an open pipeline to God.

The tongues of God require practise for their fluency,
                  require accurate emulation with the soundings of the tongue,
                  require repetition until acceptability is acclaimed to enable a
                                'moving on':
                  from a rendering of the tail end of the practice with success

and readiness to proceed—
when next brought into use.

The tongues of God circumvent the telephone,
deny the usage of morse code,
subjugate the electronic to the past,
promote the brain of man as a suitable tool for envy and
of fascination.

The tongues of God can move through the brain faster than electronic switching
can permit,
faster than a bird can cheep for help,
faster than the wind can blow a storm,
faster than the sea can curl a wave,
faster than a youth can drive a car.

The tongues of God are satisfied with their capabilities,
the ability to loosen and to blend,
the ability to expound and to enliven the discourses of both
man and God,
the ability to sing and to extol the praises for infinity,
the hymns of grandeur and
of wonder,
the worship of the ages:
as built on participation with the marshalling of support.

The tongues of God neither clash nor shatter the intent of man and/or the support of God.

The tongues of God offer shelter to the afflicted,
hope for such repair,
integrity with a purchase,
summations with returns.

The tongues of God are not subject to excuses,
are not interested in reasons whether factual or imagined,
whether practical or reasoned,
whether winsome or disjointed.

The tongues of God express The Will of God,
convey the thoughts of man,
recycle justifications for the outcome encountered in the application
of Freewill.

The tongues of God are surprised in the presence of gratitude expressed,
are surprised where innocence is present,
are surprised when a child is heard on the circuit released to those
who know and care:
enough to learn and teach the highway to the stars;
hand in hand with a synopsis of an existence away into

the future;
where Righteousness and Truth confirm a future birthed
of commitment;
as found within The Fields of Faith and Grace—
with promises of attendance in the gardens as opened,
for expressing The Delight of God.

The tongues of God carry the secrets of the centuries:
from the shameful and the proud,
from the criminal and the insane,
from The Captured and The Free,
from the abused and the mourning,
from the joy-filled and the smiling,
from the pleasant and the thankful.

The tongues of God teach and rebuke,
encourage and uplift,
access the locks and handles:
with The Keys sustained by Faith,
when a call to bind or loose is heard within the halls of Freedom
or obscurity,
as angels are directed to attend with urgency such requests;
so matters of great importance to God may not be unnecessarily
delayed before becoming current and enabled;
to so attend the enlivened server with the reported actions as
requested and enacted.

The tongues of God once signified the beginning of a new covenant,
now are called to indicate the onset of finality:
of The E nd-time of Faith and Grace.

The tongues of God await The Triumphant Fanfares,
denoting The Call of God,
on A New Day of Change."

My Content Study Aid

_____
_____
_____
_____
_____
_____

The Orphanage of God

And I hear The Lord Jesus saying,
"The orphanage of God is a home away from home,
                is a home among the heavens,
                is a home of sequestered love.

The orphanage of God is separated from the influences of man.

The orphanage of God is based among the angels,
                is based with due regard to privacy,
                is based with a due regard for lineage,
                is based on the ability to bless the very young and dependent
                                where parenting is not able to exist.

The orphanage of God is where the endangered in the womb
                are sequestered for development,
                are sequestered for repair,
                are sequestered where the mother can no longer reach and hinder:
                                from a womb of unforgiveness.

The orphanage of God gathers in the 'cot' deaths of stupidity and carelessness:
                and tucks them up in bed with a bed-time story from an angel.

The orphanage of God attends to the children of misadventure,
                  the children of disasters,
                      of accidents,
                      of rejection,
                      of earthquakes,
                      of fire,
                      of the perils of the waterside witnessing
                              the submersion of the face,
             of insufficient food where starvation rears its ugly head:
                to take away a shadow and leaving no replacement,
             where there are no daily scrapings left within a pot or pan.

The orphanage of God holds the children falling foul of murderers,
                    together with the victims of the finality of violence,
                        and the acting out of hate.

The orphanage of God is filled with love and care,
                is filled with hugs and kisses,
                is filled with genuine affection unknown upon The Earth.

The orphanage of God is filled with supervision where an eye is never blinded,
                        where a tongue is never harsh,
             where the enfolding arms are always loaded with delight,
            where the secrets and the love notes have their beginnings as the

whispering quiet voices:
sharing their love and storied love notes in extremely
close proximity,
to the keen and listening ear.

The orphanage of God has neither sighs nor whimpering,
has neither tears nor frustrations,
has neither enforcements nor restrictions.

The orphanage of God has amusements filled with blessings,
has the truthfulness within the care and counselling of angels,
has the loving and the kindnesses as showered upon the young:
who no longer dwell in wariness or fear,
of either the hard eyed glance,
or what is hidden at an arm's-length,
while staying out of sight.

The orphanage of God has a lot of parties,
has a lot of singing,
has a lot of story telling,
has a lot of dress ups when meeting with the clowns.

The orphanage of God is a place of wonder filled with happiness,
is a place of learning and of teaching,
is a place of preparation for a life committed:
within the dwelling place of God.

The orphanage of God is ablaze with the active gifts of God,
is ablaze in an environment so filled with the vocality;
of expressing the very fullness of agapé love.

The orphanage of God is a wonderland for children,
is a wonderland applied to the innocent in both form and thought:
in mending the circumstances within surroundings as activated;
by the wounding of the welfare in denial of the gifts of God;
in the demonic sixth estate of man;
entailing suffering and actions in a life cut short;
where the envelope was opened well before the postage
was completed;
leaving the delivery impaired and impossible to complete.

The mother and the father of the deliberate dead,
who denied a sojourn in a working womb,
with be held to account for the act of Freewill which produced a hired executioner,
to forsake the oath in the quest for a purse already weighted;
to carry all the involved to Hell.

There,
to stand beside a bed and watch as an infant being,

trying desperately to escape the tongs;
those bent on thwarting the integrity of new life:
while still within the womb.

The parents of the deliberate dead felt the implant in the passion of the moment,
later choosing to purchase the multi-accepting folded ticket of destruction:
as it consents to the killing of the innocent—
in the confirming of the price paid for a life,
resulting from the former pleasuring of the parents.

So,
in turn,
the gates of Hell are opened for the conspiracy of killers:
for the killers in complicity of both the deed and prior knowledge.

The orphanage of God attends to the accidents of The Earth,
the unforeseen yet sudden deaths where mourning is both sincere and prolonged.

The orphanage of God attends to the foreseen and gratuitous deaths
in the plucking of the womb,
in the emptying of the womb,
in the denial of the fruit,
in the forsaking of a life,
where a whim within the time frame is both fragile and ill-advised
as a basis for enactment,
as it becomes impervious to reversal for the regaining of the innocent.

The orphanage of God willingly accepts the contributions of The Earth.

The parentage of man walk the battlefield of God with denial of reality in
cuddling up
to the belief that the purse of man can overcome and offset the morality of God."

My Content Study Aid

_____

_____

_____

_____

_____

_____

_____

_____

_____

The Approach of God

And I hear The Lord Jesus saying,
"The approach of God to His People is sacrosanct and holy.

The approach of God is straightforward and direct,
            is authoritative and honouring,
            is announcing and relating.

The approach of God minds the details for the soul,
            minds the entries for His Book of Life,
            minds the circumstances of relationships in development.

The approach of God is to observe and to record until maturity is achieved,
                        until responsibility is assumed,
                            when generations re-align:
                in the light of a new fully fledged member as received into,
                        and now at ease within the family.

The approach of God oversees and encourages,
            blends the spiritual into the natural,
            checks the devil on a prayer request.

The approach of God is a blessing to man,
            is a reality check upon the tableau of life,
            is a reference point to man which he would be foolish to forget.

The approach of God is waiting for a commitment,
            is waiting for a prayer of sincerity,
            is waiting for the blaspheming to stop.

The approach of God signals in the dream time,
            signals in the lifetime,
            signals in the daytime.

The approach of God signals and awaits,
            signals and listens for a response,
            signals and knows when the senses of man are alive and well:
                            with settings to ignore.

The approach of God should be the high point of a life,
            should be as a clap of thunder which follows on the flash,
            should be the introduction to what is supposed to be.

The approach of God is not expecting to be rejected,
            is not expecting to be set aside to wait,
            is not expecting to be lied to and trod into the dirt.

The approach of God is worth the tears of joy,
            is worth the day of greeting,

is worth the time when the baby is set to climb out of the cot.

The approach of God is signed by the angels in accompaniment,
               is signed by the hosts of heaven dressed in full regalia,
               is signed by the wind and the scent of My Spirit as when passing
                       around the invitations:
                             to participate within the calls of God.

The approach of God is magnified by silence,
               is magnified by holiness,
               is magnified by being prepared to listen—
                       to all He has to say.

The approach of God is not with Him on tiptoe,
               is not with Him with hands within His pockets,
               is not with Him in bringing a sternness of expression.

The approach of God indicates a message for His People.

The approach of God is measured in His approach,
               is measured in His retreat,
               is measured and determined as success is measured by His will.

The approach of God can have His counsel understood by His 'will' and 'shall',
                     together with His 'may' and 'can' and 'should' and
                                 'would' and 'could',
                             as His presence so requires.

The approach of God is not as a bee humming in a hive,
               is not as a salmon leaping on the falls,
               is not as a swan with all the wings in tune,
               is not as a goose flapping for dear life.

The approach of God is dramatic and sincere,
               is honouring and reliable,
               is confident in which holiness is personified and does not
                                fade away.

The approach of God follows in His Spirit's way,
               follows in the call for help,
               follows in His calling for commitment to a future known to Him:
                       as valued highly by His short term guests.

The approach of God is attentive and transfixing,
               is commanding in leading,
               is kindness before the injured,
               is loving before the tearful and upset.

The approach of God enters into all the emotions of man as He relates and participates
                              in the trials of man.

The approach of God knows the heart of each,
>> is doubtful when the heart is seen to vacillate,
>> is disturbed when He hears the 'yes' and 'no' of man making
>>> nonsense of The Truth.

The approach of God should be enjoyed and longed for in a life of rectitude
>>> and happiness,
>> in a life of endeavour and of satisfaction,
>> in a life of worship and of praise:
>> in confirmation of man's gratitude for the showering of His gifts,
>>> as brought by His Spirit for man's body soul and spirit.

The approach of God is not empty-handed in His approaching of a King or of a Queen,
>>> of a prince or of a princess:
>> the royalty of His kingdom as to be placed in their positions of responsibility.

The approach of God is a delight to attend,
>> is a marvel to encounter,
>> is a wonder to be engaged—
>>> with a two way conversation with The Mastermind of Creation.

The approach of God stirs a cup to overflowing,
>> enlivens The Communion as prepared and offered,
>> attends the second birth with both meaning and approval,
>> brings Righteousness to the fore and lays it on His altar:
>>> to be the valued fare of man in conjunction with The Truth.

The approach of God lights The People of God,
>> lights the radiance of eternity,
>> lights the joyous and the celebrating with their very special smiles.

The approach of God can be the starting point as a step off:
>>> into The Discipleship of God,
>>> into The Way Stations of The Lord,
>>> into the counselling and gifting of The Holy Spirit—
>> as He brings a new way of existence before the gratefulness of man,
>> as intertwined with the agreement of The Father."

My Content Study Aid

_____

_____

_____

_____

_____

The Planting of The Vineyard

And I hear The Lord Jesus saying,
"The planting of the vineyard is planted securely and with thought,
is the lasting into eternity,
with the initial enabling of man,
to grow into all he is intended within the culture of His God.

The planting of the vineyard grows in meeting the demand to be planted with precision,
to be planted where placed,
to be planted within the oversight of God.

The planting of the vineyard has vines of strength and character,
has vines stretching out to The Son light,
has vines filled with exuberance and determination,
as commitment is birthed within the roots:
in order that the fruit can recount their life stories—
as the fruit of the planter with The Son.

The planting of the vineyard is an ongoing facet of the workload of God,
following on the insetting of belief into the soul of man,
followed by the changes wrought of the spirit,
as the spirit assumes the captaincy of the soul within The Temple:
now seen as under the finality of construction,
now seen as where The Spirit dwells,
with His gifts accepted and operational;
in a life now deemed to live in Righteousness—
for the ultimate destiny of both honouring and of choice.

The planting of the vineyard has an enduring lifetime,
has a handshake with eternity,
has a grasping of belief in patterning the lifestyle of success.

The planting of the vineyard acknowledges the existence of commitment,
the pointing of The Freewill of man into a voluntary recognition appreciating
The Sacrifice of God:
of the reconciliation implicit in The Inheritance of The Cross;
of the adoption into The Family of God,
of life beyond the grave,
of life assured by a promise of a place prepared.

The planting of the vineyard opens up the avenues of intersection with their supports
in place,
the express ways of the plantings where the vines
are on display,
the seasoning where the fruit does come as buds:
destined to burst into the fruit of ripeness;

which spreads out in commissioning as it leaves its vine behind.

The planting of the vineyard is a central part of The Foresight of God.

The planting of the vineyard is pruned and trimmed by the faith-filled as selected
by God.

The planting of the vineyard is weeded under care by the at home within The Family
of God.

The planting of the vineyard is matched for the success of the objectives of the vines:
of the sizing of the fruit,
of the absence of the objectionable in affecting growth,
of the absence of the stress levels which denies a withering,
of the absence of the birds—
the consumers of the near future—
as built on expectations for the season of the ripening,
followed closely by the bounds of harvesting with the bounty of The Lord.

The planting of the vineyard is at the threshold of establishment,
is at the boundary of acceptable behaviour of each vine,
is at the presenting of a resource for both the small and
the mature,
around which they can both play and develop
within The Wisdom of the sheltering.

The planting of the vineyard keeps and holds its place:
free from intrusion of false belief,
of doctrine running wild,
of integrity attacked,
of attentive care withheld,
of the poaching of The Lambs from the
Shepherd's flock upon a rise:
where the dining field,
with its feeding rhythm,
is broken by a change in pace,
as measured by the intent of the encroaching wilderness
with its fixation:
on the ethics as bred of man,
with woman at his side,
within his overall foolishness wherein he denies his God.

The planting of the vineyard is a significant part of The Earthly Edifice of God,
has the ongoing interest of God,
lies within the future expertise of God,
displays within The Will of God:
as God is honoured worshipped and remains
within the prayer field of His vines.

The planting of the vineyard is the envy of the others,
<blockquote>is the envy often present with the level of success,
where numbers are released as a measure of acceptance.</blockquote>

The planting of the vineyard is now advancing,
<blockquote>like no other season,
as the end-time season gathers understanding and adherents,
as there is a closing-in on how to become a vine while it is
still today.</blockquote>

The planting of the vineyard requires no actual space upon The Earth.

The planting of the vineyard is accompanied nearby with a constructive part of The
Edifice of God,
<blockquote>where with praise with worship with teaching with commitment,
is The Work of God advanced within The End-time of Faith
with Grace.</blockquote>

The planting of the vineyard holds sway within The Faith fields of religion,
<blockquote>holds sway within The Call to Christianity,
holds sway within the eternal existence of The Living
Loving God of all creation.</blockquote>

The planting of the vineyard owes reverence with honour to The Apostles of The Lord,
<blockquote>to their attention to The Gentiles,
to their sharing to form a base
from which the vineyard could be born,
from the eventual outreach of a founded church,
which touched upon the wife of an emperor,
and thereupon the emperor,
via the scenes of battle subjected to a vision of intensity:
with the attaching of the symbol from The Day of Faith declared."</blockquote>

My Content Study Aid

_____

_____

_____

_____

_____

_____

_____

_____

The Worthwhile and The Lost

And I hear The Lord Jesus saying,
"The worthwhile and the lost have much in common within the sight of God.

The worthwhile and the lost are not seen as opponents:
>> in competition for the love of God,
> are not seen as competitors:
>> for seats within His presence,
> are not seen as having trampled:
>> on the rights of others.

The worthwhile and the lost both come to God as united friends—
> waiting to learn The Way of Discipleship:
>> The Way of Unity of Purpose and Belief;
>> The Way of Trust and Servanthood;
>> The Way of Integrity and Truth;
>> The Way of Shedded Sin;
>> The Way of Grace and Favour;
>> The Way of Sharing Testimonies;
>> The Way of Thankfulness and Gratitude—
>>> to be within The Adopted Family of God.

The worthwhile and the lost know their way within the need to search and find,
> know their way to garner and replenish,
> know their way to furnish and supply.

The worthwhile and the lost evaluate and discard,
> prize and keep,
> accumulate and store.

The worthwhile and the lost are only known to God,
> are not known to one another,
> are not the sum totals of humanity which are known—
>> to and by The Living God of Love.

The worthwhile and the lost are the main practitioners of Discipleship under God,
> are the main seekers of His stewardship,
> are gathered as the potential keepers of the new covenant,
>> joining readily with all the other seekers in selecting,
>>> in achieving,
>>> in qualifying:
>> for the destiny of choice,
>> a presence in The Bride of Christ,
>> an inheritance in waiting upon a resurrection,
> in following the counsel as to the application held under accountability—
>> with full responsibility for the usage of Freewill as gifted to each soul.

Anthony A Eddy (Scribe)

The worthwhile and the lost come to love the call to travel,
to accept the opportunity to share and testify,
to be The Proxy Ministers of God:
as each is assigned unto the eager and committed—
to seek and change the lives of the willing and the open:
as each decides to join The Ongoing Scouts of God."

My Content Study Aid

_____

_____

_____

_____

_____

_____

_____

_____

_____

_____

_____

_____

_____

_____

_____

_____

_____

_____

_____

_____

_____

_____

_____

_____

_____

_____

_____

_____

_____

The Time for Witnessing

And I hear The Lord Jesus saying,
"The time for witnessing approaches.

The time for witnessing approaches.

The time for witnessing approaches.

The time for witnessing unfolds its doors as it approaches,
                    unfolds the shelter from the storm,
                    unfolds the mantle of The King.

The time for witnessing is the shout of victory,
                    is the war cry of The Lord,
                    is the shout of attention as the heads all turn,
                    is the shout which shatters doubt,
                              which affirms the call to arms,
                              which confirms intent to validate,
                              which seeks the present Truth.

The time for witnessing disturbs a sleeping landscape,
                    disturbs the basking in the sun,
                    disturbs the lounging in a chair as laid upon a sandy shoreline,
          with the lapping of the waves as they gently halt and then retreat.

The time for witnessing approaches and departs,
                    follows in the imprinting of the sun on a land of heat and toil,
                              on a land of suffering and exhaustion,
                              on a land of death and of disease.

The time for witnessing is when heating is most comfortable.

The time for witnessing excludes the roasting and the freezing.

The time for witnessing encourages dressing for the season.

The time for witnessing spreads a hand of invitation,
                              puts a smile upon a face,
                    places The Words of God in readiness for an invitation,
                    provides an atmosphere in which a welcome dwells
                                        and is at home.

The time for witnessing breaks the grounds for doubt,
                    confirms the intensity of prayers,
                    sees the results of The Agapé Love of God in action,
          as healings descend in answer to desires,
                              in answer to the needs,
                              in answer to the pain and suffering,
                              in answer to the sheltering and the feeding,
                              in answer to the attacks of lifetime disabilities.

ANTHONY A EDDY (SCRIBE)

The time for witnessing is evident by the inspection of surroundings,
>by the health levels which leave much to be desired,
>by the facilities not fully operational:
>not properly available nor repaired when required,
>neither checked nor duplicated as the need expands,
>neither fixed nor maintained as facilities are seen to fail,
>as services can no longer lift their heads with the smiles in place,
>in readiness to perform.

The time for witnessing sees the passing of opportunities,
>sees the failure of commitment,
>sees the passing of a sojourn with neither a focus nor
>an application.

The time for witnessing is decreed by The Call of God,
>is accepted by the keenness of anticipation,
>by the onset of contact with the planning,
>by the demonstration of a willingness to attend
>with full participation.

The time for witnessing is in the here and now,
>is in the will of Sacrifice,
>is in the scope and vision of The Lord,
>is in the imparting of the knowledge and The Wisdom,
>of the authority and prayer life,
>of the familiarity with the gifts of God.

The time for witnessing will not pass on by,
>is here to welcome The Advent of The Lord,
>has an innate ability to express The Word of God:
>as implanted within a heart,
>to express The Word of God:
>as expressed within His Word,
>to express The Word of God as heard
>and carried:
>into the locality as determined for release.

The time for witnessing raises the fruit up from The Earth,
>establishes the fruit within The Monarchy of God,
>introduces the fruit into the knowledge base:
>of the widest of wide families;
>enables confirmation of the reality of the importance;
>in selecting the destiny of choice.

The time for witnessing leave specific locations better off because of visiting,
>as called at the behest of The Lord:
>where the doors are opened;
>where the greetings are eagerly awaited;

where the miracles are aligned for due release,
by the speaking servants of The Living God.

The time for witnessing culminates in the achieving of The Will of God:
in the spreading of hope and commitment,
both reinforced and replenished;
in the flow-on marvelling at the wonders of
the miracles:
with the changing of the lives,
as matched by the capability of the willingness of God;
to display His fullness of His reality,
to manifest within each life awaiting healing:
in earnestness of Faith with the attendant liberation,
from the crippling pain.

The time for witnessing now is in The End-time of Faith and Grace,
now is in The End-time full release of My Spirit,
now is in The End-time experiencing an open heaven:
for communication with The Lord of Hosts as a return approaches,
as God redeems His Promise,
as God enhances His succouring of the requests for Healing,
with a linkage to The Knowing of His Loving Presence.

The time for witnessing brings forth the fruit of God from His orchard of supply.

The time for witnessing brings forth in abundance The Healing Proxy Authority of God.

The time for witnessing brings forth the approval of The Father,
the willingness of the attendance of My Spirit,
The Blessings with the cures of all which ail
My People and their friends,
as I,
The Lord Jesus,
attend to the prayer requests as submitted for attention by My servants:
from within their fields of life."

My Content Study Aid

_____
_____
_____
_____
_____
_____

The Righteous Growth of Man

And I hear The Lord Jesus saying,
"The righteous growth of man is a credit to a character,
is a credit to a childhood,
is a credit to the parents.

The righteous growth of man is beyond the negative criticism of a sinful life,
of a life with hope foregone,
of a life with despair around the corner,
of a life where violence lives in the presence of a broken Peace.

The righteous growth of man is patterned on The Son Light of the day,
on the teachings within the jurisdictions of the schooling,
on the concepts brought alive from within The Bible,
on the hopes and dreams aspired to by the heroes,
as read between the leaves of testimony:
where Truth can also both exist and prosper.

The righteous growth of man is led by his spirit,
is confirmed by his soul,
is testified in health by his body free from drugs.

The righteous growth of man is the evidence arising from the support of family values:
as controlled and understood.

The righteous growth of man is evidenced by a vocabulary,
which brings no shame upon the tongue,
brings no flush unto the cheeks,
puts no stress upon the lips.

The righteous growth of man is a seeker of like with like,
invites comparisons in the selection of those entitled to wear the tag of 'friend',
of those inviting the companionship where
love has stirred the mix,
of those chosen to be present when the knot
is tied,
as the vows are made,
within confession of their Faith and the presence of The Loving God:
as man and woman are united before the face of God.

The righteous growth of man is rewarded by witnessing the springing forth of life:
as a family is generated with the oversight of God.

The righteous growth of man is adamant on responsibility
which will preserve the way of life,
which will welcome close relationships,
which will lead into a relationship with the honouring of God.

The righteous growth of man verifies his starting point,
> verifies his willingness of intent,
> verifies his commitment within a life with God.

The righteous growth of man leaves a trail of onward gain,
> leaves a trail within the jungle of The Earth,
> leaves a trail which points to God.

The righteous growth of man shepherds the young at foot,
> shepherds the interested and the yearning,
> shepherds and assists with the walk into the eternity as
>> promised on The Cross.

The righteous growth of man has eyes on continuity,
> has eyes in focus and alive with absorbing and declaring,
> has eyes accompanied with a smile at where his heart does lie,
> at where his bed is bounced each morning by an early visit,
> at where his life is centred with responsibility accepted
>> and adored.

The righteous growth of man holds The Pearls of God within his heart,
> holds the conceptual truths as valid for his future,
> holds the gifts of God with heartfelt appreciation,
> as he witnesses with participation the gifts of God in action—
> in demonstration of the reality of God when coupled to a life
>> within mortality.

The righteous growth of man installs a hedge of protection around his family residence:
> in achieving the affirmation of the outreaching of the love of God,
> with the dedicated bands of angels,
> with the allocation of the rear guards of the hosts of heaven.

The righteous growth of man celebrates his life with God,
> welcomes and acknowledges The Peace within his heart,
> his outreach to his neighbours,
> the love and care as lavished on his home,
> with the happiness and gaiety deserved and experienced,
> with The Temples of The Spirit protected and secure.

The righteous growth of man sees his effort rewarded and replenished—
>> within the time frame of a life,
> sees small feet again running across a lawn,
> sees the games of hide and seek re-instated from his days
>> of early memories,
> sees again the vigour and the intensity in the playing of the
>> games of childhood and of youth.

The righteous growth of man attends the gatherings,
> where sendoffs are scheduled and achieved,

ANTHONY A EDDY (SCRIBE)

where the third generation have the beaux and damsels
as selected and cherished for an ongoing life together.

The righteous growth of man reflects The Righteousness achieved,
witnesses its spreading and developing within creation's
pool of love.

The righteous growth of man has nursed it on his knees,
has held it in his arms,
has run and jumped and hidden,
within the sound reach of erstwhile achievement and of satisfaction:
as confirmed in the laughter and the glee.

The righteous growth of man knows Peace within his heart,
knows the joy and the bounty within a life which overcomes,
which perseveres,
which knows and welcomes God into the home of angels,
into the home of agape´,
into the home of prayer
and of reconciliation,
into the home where God is both welcomed
and appreciated:
for all He has contributed to the lives within mortality,
and the prospects of eternity within The Ongoing Family of God."

My Content Study Aid

_____

_____

_____

_____

_____

_____

_____

_____

_____

_____

_____

_____

_____

The Questing for Peace

And I hear The Lord Jesus saying,
"The questing for Peace is a difficult objective.

The questing for Peace searches for a way forward,
                  has uncertainty enchained as an encircling of the neck of man,
                  has a gamble for achieving the finish line of life secured in
                                  its keeping.

The questing for Peace is not an overall objective of The Settlers on The Earth,
                  is not an objective of either the young or the old,
                  is not an objective which can be passed by a vote,
                  is not an objective which can be imposed by force,
                  is not an objective with a time frame for achievement.

The questing for Peace sits awaiting as a golden opportunity to open up the future.

The questing for Peace resides within the hearts of tears,
                      within the hearts of fears,
                      within the hearts of sears,
                          where man in his ineptitude is grasping at the straws.

The questing for Peace is a goal where the mountain must be climbed,
                      where the landslides must be dodged,
                      where the earthquakes must be survived.

The questing for Peace is not a simple find and sieve,
                  is not a simple do and give,
                  is not a simple trust and live.

The questing for Peace is not a committing to the robots,
                  is not found in a sequence bound by hope,
                  is not curtailed by a plan for war.

The questing for Peace must expound the logic,
                  must expound a history,
                  must expound the viability with longevity.

The questing for Peace must declare progress to the uninitiated,
                  must promote the way into the future,
                  must retain the sensitivity to meet with the warlords,
                          and the would be conquerors at large.

The questing for Peace must overcome with an attractive proposition,
                  must compound the concept of co-existence
                        within the livelihood of all,
                  must seek and detail the basis of agreement—
                  as distinct from the flights of fancy,

as birthed without the application of a dose of common sense.

The questing for Peace is not the rotten apple in a barrel,
                              rather it is the golden orb of life—
              as glistening and floating above the heads of the intelligent—
                     currently just out of reach yet hoping to be captured.

The questing for Peace is the rosebud waiting to bloom,
                   is the scent of victory waiting to be enjoyed,
                   is the acknowledgement of the casting away of the wreath
                                                            of death:
                                        either premature or mortal.

The questing for Peace requires Justice and Truth on both sides,
                     requires access and freedom of movement among the stars,
                     requires acknowledgement of each other's lifestyles with a
                                        respecting of their privacy,
                     requires room for development and preservation of the right
                                                 to existence,
                     requires a coalescing of objectives together with acceptance of
                                                 the status quo,
                     requires a negotiation where a divergence is proposed:
                          without prior consultation of the board of modulation.

The questing for Peace is not a haphazard affair,
                   is conducted with much foresight,
                   is conducted with much goodwill,
                   is conducted within the bounds of Righteousness—
                                        The Harbinger of Peace.

The questing for Peace is not a case of trial and error,
                   is not a case of imposition,
                   is not a case of self-aggrandisement,
                   is neither a case of might nor majesty,
                   is neither a case of surveillance nor of poaching,
                   is neither a case of wanting nor demanding,
                   is neither a case of stealing nor of pilfering.

The questing for Peace is a case of honesty with integrity,
                   is not a case of betrayal with deceit.

The questing for Peace is a measure of conciliation,
                              of acceptance and assistance,
                              of marketing and growth,
                              of the vested interests in the pride of achievement:
                   accompanied by a rosy outlook for the honouring of promises.

The questing for Peace must have feedback methods installed and operational:
                   for when dissatisfaction rears its head to upset the applecart;

to achieve nothing but an echo of denial in reply;
whereby is generated the motivation of the call to division
and separation:
the instigation of mischief on a growing scale.

The questing for Peace is affirmed as within The Will of God,
puts an end to the 'I's' and 'me's' of life:
with society sounding the drums of imperialism,
on demands arising from the pow'r and envy;
and substitutes the 'we's' and 'us' of love:
into a society encouraging the greeting of humility
with care,
and where agapé love abounds as a new experience,
assisting the desires of both.

The questing for Peace promises the birthing of new relationships,
The Seeking of new friendships,
the encouraging of new sources of knowledge and
of Wisdom:
the recreational and craftwork of the past,
setting a seal upon the enlightened and investigating,
the enthralled and the content,
the wise and the reflective,
the joyous and the celebrating;
in order that life,
as on The Earth,
may reach out to the distant realms of space to return
much wiser:
to so recount the episodes of discovery,
as impressed upon,
the memories and cameras of the day.

The insight of the potential future of The Earth:
is seen within the possible and the probable of achievement;
so endorsed by God as being within the scope of activities—
as offered to The Bride of Christ."

My Content Study Aid

_____

_____

_____

_____

_____

Encountering Death

And I hear The Lord Jesus saying,
"Encountering death within mortality can be instant oblivion with the loss of entity.

Encountering death can be long and drawn out as the body slowly runs down,
        can be short and sweet during a sleep in bed,
        can have many different introductions to the farewelling of mortality,
        can have the pain-free and the pain-full,
        can have the fast and the slow,
        can have the lingering of organs becoming weary,
        can have the release from the wasting of sickness and disease.

Encountering death sweetens with the ageing of man,
        increases in appeal as the body slowly dwindles in activity.

Encountering death becomes more frequent with the climbing of the years,
           as relatives and friends succumb to the inevitability of death.

Encountering death has many portals open to an entrance.

Encountering death has many avenues of escape prior to an ultimate scene of capture.

Encountering death often has delaying tactics:
        built on medication;
        built on visits to a doctor with a pad of subscriptions readily at hand,
          as allocated to specific items for the assisting of the glove of man;
        built on visits to a surgery
             when matters are more serious and time is not a friend,
        built on the samples taken for analysis of the contents from within
                 the glove.

Encountering death raises questions not previously raised in any detail,
        requires answers for the location of the grave
              or the enveloping of flames,
        requires answers in the addressing of a will,
            both seen as current and in touch with reality,
        requires answers to the count down preparation,
        requires details of the care and upkeep with the attention of
             the next of kin,
          prior to ultimately attending at the destiny of choice.

Encountering death seals a way of life in readiness for the final rebirth,
        seals a way of life with The Freewill intact,
        seals a way of life where commitment is retained and
               carried forward,
          where a commitment one way or the other,
          where The Freewill one way or the other,

where the decision powers of man one way or the other,
sum up the residues of life as they tip the scales one way or the other—
to the destiny of eternal life as chosen with God,
or of eternal life as settled by default.

Encountering death is not an incurrence within a life when in line for transitioning—
from life within mortality to life within eternity,
where the scales of influence still are brought to bear—
with registration upon the destiny—
which carries the majority of weight.

Encountering death can be bypassed by those present at The Timing of The Second Advent,
at The Clarion Call of God,
at The Sounding of The Trumpet,
at The Calling of The Shofar,
as when at the arrival of The Dawning of The New Day of The Lord.

Encountering death is soon to be remitted from The Earth,
is soon to be removed from the experience of man,
is soon to no longer be the lead-in to The Resurrection.

Encountering death will become a memory from the past,
an experience of going through a different portal,
an entry into the companionship of God through
a much wider gate.

Encountering death is presently a relief to some who are bound with pain,
who are bound with disabilities,
who are bound in need of attendance
for the comforting things of life.

Encountering death is The Earthly Call to The Heavenly Realm.

Encountering death is the absenting of tears for the spreading of the smiles.

Encountering death holds the soliloquy of man's farewell;
holds man's welcome call from God.

Encountering death is the claimant of man's mortality,
is the shepherd of man's eternity.

Encountering death is the switchover point on the rail track to the stars.

Encountering death is not the bearer of a feared residue ending in extinction,
is not the fresh start of a repeating life in a different guise,
is not the situation which meets with a fatality—
arising from a self-inflicted death.

Encountering death is not to be feared by the faith-filled.

Encountering death is not to be converted from being the welcome mat of Heaven, into becoming a lost shroud without its bones upon The Earth.

Encountering death is that envisioned by God,
                    is that encountered by God,
                    is that overcome by God,
                    is that which left footprints on The Earth,
                    is that which showed and demonstrated the pathway home to God.

Encountering death on The Cross was the meeting place of God with man,
                    was the place of the reconciliation of man back into
                                        The Family of God,
                    was the place from where My Spirit was released,
                    was the place from where the gifts of God were nurtured:
            in preparation for man's proxy ministry across the totality of The Earth.

Encountering death was the only way forward for man—
                    until The Cross of God stood upon the hill of Calvary—
                    and Golgotha shared its message of Resurrection
                                        with the world."

My Content Study Aid

_____
_____
_____
_____
_____
_____
_____
_____
_____
_____
_____
_____
_____
_____
_____
_____
_____
_____

The Reservoir of Oil

And I hear The Lord Jesus saying,
"The reservoir of 'Anointing' oil or 'Holy' water may be coming to an end.

The reservoir of oil rests within a stoppered bottle,
                may no longer be an adjunct to a blessing as recorded,
                may no longer be an accessory to a worthy priest of note.

The reservoir of oil,
            stands in significance of instruction,
        should be as ordered by God for The Wisdom of the priests in consecration,
                            of the furnishing at home within
                                The Temple,
              as started and prolonged in Faith,
              as selected and confirmed with blessings,
              as applied and carried forth in prayer,
              as an adjunct approved and cherished by God.

The reservoir of oil has its historical recipe included in the record,
            has its origins recorded with a profiling of a blessing,
              a profiling of the healing of the sick when seeking the presence
                                of The Elders,
           shares in the oil's misuse after the destruction of The Temple,
           may have a profiling of assistance in the sequestering of the demonic,
                  from an expected or present Temple of My Spirit.

The reservoir of oil is not a creature comfort for widespread use,
           may now be a mystery of existence,
           may now be a cry unto the wilderness,
               as the activities of time and history have united in the passing:
                       of the levitical priesthood of The Temple;
         together with the resources available in line with The Will of God.

The reservoir of oil may not now be deserving of an altar,
           may not now be fitted to a high place as with a likely lowly stature,
           may not now be susceptible to replenishment nor to further selection
                            of the bidden type:
              where the addition of some perfume for a noticeable effect,
              disqualifies the blend for the determined use.

The reservoir of oil clings according to its history,
           holds fast with a clinging to a pocket,
               a clinging to a bag,
               a clinging to a safety net where it feels secure,
     where its history bears no relationship to the finished product as available and used.

The reservoir of oil serves as if a mirror for a magician,

ANTHONY A EDDY (SCRIBE)

as if a system bred for distraction and for emphasis:
when reaching out as 'holy water',
when reaching out by sprinkling or by the drop well placed and out of sight,
or when rubbing is deemed necessary so the drop is not inclined to run.

The reservoir of oil and/or 'Holy' water are both the subjects of serious overcharging,
have no relationship to the quantity supplied,
have no relationship to the cost of preparation with delivery,
have no attempt to honour God as evidenced by those who set the prices of extortion.

The reservoir of oil has an open background,
has an appeal unto the senses,
has an appeal to that which is considered suitable,
is selected for a mostly irrelevant suitability,
where standards are no longer called into existence,
where history does no longer have a bearing,
where similarity has no qualified basis of comparison,
where viscosity is unconsidered,
where the sensing properties have more relevance within the
kitchen cupboard,
where cooking generates an interest with a call to service.

The reservoir of oil is oft treated as a repository of sacredness,
is oft treated as an essential item to a ministry,
is oft treated as having healing properties inherent in its nature,
is oft treated as essential to affirm a healing anticipation in the
completion of a prayer.

The reservoir of oil can be the backstop to idolatry,
can be an idol in disguise,
can be idolatry in action,
can be of no effect at all except to sometimes make a mess,
to sometimes bring a query,
to sometimes run-out with the bringing of much concern and trepidation:
as to the effect of absence with the association as linked to Faith.

The reservoir of oil is not a good investment for a proxy ministry of God;
has overtures of a perceived insufficiency in need of boosting,
where such a tendency may lead to a distancing from God,
has overtures of charlatans as working at a sideshow:
where the crowds do gather for amusement with trickery,
as the dominant force seen on display.

The reservoir of oil has its contribution challenged when applied by the faithful Elders:
to the faith-filled in the suffering call of the sick.

The reservoir of oil may not be published as if acting as the reservoir for attaching blame,
may not bring and lay ridicule or failure at the footstool of God,

may not attack the foundations of belief through the ministry of man:
where The God of Nations has an avid interest in The Truth,
as manifested in the segregating of the profane from the holy.

The reservoir of oil can be an example:
of idolatry in action,
of a carelessness in approach,
of the following of false emphasis,
of the establishment of historical obedience where the rite is not a right,
of a rite which is a wrong,
of a tradition where the rite is well past due for a sacrifice with honour.

The reservoir of oil can manifest from a habit,
can manifest as a habit,
can manifest from the tired and worn,
from the unthinking and the careless,
from the elderly embedded with the customs of the past.

The reservoir of oil speaks volumes in its presence,
may be shunned and discarded,
may not be necessary within a true dependency on God.

The reservoir of oil when tendered or prepared:
can have an application denied or questioned by the wise;
denied or affirmed as the experience being planned for the uncertain;
denied continuously while in the process of being offered to the
trembling and the nervous.

The reservoir of oil may not be an instrument of God entailed for the presence of
His healing gift.

The reservoir of oil may not be a conscript in a process where idolatry reigns regardless
of the consequences.

The reservoir of oil can sound the warning notes of common sense,
can be countenanced with any properties accruing from God,
can be so placed upon the skin of man,
can be carried in a proxy ministry of God.

The reservoir of oil can be a wakeup call to the observant,
can be a shout of disbelief upon a ministry not operating in a close
relationship with God,
can be the farewell to those who carry the impostors of fake references:
with attempts to call on the inherent Truth of God,
when using the composite lies of man.

The reservoirs of oil and water will lose their relevancy at The Second Advent
of The Lord."

ANTHONY A EDDY (SCRIBE)

The Patter of The Rain

And I hear The Lord Jesus saying,
"The patter of the rain should be of comfort to man.

The patter of the rain is not something to be feared,
is not something to be avoided,
is not something to be denigrated within the experience or memory
of man.

The patter of the rain is a sign that all is well,
is not exerting wrath,
is steady in the witnessing of control.

The patter of the rain is enjoyed by the vegetation invested in by man,
is enjoyed by the greenery invested in by God.

The patter of the rain is welcomed by the seasons of The Earth,
is welcomed by the thirsty and the withered,
is welcomed by the dusty and the dry.

The patter of the rain is the sounding of the release of heaven,
is the sounding of a gentle beat upon a roof,
is the sounding of the quenching of a thirst,
is a sounding of the sprouting of the seeds as sown by man.

The patter of the rain is enjoyed by the animals of the fields,
by the animals watching from the shelter of the trees,
by the animals who want to wash their coats.

The patter of the rain speaks to the fish of 'a fresh' within a stream,
a deepening of a river running low,
a cooling of the warmth within the flow,
a time to prepare to await the washing of
the overhang—
with a meal into the water—
as delivered from the sky.

The patter of the rain is gentle and forgiving,
is soaking and absorbed,
is appreciated and relieves—
the concerns of the planter of the crop.

The patter of the rain knows it can overcome,
that it can quietly invade and capture the gratitude of man.

The patter of the rain is a welcome sound at night,
cures the tossing and the turning with the fullness of a night of rest,
fills the closing eyes with the light of expectations for the benefits:

to be so welcomed in the landscape of the dawn.

The patter of the rain does not create the puddles,
does not create the mud,
does not drown out what it has been sent to nourish and so to save.

The patter of the rain brings the gleam of dollars back into a livelihood,
puts a smile upon a visage and removes the lines of worry,
places shopping hands in pockets while waiting for completion—
with a visit to the town of servicing where favour is encountered:
with friendships confirmed by greetings in the raincoats sprinkled
with the rain.

The patter of the rain is not a flood in the making,
is not the forerunner of a washout on a slope,
is not a surplus gone to waste in the drowning of a crop.

The patter of the rain speaks of replenishment of the stockpile in a tank:
in feeding from a roof.

The patter of the rain spreads the gift of God in a region waiting for its turn,
in a region serviced by the mountains,
in a region serviced by the rivers—
the pathways of the rain,
the highways of the fish,
the waterers and conveyancers—
in their returning of the surplus to the seas.

The patter of the rain is felt and enjoyed by those with understanding;
is received and welcomed in the nurturing—
of what is later expected to be reaped or gathered;
is to be treated with due honour for its major role within creation:
as creation comes to drink from the waters bringing and maintaining life—
within its capsules of containment.

The patter of the rain varies with the concentration of the clouds,
the height and depth accompanying,
the turbulence involved,
the churning due to the heating of the sun.

The patter of the rain sends the timid seeking shelter,
sends the young seeking comfort under wings,
sends the time-released and the targeted attending to supplies.

The patter of the rain is measured and reported,
is assessed within the range of scarcity and surplus,
brings smiles when judgment reflects due satisfaction:
at the level in the rain gauge.

The patter of the rain causes sprints unto the clothes lines,

ANTHONY A EDDY (SCRIBE)

applies an urgency to fast recoveries,
runs return trips until all are gathered in—
with the shutting of the doors.

The patter of the rain brings the children and the pets to similar decisions—
imposes thoughts of shelter and protection:
as evidenced by the hurried retreats from that which was holding their attentions.

The patter of the rain instigates a call for umbrellas,
a call for the protecting of the head and shoulders,
a call for a walk maintained in the presence of others
scurrying to reach the proximity:
of where the rain can no longer wet and trickle down the neck.

The patter of the rain can be controlled by man,
can be controlled in prayers,
can be controlled when thought has been given to both the start
and the ending:
together with the amount required.

The patter of rain speaks of The Loving Living God aware of man's dependency
on the cycling;
is aware of when a relationship of trust exists,
is aware of The Faith within a heart,
is aware of the sincerity expressed;
is aware of the reality of responsibility—
both accepted and discharged,
is aware of when gratitude is both expressed
and meant."

My Content Study Aid

The Fishers and The Catchers

And I hear The Lord Jesus saying,
"The fishers and the catchers usually work together,
usually have similar objectives,
usually have meaningful results
where the day is far from wasted,
where the storm is now abated,
where the residues are worthy of success.

The fishers and the catchers are good at what they do,
know the stories of the risks and hazards,
the stories for the young at heart,
the stories with the basis of The Truth.

The fishers and the catchers often have a playground built on boats,
often have to put shoe leather to The Earth,
often have to travel in:
an earthbound car,
or in an air bound cabin of a plane,
or in a sea bound cabin on a ship.

The fishers and the catchers rarely catch a fish which flaps in an effort to escape.

The fishers and the catchers seek the ones fully dressed which:
are easy to call into an open conversation,
are easy to question when time is not pressured,
when daylight brings forth the sunshine as rationed to its care.

The fishers and the catchers discuss the higher things in life—
the valued and the helpful,
the majestic and the moving,
the thoughtful and the graceful,
the enhancing and the adjuncts to a life of wonder as built for:
the receiving of the miracles,
the acknowledging of the miracles,
the thankfulness for the miracles,
as they are gathered in by the knowledgable and the needy,
by the injured and the pained,
by the sick and the hurting—
who are most interested to learn of the ease of access available,
upon a request for help.

The fishers and the catchers have the love for the fellow man at heart,
desire to share the plans for beneficence with welfare,
for Righteousness and Truth,
for both Faith and Grace together,

as they share the two fields of each in unity of existence:
as promises are upheld and needs are resolved,
prior to the onset of the sleeping of the just.

The fishers and the catchers are the gatherers and the teachers,
are both knowledgable and wise,
are both patient and serving,
are thorough and dependable,
are reliant on the spoken word being heard for both
attention and actioning:
without a word being missed.

The fishers and the catchers are experienced and confident:
in what they say and do;
in how they speak and encourage the corrective actions they request;
of how they become excited for their companion,
when requests are handled promptly right before their eyes.

The fishers and the catchers are familiar with the pain thresholds,
like to see them broken and despatched,
like to see them nullified and neutralized,
like to see the joyful expressions on a face,
when realization dawns of that which they have just experienced,
without the fuss and hoo-ha.

The fishers and the catchers listen attentively as a new testimony is born,
as a new testimony to be remembered,
as a new testimony worthy of a grateful
heart with a private word of thanks.

The fishers and the catchers do not like to be hurried,
like to include,
to bind,
to loose,
as The Spirit calls with His gifts unto the spirit:
with the gifts,
as lodged and available for an install and usage,
as appreciated in the holding of The Keys of Heaven:
as the dwellers on The Earth.

The fishers and the catchers anticipate success,
know the doors are opened by He who goes before,
recognize the divine appointment:
note the golden rendezvous-in-waiting,
await the hugs of appreciation for the changes wrought,
as the fish no longer seeks to escape,
is willing to settle in to the new life ahead.

The fishers and the catchers salute the honourable and the trustworthy,
the righteous and the truthful,
the prayerful and the worshippers.

The fishers and the catchers know the access way as revealed,
the access way
which can be traced from its beginning at The Cross of Calvary,
which can be traced through all the wonders of creation:
to a commitment which stands the final test of time.

The fishers and the catchers encourage a decision which removes the destiny of default,
which imposes Faith and Trust where
previously there was none.

The fishers and the catchers are familiar with two letters of The Greek alphabet with
very special meaning:
The Alpha and The Omega,
the first and the last,
the beginning and the end.

The fishers and the catchers invite all to attend to consummate:
the memory aroused by the bread and the wine,
that Grace may be seen in action as adoption flares in blessing,
The Committed and The Righteous from within The Bride of Christ.

The fishers and the catchers have fished and caught:
on the proxy ministry of Jesus;
have scaled and dressed the catch within the folds of The Divine;
have prepared and taught the basics in readiness for achievement;
have the knowledge mixed with Wisdom regarding the reliability:
of the evidence as both read and heard.

The fishers and the catchers are the end-time servants of The Living Loving God:
who lived through and conquered;
by His death and resurrection on and from The Cross;
with the release of man's Freewill,
with the release of Faith as tempered,
by the power and the authority of unhindered Grace;
for on what much has been written,
so much more can be said."

My Content Study Aid

_____

_____

_____

The Role/Roll of Thunder

And I hear The Lord Jesus saying,
"The role of thunder reverberates across the heavens,
        grumbles to itself as it sulks at the loss of voice,
        laughs at any echo,
        and tips the hailstones out of bed.

The role of thunder is a child of frustration,
        feels it's a one-shot wonder,
        never is given a second chance at life,
        builds up a head of steam which triggers with a bang,
                        when its back is turned.

The role of thunder keeps an eye on its surroundings,
        watches carefully the potential building up,
        is careful with the placement of its shoulders,
        weighs the loading of the rain,
        is cautious with the sleet as it attempts to break free.

The roll of thunder scares the wild horses on the hilltops,
        sees the birds flee to the comfort of the trees,
        wonders why the ponds have shivers on their surfaces,
        as the shock waves of the moment are absorbed in dissipation.

The role of thunder expresses an introduction for the followers at large,
        expresses the will of the condensers and the aggregators,
        expresses the free fall with the achievement of escape:
        from all the ups and downs of growth when trapped within his grasp.

The role of thunder does not go out with a fizzle,
        ensures all do know of its presence and intent,
        as it skirts the mountaintop which would penetrate its base,
        as it veers as guided by the wind,
        to avoid an argument with the stone walls of a chain in place,
                        both steadfast and secure.

The role of thunder neither shelters nor protects,
        neither limits nor measures,
        neither controls nor determines.

The role of thunder spreads and dumps on what is underneath,
        does not care for the landscape from a bird's eye view,
        does not care for the fruit trees or the ripening of the crops,
        sees no damage wrought,
        knows the smell of rain,
        sees the white deposits bringing the stripping of the trees,

with the bruising of The Earth.

The role of thunder is the indicator of release,
       is the signifier that weight has won the battle of the uplift:
          that now all is to be dumped on the terrain as underneath,
          that the hail stones will be fully grown and sized,
              about to be shown to all upon The Earth,
          with what appears to be a semblance of pride in what has been
               compiled and placed,
          without regard or favour on the effort of the unfortunate,
          which now may only watch in dismay as the bruising and the
               damage continues,
              until all is finally spent;
         as movement is encouraged to another venue.

The role of thunder brings no joy to the orchardists,
       brings no joy to the croppers,
       brings no joy to the sensitive of that which is laid out on The Earth.

The role of thunder may wipe out a year's returns,
       may cancel all the expectations,
       may destroy the cash flow of dependency and hope.

The role of thunder gives insufficient warning,
       speaks of instantaneous release,
       does not stay to repair the damage.

The role of thunder may usurp the right to dominion,
       may usurp the effort of Freewill,
       may usurp the controls of man.

The role of thunder needs to be curbed and controlled in its infancy of formation,
       needs an appeal to God,
       needs the call from a dependent heart with the declaring of desires,
       needs the call to remove the threat before it becomes unmanageable,
          and the damage has been done.

The role of thunder can be prevented and upheld,
       can be discharged from the inspections and sent on its way:
       still embroiled and searching for a place to stay,
          where appreciation reigns.

The role of thunder sips but does not drink,
       tastes but does not swallow,
       may harm or help but should not bring despair.

The role of thunder supplies the distance from a target,
       indicates the energising of the family,
       announces the battle plans as drawn for the fiercest of fierce storms.

ANTHONY A EDDY (SCRIBE)

The role of thunder awaits the flash to play its part,
  can bring bystanders to stand and watch the battle in the sky,
  can send a hint to the exposed and uncovered in its sending of
      the scurrying to shelter.

The role of thunder cannot change its course without some worthwhile interference;
  cannot change its potential for delivery without the interference:
    of the seekers of recourse with an action plan in play;
  cannot drift away without the seeking of a replevin bringing matters
      to a head,
    where the receivers of their loss may have cause to seek
      the reparation:
    for that which was taken without due cause and notice.

The role of thunder can summon rain to the unwatered seeds,
  can bring rain to save the thirsty in their growth,
  can fill the reservoirs of storage and availability—
    as they even out the supply chain of measurement and demand.

The role of thunder is often a welcome sound upon the landscape,
  is often an answering of prayer,
  is often valued for the bringing of a much needed fall of rain,
    upon a cracked and barren land where the cattle are at risk,
    as poverty raises its ugly head in surveillance of the scene.

The role of thunder gives notice to man for the options of delivery,
  invites man to take control in the prayer field of consulting,
  seeks man to be aware of The Wisdom within The Counselling of God."

My Content Study Aid

_____

_____

_____

_____

_____

_____

_____

_____

_____

_____

_____

The Scribes of God

And I hear The Lord Jesus saying,
"The scribes of God are cherished and protected,
>>are valued with independence,
>>are teachable and truthful,
>>are Righteousness personified within their Temples of The Spirit.

The scribes of God are each called by The Lord,
>>are the first to hear to see to detail with implicit accuracy
>>>>the speaking of The Lord:
>>>as intended for the ears or eyes of man,
>>>as intended for His People,
>>>as intended for the senses of earthly
>>>>royalty with their thrones as filled.

The scribes of God are reached with the imagery of visions,
>>>the songs as dwelling within the field of music,
>>>the choreographic scripts as they trip the body feet
>>>>and hands—
>>in filling a presentation with both Grace and timing,
>>>the counselling from within the field of Wisdom
>>>>reaching out in consolation,
>>>the interpretations of the verbal gift of tongues—
>>>as coming forth with understanding and
>>>>with accuracy:
>>>of the tenor of His calling within the field
>>>>of servicing,
>>>the communication needs of divinity in action;
>>>as the scribes attend their recording functioning
>>>>enacted for delivery,
>>>with neither fault nor explanation.

The scribes of God are the preservers of the time fields of the past,
>>>are the keepers of the scrolls of God,
>>>are the expositors of God selected for their skills,
>>>are the establishers of the record of The Word on which a populace
>>>>does feed,
>>>are the assemblers of the recorded intent of Divinity as timed and set
>>>>and sent by God.

The scribes of God are scattered but reachable,
>>are conscientious but perfectionists,
>>are time sensitive but reliable.

The scribes of God have attributes aligned with their perspectives,
>>have close relationships with God,

ANTHONY A EDDY (SCRIBE)

do not procrastinate their work load,
have connections open 24/7 into the relay stations of The Lord—
where thought transference is inlaid into a brain-set with connectivity,
through The Holy Spirit within a Temple of The Lord.

The scribes of God are Followers of The Ways of God,
are Adherents to The Will of God,
are Disciples in their Walk with God,
are The Exercisers of their Freewill within The Objectives of God,
are Participants in Communion with God,
are perseverant in targeting completion.

The scribes of God can be The transmitters of The Wisdom of God,
can be The Resource Fields for The Gifts of The Spirit,
can be The Conduits for Answered Prayers.

The scribes of God are not seekers of publicity,
have their fruit readied for display,
where The Holy Spirit both guides and directs
as the doors are opened,
as the fare is laid upon the tables,
as choice comes to the fore with inspection,
as to acceptability of the content in the directing
of a life:
as activity responds within Freewill.

The scribes of God are the retailers of The Truth,
are The Opponents of Evolutionary Theory denouncing God,
are The Links to The Word of God destined to stand for all eternity:
without adjustment to The Truth Statements as initiated by God.

The scribes of God are blessed with common sense,
are blessed with access to The Living God,
are blessed with The Trust of God,
are blessed when walking within the fields of need,
are blessed within the affirmations of God,
are blessed within the prayer contacts where healing is requested,
are blessed within the constructs where intent comes to the fore
as dictation is received.

The scribes of God are visionaries of the future,
are the warning bells of approaching conflict,
are the alarm sounders for the coming trials of man,
are the upholders of the heavenly courts of justice on The Earth,
are the advance warners with the calls to man,
where The Wrath of God is soon to settle in His cleansing motions,
of where God is no longer honoured as blasphemy rules the day
and the night,

as the utterances by the thoughtless and the fools,
confirms the approaching intent of God.

The scribes of God are acceptable to God,
are acceptable for the ease of intercommunication,
are acceptable for the rendering of the initiations as offered up by God.

The scribes of God are talented and capable,
are thoughtful and consistent,
are secure and unimpaired.

The scribes of God are native speakers of the tongues employed,
are tongue speakers of The Heavenly endowed,
are confidential in the preparation of their work loads,
are close confidants of God.

The scribes of God are forward thinking and explicit,
are familiar with the safety checks for the uncovering of interference,
of insertions without the affirmations of validity,
of spontaneous comments without due relevancy
to the subject matter.

The scribes of God are aware of the necessary checks and balances,
are aware of the sensitive nature of their calling,
are aware of the protective nature of The Loving God of man,
are aware of the reality of The God of man alive within The Trinity,
with the deepest of concern,
for the welfare of man's body soul and spirit
on both sides of the grave."

My Content Study Aid

_____

_____

_____

_____

_____

_____

_____

_____

_____

_____

The Hero of A Revolution

And I hear The Lord Jesus saying,
"The hero of a revolution is a statesman motivated by statehood,
　　　　　　　　a statesman who is firmly fixed on looking to the future.

The hero of a revolution is not concerned about the present,
　　　　　　　has learnt from the past,
　　　　　　　will not suffer a repeat of practices which have gone before.

The hero of a revolution is the tall poppy who refuses to be trampled
　　　　　　by the mob composed of mediocrities;
　　　　　　　　composed of sin in seeking financial opportunities;
　　　　　　　　composed of cronyism and the getting of a cut;
　　　　　　　　composed of the here and now with everyone for themselves;
　　　　　　　　composed of a lying tongue to convince all:
　　　　　that butter would not melt within their mouths,
　　　　　that they are knowledgable and caring within the pocketing of their votes,
　　　　　that they are forthright and reliable in all they say and do,
　　　　　that they are not participants in the club of the shady and dishonest,
　　　　　that they are not prone to linger in the filth available—
　　　　　　when unaccompanied in the promoting of their endeavours of the night,
　　　　　that their greatest fear shrieks in trepidation at the likelihood of exposure.

The hero of a revolution often quickly gathers the servile and the hitchers of a ride;
　　　　　　　often gathers those with an eye as to a meal ticket;
　　　　　　　　with an eye as to a free ride to 'success',
　　　　　　　　with an eye as to a secret motivation which if declared—
　　　　　　　　　　would bring others to run for cover without delay,
　　　　　　　　with an eye which only sings the praises of the self—
　　　　　　　　　which is ignorant of the details and how they may
　　　　　　　　　　　　be achieved.

The hero of a revolution needs to sort the rats and mice from The Committed and
　　　　　　　　　　　　The Free,
　　　　　　　needs to resolve the stairs of authority,
　　　　　　　needs to know the backgrounds to the would-be supplicants,
　　　　　　　　　to the would-be joiners for a journey,
　　　　　　　　　to the would-be architects—
　　　　　　　　of what they have previously failed to understand,
　　　　　　　　　　nor been able to construct.

The hero of a revolution does not fade away when the road deteriorates—
　　　　　　as it starts to pour from clouds which obscure the presence of the sun.

The hero of a revolution perseveres until he overcomes,
　continues until the end comes into sight,

continues until the horizon is reached and seen to be already compliant with his vision.

The hero of a revolution marks the goalposts as being upright and fully centred,
of being vertical and true,
of being strong yet swaying in a gale,
of being permanent fixtures within his
mindset for fulfilling The Keys of
Righteousness and Truth—
which are repeatedly seen to sail between the goalposts set in
judgment of determination:
for each day of progress and salutation in its valued
contribution to the future.

The hero of a revolution dances to no one else's jig,
is tied to no one else's lead,
is free from indebtedness and subservience,
is free from the tugging of control,
is free to pursue the golden dream,
is free to vanquish the users and usurpers from positions they
have long since envied:
with their postings of rewards.

The hero of a revolution knows to move and to gather within the close proximity of God,
knows the trustworthiness of the counselling of God,
knows the widespread access to both the knowledge and to The
Wisdom borne of God,
knows the satisfaction in the completion of a task installed
by God,
knows the assistance made available on applying The Keys of
The Kingdom to the gifts of God,
knows the foresight and the success rate in listening to God,
knows the destiny of promise as entered into by The King
of kings.

The hero of a revolution does not encounter violence—
when his trust is placed upon a ballot box:
which is highly valued for the record kept within,
for the record holding change,
for the record sustaining a new direction,
denoting confirmation of the oversight of God,
upholding the acceptance of a review of policies of value
within The Edifice of God.

The hero of a revolution remains so because of the marked absence of blood,
because of the will of the people being followed,
because of the supranumeracy of The Caring Loving God.

The hero of a revolution forges a new way forward,

declares a forsaking of the past's inaction,
churns the wheels throughout the land to operate at a much
faster pace,
applies the hands to busyness in earning fresh rewards,
ensures Faith with Righteousness are reinstated as objectives
worthy of aspiration.

The hero of a revolution keeps the goalposts securely in place,
prevents them from being moved,
enhances their appearance:
in their becoming worthy to be hugged with full acceptance of their Promises—
established in fulfilment.

The hero of a revolution sees wonders and miracles descending
within the cloudbursts of God."

My Content Study Aid

_____

_____

_____

_____

_____

_____

_____

_____

_____

_____

_____

_____

_____

_____

_____

_____

_____

_____

_____

_____

The Triumph of Man

And I hear The Lord Jesus saying,
"The triumph of man speaks of his ability to overcome the hazarding of life.

The triumph of man rests in his alliance with his God,
>> his approval of The Father,
>> his adoption of My Spirit,
>> his reliance on My guidance as born of Sacrifice and pain.

The triumph of man speaks of recognizing and adopting the example set by
>>> The Son of God,
>> of recognizing and adopting the gifts of The Risen Christ,
>> of recognizing and adopting the mission fields as set by God.

The triumph of man speaks of the recognizing and adopting The Discipleship of The Son,
>> of Faith in The Promises of God,
>> of Faith in The Living Loving God,
>> of Faith in following in His footsteps,
>> of Faith in testifying of His Earthly Deeds,
>>> as examples to be learnt,
>>> as examples to be taught to the children of the day.

The triumph of man was not achieved by his surrendering to Satan,
>> was not achieved by fragmentation with the splitting of the vote,
>> was not achieved by raucous and uncouth behaviour,
>> was not achieved by lying and deceit,
>> was not achieved by ignorance and passivity,
>> was not achieved by labouring within the field of idolatry.

The triumph of man was achieved by commitments of sincerity,
>> by passion for the message,
>>> for the recognition of the reality of the destiny
>>>> of choice,
>> by the first hand experiencing of the love and proxy
>>> ministry imparted,
>>> as received from The Saviour of the lost.

The triumph of man speaks to his environment,
>> speaks to his growing awareness,
>> speaks to his solicitation for the joining of endeavours—
>>>> to benefit The Earth,
>>>> the sea,
>>>> the sky.

The triumph of man has many and varied aspects by which he may be rated—
>> either with a swing to the positive—
>> with assistance of recovery:

ANTHONY A EDDY (SCRIBE)

with improvement being offered to the weak
and threatened;
or a swing to the negative with the resultant extinction
of species—
once either met the wants or needs of man,
or got in his farming way.

The triumph of man tends to evaluate his success by measuring his progress over time—
the discoveries and inventions,
the complex and the transparent,
the agricultural and the industrial,
the labouring and the opening field—
where technology reigns to stretch the imagining of man,
and the expanding longevity of life itself,
within the effects of medicine,
on the mortal life of man.

The triumph of man would like to have it thought that it is proven in the reality of his
reaching for the stars,
would like to have it thought that it is proven in the reality of
visiting the depths of marine life,
from the shore line to the touching of the bottom,
would like to have it thought that it is proven in the reality of
advances in the applications of his knowledge—
where Wisdom really needs to increase its headway—
so it can be felt as both strong and active within the current reach of man.

The triumph of man can be dramatic depending on the basis of comparison—
where he either stands or falls.

The triumph of man may just be a flimsy shadow getting in the way,
where past civilisations are concerned—
still able to show off their achievements to the amazement of man in his currency:
that which still puzzles man as to enactment of a vision;
standing still as an affirmation of a monument of fitted stone;
or of concrete as formulated in the distant past.

The triumph of man may easily be seen as a fizzle on a stick-end;
where the technology of others far surpasses the still green and the naïve:
in terms of man's achievement within a time frame of a partial blink.

The triumph of man may well be written off as a non-event:
when judged in full knowledge of the past;
and as mixed within the present;
as a secret protected by the lies of man—
in the power play of the ages where ignorance is bliss."

The Upward Path of Man

And I hear The Lord Jesus saying,
"The upward path of man depends upon his willingness to walk,
> to learn,
> to understand,
>> the pathway to the stars.

The upward path of man depends upon his relationship with God,
> his Faith as seen in action,
> his deeds fulfilled within his tasking,
> his immediacy of response to The Golden Words
>> of God,

the closeness of his prayer life in following The Will of God,
the out-turn of his fruit when marked by an initiation seeking the assistance of God,
> with His move into reality,
> with the answering of prayer.

The upward path of man moves and shakes:
> those seeking ministry within The Will of God.

The upward path of man follows closely the path of Trust,
> of Truth,
> and of Experience handed down.

The upward path of man distributes Faith to all encountered on the way,
> shares with those of like Faith unshadowed by the mindset
>> of unbelief,
> builds upon the taskings of the past to secure the unexplainable
>> for attending to—
> the distraught and tearful,
> the pained and the uncomfortable,
> the ageing with afflictions—
> those which only Faith in The Loving God can address
>> and mend.

The upward path of man takes man through the vagaries of life,
> takes man through the seasons of shouting and of recrimination,
> takes man through the times of gentleness and whispers,
> takes man along the pathway of acquisitions
>> where he can pick and choose,
>> where he can select Wisdom as a worthwhile attribute
>>> to match up with his knowledge,
>> where he can come and go,
>> where he can rise and shine,
>> where he can assemble and progress,
>>> as knowledge fortifies and strengthens—

ANTHONY A EDDY (SCRIBE)

the onset of Wisdom;

where he can fall and suffer,
where he can shrink and wither,
as courage fails and Faith departs in waiting for
the turning of a leaf.

The upward path of man sees the spurts of inspiration,
feels the warmth of companionship,
senses the sharing of responsibility—
the amalgamation of the effort which ensures the onset
of success.

The upward path of man is evident in man's mortality.
The upward path of man is likewise evident in eternity.

The upward path of man leads to the wonder of a homecoming
where wonder and gratitude are both beset with beauty.

The upward path of man has no end prior to eternity,
has no end within eternity,
has no end within the time frame of man.

The upward path of man ventures into areas of magnificence,
ventures into arenas of the large and small,
ventures into the concert halls of theatre and of song—
where makeup satisfies the presentations of participants.

The upward path of man has neither somersaults nor about turns surfacing as distractions,
has neither calls nor shouts interfering with concentration,
has neither trips nor stumbles to create unsteadiness,
has neither light flashes nor excessive noise to overcome
the senses,
has neither the flailing of the arms nor the kicking of the feet
to dislodge the balance:
for when balance is both critical and sensitive.

The upward path of man grows and develops in security,
passes through the storms of life unscathed and full of hope,
secures the ropes to hold when rolling all at sea,
tempers haste with safety when in an unexpected presence—
while uncertainty prevails.

The upward path of man offers sensational views from vantage points—
designed as rewards for effort.

The upward path of man does not tolerate veils to hide the face–
either on companions or on strangers encountered on the walk.

The upward path of man keeps man above the mire,

keeps the head of man above the waves at large,
keeps man in his completeness above the fields of
excessive danger,
keeps man above the imminent concerns of those not on
the upward path of man."

My Content Study Aid

_____

_____

_____

_____

_____

_____

_____

_____

_____

_____

_____

_____

_____

_____

_____

_____

_____

_____

_____

_____

_____

_____

_____

_____

_____

_____

The DNA of Man

And I hear The Lord Jesus saying,
"The DNA of man should be of great interest to man,
> holds the history of the development of man as if in a nutshell,
> holds the ancestry of each man as spread across the national
>> boundaries of history.

The DNA of man is now yielding its former secrets into the knowledge base of man,
> is now tracing each ancestral journey to this day of existence,
>> to this day of a released identity,
>> to this day releasing influence and posture,
>> to this day where the uniqueness of identity is revealed
>>> in readiness to seek and find:
> all ancestral relationships which have ended up placing each within the nationhood,
>> where each may now be found.

The DNA of man is as if the ticker-tape declaring each parading of man,
> as each accrues and builds within his registered achievements,
>> of all prior generational building blocks,
>> viewed in survival mode,
>> within the stepping stones of history.

The DNA of man is able to identify like with like,
> is able to enable families to coagulate into the closeness of embrace,
> is able to acquire the knowledge of importance in the decision making
>> of the past,
> is able to bring full understanding to the initiation of journeying,
>> beyond the boundaries of their birth place:
> as such brought change and circumstances afresh;
> as within the lives of those eventuating into a future time and space;
> as accruing from such effort;
> as evidencing the relating of the transfers of success.

The DNA of man measures the success of the reproducers,
> measures the extent of families,
> measures their willingness to separate and to adopt,
> measures their willingness to seek a better way of life,
> measures the necessities encountered in avoiding starvation
>> and the tolling of disease,
> on families without the measures to counter and to overcome,
>> their present situations of suffering and heartbreak.

The DNA of man measures those prepared to take a risk:
>> with a leap of Faith into the unknown,
> where willingness and determination will justify and benefit
>> the welfare of a transferred family:

now separated by distance and the unwillingness to return,
until well established in a setting judged as a success;
without the trials and tribulations as previously encountered:
being without reward,
as daily drudgery with hunger accompanied by ill health
continued unabated,
as families were seen to generate nothing—
except entries in the local churchyard cemeteries.

The DNA of man stems from the record keeping of God,
stems from the design of God,
stems from the preservation of uniqueness within families,
of uniqueness across the generations—
where blood lines are not constant,
stems from the necessity to minimize the cloning
of the spirit and the soul:
as when shared by the split embedding in the birthing of identical twins—
both sharing their identity.

The DNA of man can indicate a common ancestry in the extremely distant past,
can indicate what occurred beyond the present memory of written
family history,
before literacy was attained in making record keeping possible;
before when the family histories were only verbal:
as maintained down through the generations through recounting
by the elderly,
when seated round the fires providing warmth and food.

The DNA of man is a very recent revelation:
now moving into the memory banks of man,
where it was still unknown within the present living memory,
as generations previously were reliant on the written records,
as recorded by the establishment of the writing tools of man.

The DNA of man still has a much greater amount of knowledge to impart to man,
as man learns to read with full understanding that which maps
the development of man,
as man can break the mapping code into smaller and
smaller segments,
so the knowledge base of man will increase in leaps and bounds,
as sensibility dawns in all its fullness of potential,
with the understanding of the content of the creation sequencing
of man.

The DNA of man brings historicity to the present,
places all the detail into the hands of man as guided
by man's inherent curiosity.

ANTHONY A EDDY (SCRIBE)

The DNA of man dates from the origin of man when The DNA was first adulterated:
>by man's cross-breeding with a species of manufactured compatibility.

The DNA of man,
>as now being unravelled upon The Earth,
>holds the key to man's earthly supremacy,
>holds the key to man's increase in brain capacity with the shell wherein
>>such dwells,
>holds the key to man's present level of intellect with the extra capacity
>>lying dormant:
>>as yet unused—
>for great is man's mental capacity when the brain is fully formatted:
>in readiness for the acquiring of the database still awaiting input,
>thereby achieving the completion of the mortal preparation of man
>>for his entry to eternity;
>with the updating input of God to be so installed in fullness,
>for the onward guiding of activity in an approaching expectant life.

The DNA of man travels with man wherein such stands as the record of the completion
>of mortality."

"The Neandertals supplied the basket holding The DNA of Man."

My Content Study Aid

_____

_____

_____

_____

_____

_____

_____

_____

_____

_____

_____

_____

_____

_____

_____

The Seasoning of Man

And I hear The Lord Jesus saying,
"The seasoning of man speaks of the attaining of maturity of outlook.

The seasoning of man indicates a change of attitude within the mindset,
indicates a welcome to the stars at large,
indicates a status due in the respect or honouring of man's Freewill
as tabulated and retained,
indicates the achieving of a milestone in the life of man to augment
the future,
highlights the storing of the keepsakes reserved as 'Responsibility'
becomes married with 'Achievement' so to cuddle up in bed.

The seasoning of man enlarges opportunities,
fulfils ambition going forward,
steps upon the matters deserving to be squashed.

The seasoning of man verifies the effort and the learning,
justifies the teaching and the rewards,
encourages progression further into The Family of God.

The seasoning of man is not a haphazard affair,
is not a mistaken measure of success,
is not the totality of life,
is not the summation of experience,
is not the antithesis of failure.

The seasoning of man is as a milestone of achievement added to the lockbox of
Trust and Faith,
is the recompense for the absorption of information as it opens
the horizons for a better view.

The seasoning of man does not trip over spices,
is not garnered for a plate,
is not questioned about the application of the salt and pepper.

The seasoning of man measures the robustness of the spirit,
the intensity of the soul,
the security of the body—
in displaying the attributes of manhood in his daily walk within the statutes of life.

The seasoning of man can stand up to the weather,
can bounce the hail off without an injury,
can willingly partake in the jocular and friendly efforts
to initiate a smile,
to terminate in the breeding of a laugh when laughs are very
scarce in the middling of a winter.

ANTHONY A EDDY (SCRIBE)

The seasoning of man is not as if a bluegum log dried in readiness for the fire,
        is not the repository of sparks,
        is not the status holder calling for explosion within a showcase
                of combustion.

The seasoning of man is not a welcome to senility,
        is not the onset of selfishness,
        is not the installing of desires as gathered casually in the passing by,
        is not the stops upon a highway for rest and relaxation.

The seasoning of man is there within a handclasp,
        is there in the offer of assistance,
        is there in the unbidden generosity towards his fellow man,
        is there in the commitment to a promise awaiting its redemption.

The seasoning of man is there within his change in lifestyle,
        is there within the forsaking of his games of childhood:
                to concentrate on the new needs of a growing family,
        is there when toys are discarded to a basket:
                as having lost all their former appeal resulting from
                        childhood addiction.

The seasoning of man does not bring backward glances,
        does not bring grievances afresh,
        does not bring the stirring of the pots—
                to the front and centre.

The seasoning of man knows the value of introspection,
        knows the value of meditation,
        knows the value of due consideration prior to the rush to arms.

The seasoning of man values the sidestep in the avoidance of a puddle,
        the jumping of a ditch,
        the climbing of a fence,
        the cautious approach deemed necessary:
                when insulators are on view,
        the resultant clambering over a wooden gate.

The seasoning of man is as grist in overflow from the mill of experience,
        is as grist drawn from the bank of capability,
        is as grist released from the bank of enthusiasm,
        is as grist gathered from the banking of awareness,
        is as the grist of Wisdom as it increases or retreats within the bank:
        which holds the residues of common sense.

The seasoning of man resets the preparedness of man,
        resets his thinking in advance,
        resets his avoidance of the errors of the past,
        resets his attitude when installed in an adventure.

The seasoning of man sees him camp with care,
>> not get flooded out,
>> not forced to pack up in haste,
>> not lashing out in anger or frustration as a pet gets in the way.

The seasoning of man sees his vocabulary controlled,
>> sees his regard for others established and manifested with a degree
>>> of service,
>> sees his garb appropriate to the circumstances of surroundings.

The seasoning of man does not violate a trust,
>> does not violate the law,
>> does not short-change the aged and the dependent,
>> does not upset a kindred character at home within belief.

The seasoning of man does not make a spectacle of himself,
>> does not suffer the lolling of his head,
>>> the slurring of his speech,
>>> the handling of a vehicle—
>>>> with a tainted breath,
>>> the stumbling of his step with the loosing
>>>> of control.

The seasoning of man does not trigger confrontation,
>> does not bicker into disjointed conversations,
>> does neither discuss nor argue when the cause is immaterial and
>>> it is a lovely day.

The seasoning of man appreciates The Works of God,
>> appreciates the beauty of His finished sculpturing of man,
>> appreciates the gifts of God as enhancements to the breathing
>>> and self-aware.

The seasoning of man knows the destiny achieved by choice,
>> The Wisdom in deleting the destiny approaching in default,
>> the importance of deciding on commitment,
>>> with a happy ending,
>>> while it is today."

My Content Study Aid

_____

_____

_____

_____

The Freewill of Man

And I hear The Lord Jesus saying,
"The Freewill of man is exercised with forethought.

The Freewill of man is exercised in selfishness,
>> is exercised in generosity,
>> is exercised in caring for his neighbour.

The Freewill of man surfaces in love,
>> surfaces in hate,
>> surfaces in life spent nearest to an altar.

The Freewill of man surfaces within the will of demons,
>> surfaces within the will of self-aggrandisement,
>> surfaces within The Will of God.

The Freewill of man changes on a whim,
>> changes on correction,
>> changes on guidance,
>> changes on knowledge,
>> changes on Wisdom,
>> changes in the proximity of The Power and The Authority of God.

The Freewill of man is a gift of God,
>> is freed from the controlling laws,
>> is freed from the forced enslavements.

The Freewill of man carries man to the heights of achievement,
>> carries man to the depths of despair.

The Freewill of man carries man throughout his lifetime in mortality,
>> carries man within his freedom in eternity,
>> carries man within his restrictions birthed of judgment:
>>>> when leading to the destiny of default.

The Freewill of man varies with his health,
>> varies with his age,
>> varies with his workload,
>> varies with the chosen pursuits of his life.

The Freewill of man varies with his standing before God,
>> varies with His companionship with God,
>> varies with The Promises of God,
>> varies with the objectives of man,
>> varies with the achievements of man,
>> varies with the desires of man.

The Freewill of man is capable of being weighed,

of being adjusted,
of being targeted.

The Freewill of man is capable of being assigned and lost to servitude,
of being subject to dismissal when followed by a vow,
of being rewarded by a blessing when followed by
a prayer.

The Freewill of man can be served by both knowledge and Wisdom in the satisfaction of
The Accepted Will of God.

The Freewill of man can be vanquished by following a commander with the lies
and the false promises,
with the deceptions bringing frost upon the pathway of default,
with the dismay bred from the realisation of all which has
been foregone:
through ignorance and denial.

The Freewill of man either blesses or curses depending on the scales of justice:
when mixed with Love,
hate,
envy,
lust,
and how he applied his wealth in the freedom of his movements.

The Freewill of man embraces the authority of God,
embraces the dominion of Satan,
embraces a walk with God,
embraces a wandering with demons holding hands,
embraces a life projected as a life with God,
embraces a life as captured by The Devil.

The Freewill of man can bask in the rewards of a life well spent:
aspiring to the heights;
or being decried with the unfolding of his capture:
on a pathway to the depths.

The Freewill of man can vary in intensity,
can vary in obligations,
can vary in a season,
can vary in compression,
can vary in expansion,
can vary in accession.

The Freewill of man can vary in achievement even so when guided by My Spirit;
can vary in achievement when commitment is in doubt;
when commitment fails to climb a mountain,
when commitment races to the exit gate,
when commitment fails to flourish and flowering does not occur,

when commitment wilts and fades and leaves the stage of light.

The Freewill of man can be a source of great endeavour,
                can be a source for changing lives,
                can be a source where hope is reinforced.

The Freewill of man when encouraged,
                      can reconstruct a life;
           when in a mindset to overcome,
                      can dispense with all the sources of addiction,
           when walking in the field of commitment,
                      can build the empires which will shake The Earth.

The Freewill of man is the gifted power of God waiting to be harnessed,
                          waiting to be applied,
                          waiting to be measured when seated on
                                the thresholds of achievement.

The Freewill of man is the greatest gift which man can muster—
                      and to thereby bring unto the service of his God.

The Freewill of man is open,
           with its offerings,
                to The Sacrifice of God,
                to the reconciliation borne of God,
                to The Promises inherent in The Cross,
                to eternal life as demonstrated and so declared by God.

The Freewill of man should seek and retain the knowledge in His Word,
           should seek and,
                by the manner of his acceptance,
           receive and lock away within his heart:
                    his access to the stars;
                    his access to the heavens;
                    his access to The Will and Love of God;
                    his access to eternal life,
              where his commitment will ensure—
                    he reaches his destiny of choice.

The Freewill of man will have My Spirit witness to a Temple,
                that by such is Wisdom shown in readiness,
                to maintain The Companionship of God."

My Content Study Aid

_____

_____

The Squeaking of A Door

And I hear The Lord Jesus saying,
"The squeaking of a door hinders the entering of a room,
of a home,
of a garage,
of a car.

The squeaking of a door serves notice of a need,
serves notice of a lack,
serves notice on a servant with a call to serve.

The squeaking of a door speaks of much service in opening and closing:
in both the heat and the dry;
speaks of a lack of serving the needs of a door,
speaks of a shortage of both effort and of love,
speaks of a future prospect of a near-term silencing,
speaks of achieving a close inspection,
speaks of being hamstrung by a source exposed at a distance,
speaks of being shortchanged in the purchasing.

The squeaking of a door does not speak of life,
does not speak of intelligence in action,
does not speak of engineering heard at work.

The squeaking of a door speaks of the past deteriorating,
speaks of a pathway leading to decay,
speaks of a time where no-one answers a call for help—
to shore up what is surely breaking down.

The squeaking of a door announces friction hard at work,
announces a fault developing,
announces a walk on the roadway to a seizure.

The squeaking of a door awaits the checking of all motion,
awaits the sealing hand of rust,
awaits the sagging of a hinge:
as repair remains unscheduled and rust completes its meal.

The squeaking of a door foretells a resting on the hinges,
a resting on the floor,
a resting in the wind,
a resting announced by the attack of silence.

The squeaking of a door meets head-on the arresting fall of silence,
the arresting of the movement,
the arresting of all ability to open and to close
within the parameters of design—

Anthony A Eddy (Scribe)

now seen as a coming victim of the future:
as a once protective shell is opened to the flailing of the weather with the storms.

The squeaking of a door looks to the future in dismay,
with an awareness that its time is limited:
in the protecting of all which lies within.

The squeaking of a door needs assistance to recover and prolong,
to extend and continue;
does not like to suffer its graduated loss of functioning,
does not like to wait for its capturing and submission—
to the weathering forces with a focus bent on destruction of the effort:
as evidenced by construction in the past when access was controlled.

As it is with doors so it is with man.

For as the signs are there for avoiding the destiny of a door,
when subject to a lack of care and maintenance;
so the future of man may be married to such a path as well.

So man may be attacked progressively—
as each organ and the flesh suffer a weathering by time,
as movement is constrained,
as flexibility is dissipated,
as replenishment and maintenance are forsaken in the present—
with the onset of a breakdown in functionality—
of eyesight for the distant,
of dentistry for the bite,
of blood pressure for the circulation,
of the heart for consistency of pumping,
of the organs staying fresh and active,
of fat leaving the pipelines clear and open to transmission,
of exercise for freedom of motion,
of diet for the flesh,
of antidotal solutions gifting prolonged control.

As the door stopped squeaking over time,
so man is seen slowing down,
as maintenance requests are ignored,
as rust demands its fee.

So man becomes static and is stuck within a chair,
is stuck within a bed,
is stuck where time and space has placed him on a journey:
where achievements were not noted,
where warnings were ignored,
where benefits were not applied,
where God was not invited,

where destinies were limited to what was the default.

The God of invitation offers the destiny of choice:
           can fix the squeaking door;
           can mend the damaged or the retiring glove of man—
                      with the entrusted soul and spirit;
           can open the door without a squeak—
               giving access to a vista with a destiny:
                  deserving the ongoing marvelling of man."

My Content Study Aid

_____

_____

_____

_____

_____

_____

_____

_____

_____

_____

_____

_____

_____

_____

_____

_____

_____

_____

_____

_____

_____

_____

_____

_____

_____

_____

The Thinking of Man

And I hear The Lord Jesus saying,
"The thinking of man leaves a desert on the river bed.

The thinking of man leaves some water in the well,
        leaves some water for the priming of the pump,
        leaves some water so all meet with a sourced supply.

The thinking of man sometimes is in need of touching his home base,
        of uplifting an envelope as time-stamped and delivered,
        of opening carefully and reading the lines inscribed,
        for both counselling and awareness.

The thinking of man has variations in his thought patterning,
        has variations in reaction,
        has variations leading up to his conduct,
        where Freewill guides the spirit soul and body—
        within the twin fields of Righteousness and Truth.

The thinking of man is a common place achievement,
        as it leads up to maturity.

The thinking of man within The Fear of God introduces Wisdom to the scene:
        which will impact on the knowledge within the bounds therein.

The thinking of man is not as a geyser blowing steam on the icebound,
        where time is very limited before the object is destroyed.

The thinking of man should dwell upon the objective:
        where it stands within reality.

The thinking of man should address the difficulties inherent in every life:
        of how to achieve the flowing of The Living Water.

The thinking of man should rest within the harmony of God,
        should rest within The Will of God,
        should rest within the eternity of God.

The thinking of man should be modified by The Wisdom of God,
        by The Gifts of The Holy Spirit,
        by The Testimony of Jesus unto The Father.

The thinking of man should be based upon his testimony of Jesus to the world at large.

The thinking of man is not nourished by the food he eats;
        is nourished by the hearing of the speaking of The Son,
        is nourished by the encouragement of God,
        is nourished by the witnessing of the healing power of God,
        is nourished by his presence within the miracles of God,

is nourished by his being within The Grace of God.

The thinking of man can easily become twisted and distorted,
can easily become embittered and disjointed,
can easily become prideful and supercilious.

The thinking of man can be led astray:
when the focus is not concentrated on the heights of light;
when the focus is confused and not from God;
when discernment drops with the falling of a veil;
to end up in a muddied puddle,
on a very stormy and unhallowed night.

The thinking of man is rewarded for his care,
is rewarded for his attention,
is rewarded for his purity of thought.

The thinking of Man is rewarded at the highest levels of existence,
at the highest levels of retrieving,
at the highest levels of supervision.

The thinking of man is best as a retriever of his past,
of an addressing of his weaknesses,
of a confirming of his strengths.

The thinking of man is the director of his Freewill,
is the motivator building heights which are scaleable and true,
is the builder of a testimony with the baseline of The Cross:
which stands and testifies,
as required,
by The One who sanctified it and knows.

The thinking of man can save himself from ignominy,
can save himself from anarchy,
can save himself from the solitude afflicting the distraught;
in remaining unbending and unsympathetic,
in an environment of excessive heat.

The thinking of man should dwell upon The Righteous and The True:
upon The Harbinger of Peace and the destroying of the lies.

The thinking of man can live within a revolving nightmare,
contaminated by the woolly-minded,
confused by a lack of clarity,
misled by the intimidated,
on an uncertain but downward path,
which the wise and the knowledgable strive to avoid:
as the pathway to the plague.

The thinking of man in not a waste of time,

ANTHONY A EDDY (SCRIBE)

does not invalidate the effort,
does not circumvent the roadway to success.

The thinking of man knows the power of thought,
knows the power of worthwhile consideration,
knows the power of filtering attached to unimpeded growth.

The thinking of man can coalesce and aggregate,
can discover and enhance,
can shakeup and improve.

The thinking of man can bear witness and affirm,
can disprove and correct,
can shortchange and leave dismayed.

The thinking of man starts the map building of man,
lays the groundwork for the architect,
lays a strategy for networks.

The thinking of man can correct the wayward,
can oversee the negligent,
can supervise the powerful and the elite.

The thinking of man can check the plumb line for The Truth,
can check the certainty of doubt,
can verify the critical and the upright,
can check the necessity for an overhaul of a project turning sour.

The thinking of man can eliminate the flights of fancy,
can eliminate the degrees of uncertainty,
can eliminate the losing of the way,
the failure of construction,
the checking of solutions,
the weighing of the weights.

The thinking of man often fails him when thinking of His God,
when thinking of the wonderful and the process of enrichment,
when thinking of accepting a helping hand:
from The Purveyor of The Universe who knows how such things work."

My Content Study Aid

_____

_____

_____

_____

The Rescuing of Ladies

And I hear The Lord Jesus saying,
"The rescuing of ladies has rules of engagement.

The rescuing of ladies requires propriety with common sense,
    requires sensibility with forethought,
    requires a hands off approach with all but the crown of the head,
    requires a mixed environment within my proxy servants for
          a hands-on approach,
      where each should know the extent of their reach.

The rescuing of ladies is important and impartial within the sight of both God and man,
    is important to enquire as to a shortened history of
         a companionship with God,
    is important to be aware of the level of commitment—
      either one of non-commitment or when well worn and trod.

The rescuing of ladies has a tendency for tears,
    has a tendency for gentleness of attitude best to prevail upon
         the ears.

The rescuing of ladies should be done within His proxy ministry,
      involving two willing servants of The Lord;
    should be done in Righteousness and Truth;
    should be done within The Will and Sight of God;
    should be focussing on The Counselling of God,
     whose acknowledgement is the basis for the setting of the stage.

The rescuing of ladies can also involve the children—
      without undue attention creating a shrinking away,
       a partial view from behind
        a mother's dress,
      a shyness of approach to someone
       not previously encountered.

The rescuing of ladies from idolatry in action requires care and attention to details:
      within a life style at variance with God.

The rescuing of ladies requires attention to the breaking of past curses:
      accruing over many generations stretching back into
        the unknown past,
        the unknown ancestry of man.

The rescuing of ladies requires the installing of The Blessings of God,
    the forestalling of evil intent:
         to superimpose the evil,
         to overwrite the good;

ANTHONY A EDDY (SCRIBE)

requires the prayer for the receiving of all the gifts of God,
>> as a Temple is readied for occupation and administering,
>>> in the presence of My Spirit.

The rescuing of ladies is not a sexist statement in the days of femininity,
> is an inclusive statement for the widows and the elderly,
>> for the tired and the pained,
>> for the deserted and the frightened,
>> for the lonely and the uncared for,
>> for the poor and the hungry—
> that all may be blessed with protection within the caring welfare
>>> of My People,
>>> who call upon My Name.

The rescuing of ladies speaks of The Love of God,
> speaks of a future in unity with God,
> speaks of conversing with The Lord of all creation and,
>>> in humbleness,
>>> the hearing of the voice of God;
> speaks of receiving the bounty of The Lord with the
>>> ongoing counselling—
>> when placing a call bred of desperation which shouts
>>> into the heavens.

The rescuing of ladies honours and praises,
> upholds and enfolds,
> encourages and assists:
>> as the lives unfold with improvements being noted,
>> as both gratitude and appreciation overtake the hearts,
>>> now supported by the twins of Faith and Truth.

The rescuing of ladies lifts them from the 'hot water' in a life
>>> which has long since cooled and seeped away;
> now to redeposit them within surroundings,
>>> where life is filled with rewarding activities;
> and the past becomes the grounds for forsaking broken memories,
>>> with promises not kept,
>>> with the shedding of the burdens—
>>> so heavy and difficult to carry;
> as new horizons open up with doorways filled with welcomes—
> offering worthwhile adoptions into and of adjusting to
>>> The Godly endowments,
>>> as flowing within His Way of Life.

The rescuing of ladies is not a repetitive deed from amongst the ill or the sick,
>>> the distraught or the abandoned,
>>> the troubled or the unforgiven.

The rescuing of ladies speaks of caring for a lonely soul,
speaks of cheering up the spirit,
speaks of nourishing the body.

The rescuing of ladies brings the lost and the despairing,
into the fraternities of the found and confident;
brings the separated and the grief stricken,
into companionship and participation;
brings the muddled and unskilled,
into the crafts and achievements.

The rescuing of ladies speaks of lives fulfilled and overflowing,
speaks of lives growing and rejoicing,
speaks of lives of music and of fun-filled entertainment,
speaks of lives of satisfaction and of questioning:
when understanding is standing off at a distance,
in needing to be drawn a little closer to an ear.

The rescuing of ladies rewards with the distant murmur of voices relaxed
and now at ease.

The rescuing of ladies has despatched emergencies requiring attention
to the fields of resolution,
has become accustomed to the livelihood of acquaintances
now coveted and reclassified as friends.

The rescuing of ladies are set to become The Friends of God,
The Children of God,
The Family of God:
have earned The Trust and The Companionship of God,
know all is well when adopted into The Family of God,
with an assured destiny of choice."

My Content Study Aid

_____

_____

_____

_____

_____

_____

_____

_____

The Scaler of The Heights

And I hear The Lord Jesus saying,
"The scaler of the heights is a reacher for the stars.

The scaler of the heights seeks and finds all the heights disclose,
all the heights hold in abeyance,
all the heights are destined to shower—
upon the life of man.

The scaler of the heights is fit and robust both before and after,
is exacting and testing in all the practical aspects of acquiring
the summit.

The scaler of the heights has a head for heights,
does not have the spells of dizziness,
does not suffer from a misstep,
does not shrink from the chasms with their depths.

The scaler of the heights has access to the confidence and security of movement,
has access to the footwear with a grip,
has access to the hand tools as fitted for the task.

The scaler of the heights does not run and rush onto the wild or untamed,
does not step on the broken or the bits,
does not stumble on the crushed or on the crumbled.

The scaler of the heights visits without undue delay,
succumbs to inspect the visions as presented for the day,
the horizons in the distance turning blue,
the portals to the distant heights where the giants do breed.

The scaler of the heights takes one step at a time,
does not run across the scree,
does not cling to the shale,
skirts the sheer and the unplotted.

The scaler of the heights follows in the footsteps of the wise,
follows in the range of reliability for both the footholds and
the hand holds:
where a slippage should result in the swinging in the air—
on a pendulum of rope.

The scaler of the heights looks both up and down as the pathway to the stars unfolds—
to be plotted one step at a time without the urgency of haste;
judges the cracks and crevices for an ability to wedge and
to secure ropes;
and ties the anchor points on precipices to the safety of
the check fall points as discovered—

and submitted to a test of holding fast—
upon the rock face awaiting a traverse.

The scaler of the heights does not scrabble for a hold,
does not release without security attained,
does not encroach upon the unreliable,
does not commit to the trap of a waiting rock slide or
an avalanche of snow.

The scaler of the heights knows the common sense available,
for the avoidance of stupidity,
knows the static line of rest,
knows the moving line of action.

The scaler of the heights knows rescue is improbable,
knows assistance is out of reach,
knows success is self-dependent on ability and foresight.

The scaler of the heights rests prior to exhaustion setting in,
prior to deciding to abandon,
prior to the need for reversing all which has been achieved
by the effort of the day:
spent as an intruder on a mountain not wanting
to be conquered.

The scaler of the heights carries the spirit of overcoming,
the spirit calling for success,
the spirit of encouragement,
the spirit pointing out the ways both forward
and upward:
where risk is at a minimum,
while life remains unthreatened,
by any disaster in the making.

The scaler of the heights has the best of equipment,
is well prepared for the attaining of the objective,
is expectant of success,
has planned and plotted the way to the top,
has no intention to admit defeat.

The scaler of the heights knows the value of prayer,
of the sharing the intention to embark on
a pursuit with God.

The scaler of the heights anchors and examines,
checks and verifies,
manipulates and retains:
the safety of the lifeline going forward.

ANTHONY A EDDY (SCRIBE)

The scaler of the heights can see the summit not too far away,
        can see the pathway to success,
        can see the feasibility and the practicable yielding to
                the expended effort.

The scaler of the heights turns a shoulder to the wind,
        adjusts the goggles on the eyes,
        the protection on the head.

The scaler of the heights approaches and is invigorated,
        does not count the chickens while they may still escape
            amongst the snow and ice,
            or trip upon a crampon.

The scaler of the heights does not struggle for a breath,
        has all breathing under the control of tempered lungs,
        has a pulse excited by the likelihood of achievement:
          as the heart maintains its beat of perseverance with vitality.

The scaler of the heights cannot rest upon the laurels,
        has to clinch what has been a struggle to achieve,
        what has been a testing of commitment,
        what has been the result of preparation for an assault upon
            the pathway to the stars.

The scaler of the heights places hand over hand with care,
          foot in front of foot with attention,
        takes a further breath from where the air is cold,
            and mittens are essential.

The scaler of the heights has the peak within the reaching out for victory,
        moves the last few steps of ease and of attainment,
         as the grand vista of the victor opens wide to yield
            to the conquering,
        of a new view of surroundings now unblocked by:
            the mountain's flesh and bones,
            the mountain's earth and rocks,
            the mountain's blood and tears,
            the mountain's death and rivulets.

The scaler of the heights looks and looks and looks,
        stops and rubs the eyes,
        and looks and looks and looks again:
            at all which has been released,
            for on which the eyes can feast."

The Relationships of Man

And I hear The Lord Jesus saying,
"The relationships of man grow with time and wealth.

The relationships of man expand into the crevices,
                expand into the bounds of life,
                expand into the records of experience.

The relationships of man are simple when a child,
                are complex when mature,
                dwindle with the age.

The relationships of man can have a lot of false parameters,
                can have a lot of echoes without a whiff of substance,
                can be as a collection of mementos—
                                gathering numbers but very little else.

The relationships of man are time-wasters when behaving as the trivial,
                when behaving as just a few lines of text within an electronic beam,
                when behaving as a collection of sweets:
                        rolling back and forth in imprisonment within a jar,
                        in which they were left without selection or attention.

The relationships of man can now be in the thousands,
                can now be hosted and ignored,
                can now be left to roll around together:
                      as followers of entities reflecting personal success or fame,
                can now be found to stretch far beyond the outreach or the true
                                  interests of man.

The relationships of man are well on the road to becoming meaningless—
                where numbers are excessive yet some still shout for notice;
                so to gather all beneath them as if in a shadow of a clucky hen.

The relationships of man in nearly every instance,
                need to be pruned and slashed from the immaterial.

The relationships of man are best when in the hands of those:
                who genuinely are aware of the qualities of 'friendship';
                of how it is developed,
                of knowledge,
                of interests,
                of families who know and care,
                of motivations neither built on business potential,
                      nor when commission rights prevail—
                        to erase a genuine friendship,
                        to replace it with a well—

ANTHONY A EDDY (SCRIBE)

where the bucket is only attached to lift that
which is determined—
to be of benefit to the owner of the well;
where genuine camaraderie is missing;
as folk have never met in any worthwhile sense,
as distance spans the cultures of residence,
as intimacy of friendship is impractical,
where the inane greetings of less than a dozen words,
sums up the whole relationship;
without prospect of any worthwhile development;
as time interferes with its stamp of impetuosity—
on the rationing installed as meaningful and valid;
for another multi-month spaced encounter,
on the outreach crowding for attention within
the social media.

The relationships of man are building and collapsing,
are being searched and added to meaningless lists of
'friend' acquisitions—
in ignorance of what a friend is really intended to be,
when outside the bonds of close family relationships.

The relationships of man,
when classified as 'friends',
requires a close and mutual relationship of common interests,
of cross knowledge,
of contact over years,
of sincere interest and concern for welfare and development,
of where the casual and irrelevant are best shown the scissors,
which trim and tidy the shrubbery of man,
that which he keeps within his garden for ongoing,
if infrequent,
conversations of detail and of interest,
as two lives engage in exchanges of renewal and honouring
over time,
are sincere and compatible without the negative feelings associated
with the strangers who list to use,
to then ignore when found to be of no further use as contacts;
neither valid nor willing to be appointed to a group
in the drive for generating wealth,
under the guise of 'friendship' gone astray,
so to be left hanging indefinitely in abeyance.

The relationships of man should be important and significant,
should be dramatic and incursive,
should be impatient for responses,

are the modern 'Achilles heel' of man:
which searches for additions yet does not value the acceptances,
which often does not even enter an acknowledgment of requested friendship,
as silence wins the day,
as the count goes up by one,
as the seeker moves on to garner other pastures with the same objectives.

The relationships of man are of importance to God;
are of importance in the establishing of Righteousness,
are of importance in acknowledging The Fear of God,
are of importance when counselling is freed for offering,
when the respecting of Freewill no longer prevents an interruption,
when the binding and the loosing has been set or freed,
for the benefit of relationship between the would-be wise of God,
and The Counselling of The Holy Spirit,
in the fullness of opened opportunities bearing His gifts within The Seal of God,
within the proxy power of answered prayer,
within the oversight and administration of The Edifice of God.

The relationships of man within mortality have an immense effect on his life
beyond the grave.

The relationships of man carry details of mortality forward into a future destiny
as selected.

The relationships of man should be vitally interested in all that God does see hear do,
as He tabulates man's impact on either the destiny of choice,
or the default destiny due respect.

The relationships of man,
with reference to the reality of life within mortality,
can be said to be a composite,
with the components presented for consideration to The Chief Architect,
for man's future dwelling-place as an adoptee into The Family of God.

I,
The Lord,
say to man this day,
"Beware My second commandment applicable within the relationships of man:
and those who carelessly bite off more than they can chew.""

My Content Study Aid

_____

_____

_____

The Whirlwind at Play

And I hear The Lord Jesus saying,
"The whirlwind at play circles and envelops.

The whirlwind at play masters and invades,
            grabs and moves on,
            halts and reverses.

The whirlwind at play absorbs and releases,
            soaks and floods,
            inundates and drowns,
            hesitates and destroys the works,
                  the impediments,
               together with the livelihoods of man.

The whirlwind at play breathes and shatters glass,
            yawns and gobbles up the roofs,
            coughs and sprays the wreckage as birthed within a vision for
                       the future:
                as existence is destroyed.

The whirlwind at play gathers up possessions to spew them:
                  across the pathway creating the tears,
                  together with the calls for restitution.

The whirlwind at play minces up and twists the valued and the essential,
            converts the used into the lost,
               the whole into the tattered remnants displaying
                  a frenzy of destruction,
                  an incarceration of the slow and pained:
                    as the flood waters take possession;
                    as access is denied;
                    as restrictions are enforced.

The whirlwind at play is very easily bored,
            visits to tear asunder,
            distributes without favour,
            brings silence to an area where the activities of man had bloomed
                       and flowered,
                in peaceful co-existence.

The whirlwind at play is not apologetic,
            does not know accountability,
            does not repair the damage,
            does not stick to a forecast of a pathway as declared by man.

The whirlwind at play has a life all of its own,

has a life where it can come and go,
has a short life bred of preparation:
                        when desire cannot be quelled,
                        as excessive freedom is released.

The whirlwind at play cannot be quenched until exhausted:
                        when attractants loose appeal,
                        as indicated by the willingness of retreat.

The whirlwind at play has a velocity belched of excessive energy,
                has an unrestricted pathway for the doomed and the victimized,
                has a noise reflecting ferocity mixed with the howl of intimidation.

The whirlwind at play shatters the repositories of shade and beauty:
                                        into missiles for hurling to impale;
                cracks and breaks the effort and the growth into a tangled mass
                                                of branches;
                        where the roots are open to impeach the sky.

The whirlwind at play is not a time of joy and laughter,
                rather reflects a battlefield of entangled forces,
                where tide and rain and wind are the feeders and the nourishers,
                        are the protagonists within the struggles for supremacy.

The whirlwind at play does not seek a playmate:
                        seeks to dislodge a lodger,
                        seeks to unsettle the settler,
                        seeks to flood the flood-prone,
                        seeks to dehouse the housed,
                        seeks to disenfranchise the franchisee,
                        seeks to inhibit the inhabitant.

The whirlwind at play is not a harnessed specimen:
                is neither controlled nor bottled up,
                is neither satisfied nor sated,
                is neither exhausted nor is spent.

The whirlwind at play would reduce timber into matchwood,
                        transport into misshapen lumps of metal,
                        homes into the residues of hope,
                                now reduced from what once was holy
                                                and sacrosanct:
                                into the dregs of hopelessness,
                        the vestiges assigned unto the onset of despair.

The whirlwind at play leaves a trail of desolation,
                disintegrates the worn and tidy,
                enforces an inspection with an evaluation,
                brings a list into existence of the tattered and the torn.

ANTHONY A EDDY (SCRIBE)

The whirlwind at play searches out the weak spots of accommodation,
        tests the strength and the integrity of a structure standing tall and straight,
        imposes the stresses and the forces to bring it piecemeal to the ground.

The whirlwind at play has excessive force at its disposal,
        is encouraged by surroundings,
        is the trampler of a path as flattened in defiance of objections:
                as encountered on the way to satisfaction.

The whirlwind at play has a timeframe for achievement,
        has a target in its sights,
        has demolishment as its objective,
          accepts the task with eagerness in surplus,
          applies enthusiasm to the breeding of success,
                in all it visits and inspects,
                in all it sees and does.

The whirlwind at play does not play half-heartedly,
        does not invest in trials,
        settles for all or nothing.

The whirlwind at play segments the whole into the parts,
        munches on its breakfast of the day,
        continues in the search for lunch,
        majors in the evening meal prior to retirement:
              in satisfaction with a day 'well spent' on exercise.

The whirlwind at play moves onto fields afresh,
        struggles with tiredness arising from the effort,
        confirms the settling of past grievances,
          with an over-the-shoulder glance,
          as witnessed by the contentment of satisfaction:
                spreading o'er a face.

The whirlwind at play has had a busy day,
        is exhausted by the production of the evidence,
        is surprised by the lack of interruptions.

The whirlwind at play awaits the heeding of the message,
        the plotting of defences,
        the noting of delay in the envisaging of improvements:
        on the rotting and the weakened,
        on the circumspect and the praiseworthy,
        on the charlatan and the smokescreen,
        on the knowledgeable where Wisdom is still missing—
          from the company of a boat,
            which has already sailed and far from land."

The Progeny of Man

And I hear The Lord Jesus saying,
"The progeny of man have many different strains,
              have many different appearances,
              have many options in their sizing and of character.

The progeny of man is the handiwork of God.
The progeny of man is the similitude of God.
The progeny of man is the design result of The Architect of the heavens and of The Earth.

The progeny of man now circumnavigate the globe of man,
              now feature in the welfare of the synergy of The Earth,
              now subscribe to the evolution over time which forsakes the need
                                for God—
                as the originator of the stability of man.

The progeny of man speak of things on which they are not competent to declare as facts.
The progeny of man listen to absurdities and welcome them as facts.

The progeny of man adopt the inane and repeat,
              ad nauseam,
              the smoking guns of speech now firing from their mouths—
                  within their homes and work places:
              now levelled at the church of God and their fellow man.

The progeny of man prefer to close their spirits and their souls to Truth,
              to evaporate The Truth from the cauldron of the soup mix:
                which once was seen in speculation as a possible theory;
                  and now has caught on as a fancy,
                is adopted and equated as the only possible conclusion—
                  for the origins of man.

The progeny of man looks around in approval:
              at all that man has created from the workshops of his mind;
              of the tools and living spaces;
              of the facilities and life styles with their aircraft;
                their land vehicles;
           together with their ships and boats upon the waters of The Earth.

The progeny of man have eyes and ears which see and hear,
              their own creations over time,
                both patented and valued—
              yet fail to see or hear,
                or to correctly allocate,
           the design feast which meets the eyes each day of their lives:
           so to also impact on their hearing when ears are attentive—

to the beauty of the chorus of the dawn,
within the start of the presented surroundings,
with the sunlight as the early encourager
of the chorus in full throat.

The progeny of man grovels in the dust from where he thinks he came.

The progeny of man grovels in the mire which he claims as a distant relative.

The progeny of man laughs and giggles,
both in unbelief and in rejection,
at the similes available when faced with the alternative of a designer:
in every man-made item which impacts on the variant lifestyles—
with an origin acknowledged as within the capabilities of man.

The progeny of man fail to appreciate,
or to weather,
the false creeds of man for what they really are:
the false accusations via the lies to cover the factual verity,
of that which brings both Peace and harmony,
to the righteous relationships of man.

The progeny of man,
within the strains of Wisdom,
seeks and finds a relationship with God;
seeks and develops the refining of a lifestyle;
seeks and commits to a destiny—
as found among the stars of God.

The progeny of man can,
with enlightenment and encouragement,
with knowledge and the scope as found within his own Freewill,
raise himself up out of the mud of man to live within the bounds:
the beauty and the charisma,
of The Agapé Love of God.

The progeny of man do not evolve depending on environment,
live their lives within a well proven design which was impressed,
with the particulars,
upon the finished glove for man—
for as each is,
so each was;
for as each appears,
so each was constructed;
for as each appreciates,
so each was given understanding and
knowledge within the glove so placed.

The progeny of man should look closely at one another,

should see and perceive the differences imposed upon each strain
of glove,
should see the signature of perfection—
how that glove is so fitted to a particular way of life,
in a determined area of The Earth:
which has earned the title of being known as 'Home'.

The progeny of man are now becoming intermingled with neighbours and with foes,
with distant unknown cousins where differences are readily apparent,
from the gloves they were given:
so to wear within their space upon The Earth.

The progeny of man has the built-in abilities inherited from a common ancestor:
to intermingle and to marry,
to settle down in new surroundings,
to raise a family,
to fit into a society of adoption,
there to proceed to a story of change and of success.

The progeny of man has the ability to learn each other's strain of language,
of both signs and tokens,
of the ways and means whereby a living
is established,
as the dirt and dust are vanquished from the lives with visions for the future:
where the 'here and now' may be only distantly related to the past;
where the future can fulfil the wonders and potential;
as perceived and accepted for a family in transit;
as The Family waits and grows within a commitment to a promised future;
as guaranteed and supplied within a kingdom of A Coming King—
now soon appearing to be seated on An Earthly Throne."

My Content Study Aid

_____

_____

_____

_____

_____

_____

_____

_____

_____

The Vacationing of Man

And I hear The Lord Jesus saying,
"The vacationing of man leaves a hole within a job.

The vacationing of man determines the expenditure of man,
        determines the length of an absence,
                the transfer of a replacement,
                the vying of position for advancement.

The vacationing of man searches out a destination,
        searches out the means of transport,
        searches out the logic for the journey,
        searches out the time frame of decision,
        searches out the time frame of return.

The vacationing of man can be determined by companions,
        can be varied by companions,
        can be instigated by companions,
        can be settled by companions,
        can be destined for companions,
        can be attributed to the wish lists of companions.

The vacationing of man sees the world in play,
        sees the availability of the drawcards of the world:
                being shuffled in randomness,
                or selected with great care,
        sees the scope and the versatility in action:
            where satisfaction rules the day when wedded to
                the evening at large.

The vacationing of man observes the swirls and dancing,
        participates in the licenced and controlled,
        watches the risqué and the restricted,
        dances with abandon as the drinks take hold.

The vacationing of man can be as a whirlwind waiting to settle,
        can be as a triumph with both sincerity and flattery,
        can be masked in a region of popularity,
            in a region of commonality,
            in a region readied for the tourist without
                the traces and the reins exerting a control.

The vacationing of man checks the spending power of visits,
        checks the limiting force of ticketing,
        measure the length of time included in a meeting
                bridging distance.

The vacationing of man is like a hoopla on a waist,
> trusting both the spinning and the twirling,
> both the cycles and the rhythm,
> both the glancing and the gawking.

The vacationing of man seals an imprint on a card,
> satisfies by opening a wallet,
> measures by the counting of the residue.

The vacationing of man listens and photographs,
> poses and records,
> addresses and ignores.

The vacationing of man simplifies and stultifies,
> mesmerizes and stares,
> secretes and restores.

The vacationing of man is wide open to suggestions,
> is eager to join the fun,
> is immune to correction,
> is offended by an offer of support.

The vacationing of man seeks a pet to pat,
> seeks a place to rest his hands,
> seeks a time outside the limiting control of man.

The vacationing of man seeks entertainment at the cheap and tawdry,
> at the sophisticated and expensive;
> at the gaming of casinos,
>> where the loss is unrestricted;
> at the numbers called in a local hall:
>> where the rewards are modest
>> while the losses are insignificant.

The vacationing of man may seek the sport of kings with the racing of the horses,
> may seek activity with the racquet and the ball before the net,
> may seek the validation of a seat to watch and munch:
> where running is attracted to a ball as hit and waiting for retrieval:
>> to a home base readied for an 'out'.

The vacationing of man can drive and drive and drive—
> where he is equipped to be mistaken for a snail,
> can be a skater on thin ice:
> where the ending is a splash—
>> with a rescue so required.

The vacationing of man can rest upon a presence in the sun:
> where the beach awaits the invasion of the sea,
> where the waves are scarcely above an ankle,

where Peace prevails and noise is quite a rarity—
broken only by a squawk.

The vacationing of man can be interrupted:
by the interlopers,
by the distant and the ignorant,
by the static and ensconced,
by the dangerous and vicious,
by the protective with the throwers-out,
by the usurpers and invaders of a space and time:
where permission was neither sought nor granted at the start,
where coming familiarity softened the shock of identity,
and separated the wise from the foolish.

The vacationing of man can validate the past,
can validate the present fears of man,
can forecast the future activities of necessity to man.

The vacationing of man can return man without surprises,
can return him with feelings that all is well and enjoyable,
can return him to the platitudes and lying of those who know
and yet will not admit.

The vacationing of man reserves without disclosure,
preserves without diminution,
conserves the status quo where ignorance prevails,
and all is seen as safe and well.

The vacationing of man returns to fill his spot reserved,
to fulfil his attendance at his workplace,
to fulfil his hopes and dreams within the residue
of life remaining:
for his uptake within mortality."

My Content Study Aid

_____

_____

_____

_____

_____

_____

_____

The Weathering of Man (2)

And I hear The Lord Jesus saying,
"The weathering of man occurs gradually in mortality,
              stops completely in eternity,

The weathering of man is the built-in release process which enables progression:
                      to another sphere of life.

The weathering of man peaks and subsides,
          magnifies and contracts within his span of years:
                    for servicing a life.

The weathering of man expresses the wear and tear imposed upon experience,
          displays the grasping of the favours and the trials,
          carries the summation of the actioning of his Freewill—
                    within an environment of change.

The weathering of man is not sudden unless imposed by accident—
          which speaks of a lack of attention as applied within surroundings.

The weathering of man is expected to be gradual,
          is expected to be scarcely noticeable,
          is expected to be the end result of a life well lived:
                  under the bounty of good health.

The weathering of man absorbs a life of robustness based on effort:
                  with muscles to the fore.
The weathering of man signs of a life as governed by a mindset:
                  with brainpower to the fore.

The weathering of man indicates either his succumbing to and accepting,
          or his overcoming and establishing—
              the life style of his choice.

The weathering of man reflects into a mirror,
          reflects into a memory,
          reflects into the evidence accumulated:
              by both night and day.

The weathering of man is not reversible within the scope of his mortality,
          is not carried forward into the grounds of his eternity.

The weathering of man has a peaking of performance whether of the power of muscles,
              or of the application of the intellect.

The weathering of man has similarities to a seesaw—
            with its many ups and downs;
          is not conditioned by a round-about—
            with the emphasis on the repetition of a view.

ANTHONY A EDDY (SCRIBE)

The weathering of man has assists and setbacks:
>> has the gaining of experience,
>> has the onset of infirmity;
>> has the establishment of income,
>> has the loss attributed to circumstance;
>> has the growth within a family,
>> has the mourning at a centre of attention.

The weathering of man ends in rejoicing or in suffering,
>> in satisfaction or in disappointment,
>> in happiness or in sadness,
>> in contentment or in dissatisfaction.

The weathering of man ends in security or in poverty,
>> in success or in failure,
>> in the destiny of choice or in the destiny of default.

The weathering of man contains no guarantees,
>> has promises open to acceptance,
>> has promises certain to be upheld,
>> has opportunities for seizing or for ignoring.

The weathering of man has the opportunity to negotiate,
>>> very early in a life,
> either the street of integrity marked out by adherence to The Truth with honour;
> or the parallel street of lies as marked out for deceit with tragedy.

The weathering of man can protect or taint the reputation as earned for his Freewill.

The weathering of man is accountable for the enacting of his Freewill within a lifetime—
>> as assembled from,
>>> and measured by,
>> his choices which led him on:
> either upwards to exultation or downwards to despair.

The weathering of man cannot always see the obvious,
> sometimes is misled.

The weathering of man needs to ascertain the validity of his actions—
>>> so they will contribute to his overall objective—
>> that which he has chosen for his way of life;
>> that which will guide his extension into eternity—
>>> as measured by the end result with its either 'up' or 'down' -
>>> either to the destiny of choice;
>>> or to the destiny of default where choice was not selected:
> which would have to have overridden the default from remaining in effect.

The weathering of man has time to seek and find,
>> has time to accept and grow,

has time to appreciate and gather:
the end-time jewels of God—
as held for an inheritance in abeyance."

My Content Study Aid

_____
_____
_____
_____
_____
_____
_____
_____
_____
_____
_____
_____
_____
_____
_____
_____
_____
_____
_____
_____
_____
_____
_____
_____

The Synopsis of Man

And I hear The Lord Jesus saying,
"The synopsis of man is drifting into being from the cuts and tucks.

The synopsis of man climbs into existence with the styling of the womenfolk.

The synopsis of man is governed by the eyes,
               is governed by the sight lines,
               is governed by the ageing without the sensitivity of man.

The synopsis of man is not inaugurated by man,
               is not foreshadowed by man,
               is not instigated by man.

The synopsis of man has an echo of approval,
               an echo requesting affirmation,
               an echo seeking confirmation of the want,
                        and,
                        thereby,
                            the reality of the birthing of the need.

The synopsis of man is written by his companion,
               is drawn to attention so remarks can be examined
                              for a hidden meaning,
               is drawn into the conversation as an essential item of the day.

The synopsis of man precludes any comment with a hint of Truth,
               precludes any comment hinting at anything other than success,
               precludes any comment involving a comparison.

The synopsis of man requires Wisdom to survive,
               requires necessity to navigate where innuendo rules in carrying
                            its own message from the stars,
               requires a sympathetic ear for much more than a nod,
                    much more than a glance,
                    much more than a comment:
                    as reused from yestertimes.

The synopsis of man knows the approval depends upon the cost,
               knows the approval depends upon inspection in a mirror,
               knows the approval depends upon the neighbours and the friends:
              who have earned their badges of honour and paraded them just so.

The synopsis of man is not usually a disease that can be caught,
                    a disease which finds it difficult to cross the gender barrier,
                    a disease which often calls for matching 'fixes' within
                              the walk of life.

The synopsis of man varies with the time scale,
$\qquad$ varies with the skin tone,
$\qquad$ varies with the competition seen at large.

The synopsis of man circles and encroaches as space and time permits.

The synopsis of man does not appear under the spotlight of an article
$\qquad\qquad$ in a custom magazine,
$\qquad$ flinches from the fashion images of starlets,
$\qquad$ shies from the camera at an intended closeup of a face.

The synopsis of man is called so for conformity,
$\qquad$ is called so in respect,
$\qquad$ is called so for the avoiding of unnecessary attention with
$\qquad\qquad$ possible embarrassment.

The synopsis of man can bring disfigurement in its wake,
$\qquad$ can bring law suits to the fore,
$\qquad$ can see the latter dissipate,
$\qquad\qquad$ as if in a puff of smoke,
$\qquad\qquad$ where publicity is involved.

The synopsis of man sometimes puts 'the cat amongst the pigeons'
$\qquad\qquad$ by a careless comment,
$\qquad\qquad$ by a careless reference to a knife,
$\qquad$ by the giving of offence through the gullibility of the patient:
$\qquad$ now seeking sympathy with understanding as a victim dispossessed.

The synopsis of man has difficulty in tendering the condolences:
$\qquad\qquad$ with sincerity and feeling,
$\qquad$ has difficulty in knowing the best ploy to adopt,
$\qquad$ has difficulty in avoiding the boomerang now sent on its journey of return.

The synopsis of man must avoid the boomerang,
$\qquad$ must avoid the catch and hold,
$\qquad$ must avoid an excess of sympathy which will usher in the tears.

The synopsis of man may need to take a walk within a park,
$\qquad$ may need to seek some solitude,
$\qquad$ may need to console and hug.

The synopsis of man can end up with an adventure seen as one too far,
$\qquad$ seen as one without a solution deemed acceptable,
$\qquad$ seen as one where the prize bypassed the one who paid the price.

The synopsis of man can be as a nightmare on the loose,
$\qquad$ can be exaggerated far beyond reality,
$\qquad$ can be harped on continuously wherever a mirror needs to
$\qquad\qquad$ be avoided:
$\qquad$ as sensitivity waits for an adjustment with the healing of the scars.

The synopsis of man seeks and cannot find,
>seeks and cannot re-assure,
>seeks and is at a loss where Wisdom has abstained and knowledge
>>does not help.

The synopsis of man cannot uplift,
>cannot mollify the guilt-fed and forlorn,
>must not underrate the imagined loss of self-respect while intransigence is in tow.

The synopsis of man awaits the passage of time to resolve:
>the softening of the memory;
>the harshness of the judgment;
>the releasing from despair after a time of mourning.

The synopsis of man goes on a holiday for two to places afresh and unvisited,
>to places where the knowing and the sympathetic
>>are unlikely to be encountered,
>to places where mirrors are likely to be rare,
>>where no one warrants a second glance,
>>where busyness is both the filler of,
>>>and the filter for,
>>the time span of each day.

The synopsis of man progresses but cannot revert,
>proceeds but cannot retreat,
>visits but is unable to reverse.

The synopsis of man is difficult to picture,
>is a weight upon both the spirit and the soul,
>is a residual mark upon the flesh which neither embellishes
>>nor enhances:
>>where it has been placed.

The Wisdom of the ages can prevent the disfigurement of God's creation:
>when man hearkens to the counselling of God,
>when attempting to enhance the presentation of the body."

Biblical References: Leviticus 19:28, 1 Kings 18:28, Jeremiah 47:5

My Content Study Aid

_____

_____

_____

_____

_____

A Teaspoon of Flavouring

And I hear The Lord Jesus saying,
"A teaspoon of flavouring is deemed necessary,
within a recipe,
when the natural is insufficient.

A teaspoon of flavouring imposes an outreach to a cupboard,
an outreach to a shelf,
a recovery of placement,
an unscrewing of a cap,
a pouring on the graduated,
a stirring in a mix,
a baking in an oven.

A teaspoon of flavouring can be placed within a cup,
can be placed within a glass,
can be placed upon the tongue when hidden in the food.

A teaspoon of flavouring can be false or true,
can be natural or synthetic,
can be acceptable or rejectable.

A teaspoon of flavouring can put a grimace on a face in the mirroring of rejection
with sincerity.

A teaspoon of flavouring can invite a further tasting,
can put a gleam into an eye,
can put a smile upon the face,
can bring a further sampling to the mouth and tongue.

A teaspoon of flavouring has relations with the nose,
has relations of consent,
or relations of rejection,
has relations when a precursor to a very tentative and cautious
placement on the tongue;
as uncertainty of acceptance is very much to the fore and
awaiting a decision.

A teaspoon of flavouring may be far too much,
may exceed the expectations of what is concentrated for effect,
may bring a surplus of an overload which involves an offered
push away.

A teaspoon of flavouring is the essence of selection,
is the colour and consistency,
is the reading of a label,
is the inspection of the contents for the requirement of a

ANTHONY A EDDY (SCRIBE)

> mixing shake:
> to reblend the ingredients where oil separates from the water,
> as an emulsion does not carry over time.

A teaspoon of flavouring exercises the taste buds of man,
> initiates a recall of the past,
> chambers a new shell into the gun of taste bursts.

A teaspoon of flavouring should not impose upon the stomach,
> should not be an interloper destined for immediate eviction,
> should not be a source of problems generated for the bowels.

A teaspoon of flavouring,
> when handled with suspicion,
> can be the forerunner leading to addiction,
> leading to an attack upon the brain,
> leading to impressions not previously available,
> leading to exhaustion of the brain and intellect,
> leading to the effort tied to the exertion of the body.

A teaspoon of flavouring may have another name,
> may have another intention,
> may have an expensive source bordering on the questionable:
> as an infringement on the common sense.

A teaspoon of flavouring may not be truthful in its labelling,
> may be timed and ready to explode,
> may disintegrate the intentions for a date,
> may overcome and seize control without a prior warning,
> where counselling is silent,
> where there is a gleam of satisfaction attached to
> a drink supplied:
> as monitored for consumption.

A teaspoon of flavouring can terminate a life:
> where the dose is greater than the body is set to handle;
> can obliterate a memory of the happenings at large,
> can inject shame into the course of the proceedings.

A teaspoon of flavouring is not the best place to put one's Faith,
> is not the best place to be in the presence of cajoling,
> in the presence of enticing,
> in the presence of encouragement to
> walk unaccompanied down a one way street.

A teaspoon of flavouring may not have a happy ending,
> may lead to a surplus of intrusions,
> may lead to a deferred call for help.

A teaspoon of flavouring may affect an outlook on a life,
　　　　　　　　may impose a change of future,
　　　　　　　　may secrete a hidden gift which deserves not to be accepted.

A teaspoon of flavouring may,
　　　　　　　　in hindsight,
　　　　　　　　　　be the dismisser of the morality of God,
　　　　　　　　　　the dismisser of all the future plans,
　　　　　　　　　　the dismisser of joy and happiness within the
　　　　　　　　　　　　　　　　bounds of marriage,
　　　　　　　　　　the dismisser which strikes as a bolt of lightening,
　　　　　　　　　　　　leaves a charred and travelled pathway,
　　　　　　　　　　which can neither be regained nor repaired.

A teaspoon of flavouring is the bomb of demons—
　　　　　　　　　　used to shatter the composure of a child of God,
　　　　　　　　　　used to neutralise the teachings of the parents,
　　　　　　　　　　used to intimidate the endorsements of the present where
　　　　　　　　　　　　'friends' are two a penny,
　　　　　　　　　　used to soften the surroundings so criticism is silenced,
　　　　　　　　　　　　unable to penetrate the ears.

A teaspoon of flavouring can leave a nasty taste within the mouth,
　　　　　　　　can denigrate a body,
　　　　　　　　can remove decorum in an instant,
　　　　　　　　can instigate a change in lifestyle for the innocent and
　　　　　　　　　　　　　　　the gullible:
　　　　　　　　　　where lies are not discerned,
　　　　　　　　　　where intent remains hidden behind the smiles upon a veil,
　　　　　　　　　　where waking up to reality is a shock upon the system
　　　　　　　　　　　　with tears to the fore.

A teaspoon of flavouring is very expensive in compliance:
　　　　　　　　　　when attached to an offer of a purchasing of a drink.

A teaspoon of flavouring needs preventive counselling,
　　　　　　　　　　requires the oversight of God,
　　　　　　　　needs to seek advice from My Spirit as a very
　　　　　　　　　　　　　　capable organizer:
　　　　　　　　　　　　where all may be orderly,
　　　　　　　　　　not leading to self-recriminations of stupidity and anger—
　　　　when sunset brings the encountering of events beyond the ability to control,
　　　　　　　　　　as when followed by a sunrise of lost hope.

The sharing of The Wisdom of God is worthy to obtain for countering,
　　　　　　　　　　for nullifying,
　　　　　　　　　　the enticements of disaster."

Anthony A Eddy (Scribe)

The Querulous and The Signposts

And I hear The Lord Jesus saying,
"The querulous and the signposts hold each other up,
        delay each other in attending to a journey,
        follow each other as the helpless and the lost.

The querulous and the signposts fail to help each other,
        fail to follow anyone's directions,
        spread confusion and dismay on every
                scene encountered.

The querulous and the signposts visit and antagonize,
          where no-one is the wiser,
          where no-one is enthused.

The querulous and the signposts point in opposite directions,
        cannot sing in tune,
        are victims of deceit,
        can neither search nor find.

The querulous and the signposts are unhelpful to say the least,
        are forgetful and chaotic,
        are disturbing and in error,
        are neither reliable nor trustworthy,
        are both ignorant and slanderous.

The querulous and the signposts lie and misstate,
        sound the false alarms,
        serve up bitterness mixed with forgetfulness
                in the same arena.

The querulous and the signposts rarely complete a conversation,
        shout each other down,
        use tactics which ensure failure to
                communicate objectives.

The querulous and the signposts long outstay their welcome,
        long outstay a visit where the greeting is suspicious,
        long outstay a room dubbed unsuitable,
           unclean,
        too small to serve the purpose of intent.

The querulous and the signposts complain about all that they encounter on the sidewalk
                of life,
        break down to dismiss the flags and bunting at a party,
        spill and slop and trample the food and drink into the
                carpet on the floor.

The querulous and the signposts bring unacceptable behaviour to the centre front,
　　　　　　　　　bring hesitation and doubt upon a scene of conflict,
　　　　　　　　　throw accelerants onto a fire bent on destruction,
　　　　　　　　　　　　where arguing is fierce and beyond control.

The querulous and the signposts bring insincerity before the courts of man,
　　　　　　　　　misbehave at every opportunity,
　　　　　　　　　attempt to escape from the cages they create,
　　　　　　　　　salute and praise no one but themselves.

The querulous and the signposts carry no responsibility for their actions or their speech,
　　　　　　　　　carry no intent to grow or to develop,
　　　　　　　　　carry no desire to define the sacred or the sacrosanct.

The querulous and the signposts go their merry way spreading disgust
　　　　　　　　　　　　　　and disappointment,
　　　　　　　　　　　　doubt and second guesses,
　　　　　　　　　　　　withdrawal and infections
　　　　　　　　　　　　which contaminate the hosts:
　　　　　　to whom they offer very little by way of building on a character,
　　　　　　　　　　　　or serving from a reservoir of hope.

The querulous and the signposts do not have checks upon their tongues,
　　　　　　　　　do not have the thought processes where miracles can
　　　　　　　　　　　　　be considered,
　　　　　　　　　do not have a relationship with the better half of life.

The querulous and the signposts are not to be the standard bearers of decency
　　　　　　　　　　　　　and respect,
　　　　　　　　　are not to be the epitome of achievement for a child,
　　　　　　　　　are not to be the answerers of questions concerning the
　　　　　　　　　　　　possibility of life beyond the grave.

The querulous and the signposts are not the flag bearers of any cause other
　　　　　　　　　　　　　than themselves,
　　　　　　　are not the gift bearers of anything of value—
　　　　　　　　　　whether of the natural or whether of the spiritual,
　　　　　　　are not the circumspect or honourers of the valued or the offered,
　　　　　　　are not familiar with The Promises or The Discipleship of God.

The querulous and the signposts slouch and are bent over,
　　　　　　　　　are twisted and soured,
　　　　　　　　　are distorted and cramped.

The querulous and the signposts are not the ones to emulate,
　　　　　　　　　are not the ones to pity,.

The querulous and the signposts are the ones to adopt for moderation,
　　　　　　　　　are the ones to engage with offers of instruction,

are the ones to be assisted in the straightening of
their stances,
in the dealing with their traits,
in The Seeking and The Finding
of the high points of a life,
the high points worth assimilation,
the high points as a standard intended for adoption,
the high points which attach to the pathway
leading home.

The querulous and the signposts can be brought to understanding,
can be encouraged to accept the unknown,
can be the trumpeters of a message worth repeating,
can be the instigators of a new approach to their fellow man.

The querulous and the signposts can compile a questionnaire of hope and of excitement,
of Truth and of honesty,
of vision and of majesty.

The querulous and the signposts can dwell where behaviour becomes acceptable,
where the querulous become reliable and upright specimens:
of the bearers of the light to a dim and dusty world;
where signposts do not point to the distasteful and the disaster prone,
do not point to the areas of destruction,
do not point to the usurpers of Righteousness—
on the way to Peace and harmony.

The querulous and the signposts can both stand tall and straight,
can both be examples of endeavour and of trust,
can both be the sharers of the situations with appeal
to the spirit and the soul.

The querulous and the signposts can become the transmitters of a change
in circumstance,
the yielders to restraint,
the adoptees gathered to become the arrows
to accompany the bowman:
for a ride on a white horse.

The querulous and the signposts may receive a new name on a white stone,
may acquire a chest where treasures can be safely stored,
may receive The Promises leading to attendance at a Bridal Function,
may not want to return to a previous way of life,
as forsaken and overtaken:
by a future which is golden and desirable and within the reach of man."

The Likelihood of Achievement

And I hear The Lord Jesus saying,
"The likelihood of achievement is well worth the calculating,
     is well worth the supervising,
     is well worth the oversight with the imposing of control.

The likelihood of achievement is a measure of determination,
     is a measure of the fulfilment of the will,
     is a measure of commitment to the understanding of the
         target for completion.

The likelihood of achievement is the passion of the present,
     is the dedication of containment to the limits of the jurisdiction,
     is the sweeping of the floorboards in the preventing of contamination.

The likelihood of achievement is a function of the sacrilege of the time frame,
     is the insistence on continuation,
     is the working on just one step at a time.

The likelihood of achievement is swelled or hindered by the weather,
     bringing expansion or contraction,
     bringing the warmth or cold,
     bringing the need for preservation of the fine lines
         of stability.

The likelihood of achievement requires avoidance of the mess and mayhem,
     of the gain or loss implicit in a contract,
     of the finding with the preservation of
         the pathway to success.

The likelihood of achievement needs inspection of the maintaining of the quality,
     needs supervision of the accuracy of delineation,
     needs the power to alter or to switch the planning of the labour force,
         with its degrees of skill.

The likelihood of achievement depends on rising to the challenge,
     on setting the targets for the night,
     on the chain of invincibility kept current
         throughout the day.

The likelihood of achievement is threatened by an illness,
     is threatened by a health scare,
     is threatened a lack of immunization in the body of
         the workforce.

The likelihood of achievement is dependent on the calendaring of the hitches and delays,
     of the recognition of the surges and the lapses in

ANTHONY A EDDY (SCRIBE)

the core well of production,
of the sticking to the serving and attendance,
to the accidents and mishaps,
with their attendant impacts on the absence of
the critical.

The likelihood of achievement flares and subsides,
grows and enlarges,
shrinks and diminishes as enthusiasm wanes in variance
with the taskings of the day.

The likelihood of achievement should be kept in the forefront of the mind,
should be the item bearing witness of the effect of
the unexpected,
should be a measure of the effort with the out-turn of
the desired results.

The likelihood of achievement can be as a swing when mounted on a branch:
with all its ups and downs until it finally slows to come
to rest,
when the energy is spent.

The likelihood of achievement requires the input of the energy of consumption,
with the matching level of the output.

The likelihood of achievement requires the supply of all the components,
as ordered and delivered,
as approved for the consistency of quality,
with the resultant intermeshing of the assemblies of the parts.

The likelihood of achievement requires consistency of approach,
of testing and approvals,
of the measuring and containment of any moving away
from the detailed standards:
of the specifications applicable within a working shift.

The likelihood of achievement depends upon the maintaining of the standards,
within the permissible degrees of tolerance,
depends upon the accuracy as delivered with the
assembly techniques employed,
depends upon the failure rate of the finished objects.

The likelihood of achievement can be muddied by an argument born of ignorance,
can be enhanced by a discussion born of Wisdom.

The likelihood of achievement can be lost within the discards,
can be lost by carelessness of application,
can be lost by assumptions without validity,
can be lost by guesswork where accuracy is foregone in

the quest for speed.

The likelihood of achievement can be as an anthill with an elephant on top,
where compression is the problem,
can be as a thorn within a side where it pricks with great consistency:
as the standards are lowered into the widening gulf of rejection,
can be as a needle in a haystack where the day is wasted in
unsuccessful searching,
can be as an imitation of the original rather than the purity of the
original itself.

The likelihood of achievement rises with approval,
shrinks with rejection.

The likelihood of achievement is magnified by care,
is decreased by the filling of the reject bin.

The likelihood of achievement is impressed by the hum of machinery,
with the lighting from within,
is impressed by the assignment of responsibility with
the out-turn of both the day and the night,
is impressed by the achieving of the targets as the orders
are despatched,
where the delivery date was not broken,
where the quality surpassed the specification—
which could have been the stumbling blocks
for the acceptance of delivery.

The likelihood of achievement is sealed by the organized and the faithful,
where the planning is meaningful and complete,
where the knowledge base is widespread and appreciated,
where success is warranted and achieved with everyone's
satisfaction at the outcome:
where beams and smiles reward the fields of effort and
of care."

My Content Study Aid

_____

_____

_____

_____

_____

_____

The Outpouring of Success

And I hear The Lord Jesus saying,
"The outpouring of success spreads the word around among the neighbours,
with their relatives abroad.

The outpouring of success is a happy end result,
speaks of a goal achieved,
speaks of interest maintained,
speaks of affluence galore.

The outpouring of success deserves an inscription on the roll of honour,
of the days spent in coveting and plotting for success,
of the nights spent in seclusion in planning the extensions.

The outpouring of success is not as a melting ice cream in a cone on a summer's day,
is not a wasteful experience seen heading to the west,
is not the blending of exotic fruit of rarity in the market place,
as sometimes seen around the home base of delivery.

The outpouring of success occurs for very solid reasons,
where excuses and absences have long decayed and rotted:
into the façade of oblivion.

The outpouring of success sees no sign of nervousness,
sees no sign of greed,
sees no sign of envy nor of jealousy at large.

The outpouring of success used to tramp the streets of wealth,
used to call and invite participation,
used to be an annoyance which needed to be done.

The outpouring of success followed slowly with ignition at the beginning of a trajectory;
gradually gathered speed with the acknowledgment of quality,
and the growing recognition of the value for money;
soon to reach the takeoff speed where staffing was important,
as it assumed the pride of place;
the job became a business where absence at the top was
not a recipe for disaster,
where the work load was shared and readied for the
demand as buried in the future.

The outpouring of success witnessed the returns when demand was released,
had funds assigned for reinvestment:
designed to cultivate the growth just out
of reach.

The outpouring of success saw the beds of industry kept well watered and weed free,

kept access to the marketplace firmly
in the goal as dated for advancement.

The outpouring of success guarded firmly the attempted infiltration of distractions:
which did no good at all,
which were the carriers of potential to become
the wasters of much time and effort,
with neither a reward seen upon distant horizons,
nor gratitude likely to be expressed:
when held within the mindset of encroachment.

The outpouring of success increases the valuing of time,
increases with the fountaining,
increases the velocity of ejection,
increases the volume emitted,
increases the paper worth of man.

The outpouring of success portrays a picture of incredulity,
portrays a surplus running wild,
portrays the ability to purchase without a glance at
the pricing ticket.

The outpouring of success has meaning to the closely bound,
has understanding from the numerate,
has questions inviting answers as to the objectives of a life.

The outpouring of success leaves numbers changing faster than can be read,
faster than can be written,
faster than delivery can be made for
counting and for storage.

The outpouring of success continues unabated,
drives the shoppers wild as they struggle for a shirt or top,
drives the recipients to expand their vision:
of the effect that wealth beyond imagination,
can vest upon a couple.

The outpouring of success destroys the functioning of the joy of attainment of a goal,
witnesses the growing of a casualness of approach,
widens without appreciation the expensiveness of life where
money is a nuisance,
having lost its ability to limit purchasing by restriction on the
amount available.

The outpouring of success makes a nuisance of having to count the zeros and the commas
with the added demand for rubber bands.

The outpouring of success widens the scope of man,
increases the ability to travel anywhere at will,

quickly brings stagnation to the pot where the
overflow continues,
with the garages becoming cramped.

The outpouring of success often rings an alarm bell signalling a stockpile of excess,
poses questions of inexperience as to how it should be
dealt with and the discovery of an end result.

The outpouring of success sees the situation worsen with an influx of begging letters
from the far and wide,
with names of unfamiliarity affixed to epistles of untruth
and misdirection,
where the fraudulent and the thieves pester and dismay,
type and do not care,
lie in order to achieve the gain,
lie with exaggeration and discrepancies galore,
as they would beat a hole into a door.

The outpouring of success can be as a gaining of intelligence,
as a seeing with Wisdom and with skill,
as an experience where wealth becomes a tool of trade,
while evangelism surfaces with orderliness and politeness,
of requests for assistance with the travel funding and the infrastructure,
required to be present at the dawning of all appearing in a new day,
in an area where God is scarcely ever invited to attend,
although He knows it well."

My Content Study Aid

_____
_____
_____
_____
_____
_____
_____
_____
_____
_____
_____
_____

Crop Circles Studied

And I hear The Lord Jesus saying,
"Crop circles as named by man are not the names in common use,
within the ones who know and understand.

Crop circles are not intended to be destructive,
are not intended to be gazed on with awe and ignorance,
are not intended to bring fear or trepidation of the unknown.

Crop circles are difficult to fathom on inspection,
are confused by the amateurs at play,
are misinterpreted by the misleading claims of responsibility
for the simplistic,
with the photographs and the seeking of publicity,
which is neither relevant nor deserved,
as such behaviours heap false mysteries on The Truth,
where guessing does not serve the cause
for the discovery of The Truth.

Crop circles of extreme complexity with determined alignment,
with care in preparation:
carry information to those who are prepared,
carry information in the intergalactic language,
in every day usage,
by the visitors who speak such as a way of life,
as they come and go,
as they search and find,
as they travel and refine,
as they settle and procure.

Crop circles are a means of communication,
are targeted for showing on television,
are readied for an unimagined announcement,
the reading of a theme,
the composition afforded craftsmanship and beauty,
the declaring of intent on the announcing of the news on radio,
with the internet at large in synchronization with the multimedia.

Crop circles standout from the air,
are hidden in a crop,
lose their detail at the harvesting of the grain.

Crop circles are drawn and configured by different entities of existence,
by entities where man is not included,
by entities which speak in a hieroglyphic
language of the stars,

ANTHONY A EDDY (SCRIBE)

where understanding is condensed and precise,
where crop labelling does not require an answer,
where they are dictating the future rendezvousing,
among the star fields of the cosmos,
or the celestial location areas quite close to The Earth.

Crop circles are a recent startling happening upon The Earth,
are having their effect and implantations overlaid,
by the stupidity of man,
of youth,
of conniving with the evil-led
hearts of man,
as the worst confusers of the universe:
as these children play at make-believe
without the integrity to admit,
of their participations in what is non
of their concern.

Crop circles envision a much greater audience,
envision a much greater effort to crack the encodings in use,
envision a response of viable communication:
with the instigators of the crop circles,
with consistency of quality,
with consistency of application,
with consistency of the standard worthy of intergalactic travellers,
where the welcome is uncertain,
where the effort is held in the hands of secret enclaves,
where past effort is not admitted,
where denials bred of lies are seen to win the day.

Crop circles are similar to tribal tattoos,
hold the components specific to a species in-line with the language used:
without acknowledgement nor knowledge of the quest for contact,
with the would-be recipients at large;
yet filled with ignorance as to the wider significance,
which is being emblazoned on The Earth,
for inspection and reaction.

Crop circles should be appreciated as the contact points of unknown civilizations:
which are being sought with the pestering of
waves of many lengths and types,
sent hurtling and buzzing into space,
with a simplicity of structure which beggars
belief from afar,
as not considered worth the answering:
as if an infant shouting from a crib,
before the language has been

either assimilated or learnt.

Crop circles are the initial response to the searching of the ether,
of the universe for contacts:
have not been recognized for what they really are,
as they carry the clues to understanding
the language of the stars,
the language of the sublime and well thought out,
the language of The Committed and The Travelling,
the language which has no effort being made to appreciate,
or to learn from the crop circles as instated on The Earth:
with genuine authority,
with patterns of significance,
with the simple leading unto complexity
as understanding dawns,
with knowledge as accumulated,
with application as bound by Wisdom,
with meaningful emulation,
being the confirmation of intelligence achieved.

Crop circles are there to be studied in detail of inscription,
are there to be studied as the openers of the pathways,
to companionship of being,
are there to be studied so preparation can be started,
so learning schools can be commenced,
so questions can be formulated and applied,
as questions in the responding crop circles,
as originating from The Earth,
with due intelligence to make them
meaningful to the senders,
as well as those on the party lines in space.

Crop circles are the opening overtures from afar:
to competent and meaningful communication,
without the need to leave The Earth."

My Content Study Aid

_____

_____

_____

_____

_____

Crop Circles Investigated

And I hear The Lord Jesus saying,
"Crop circles examined yield very few clues as to the origin,
    have speed of execution,
    are completed in the darkness,
    would indicate a prepared template with the image close at hand:
    for reproduction on the crop with physicality of presence and
        of quality.

Crop circles centred and completed,
    centred and transcribed from an image to a presence in a field,
      leave much to be explained,
      leave much to be determined,
      leave much to be forsaken when the accusations
        are false,
   are seen without credence of belief where the claimants of the crown,
        for the layout in a field,
      cannot reproduce the complex and perfected,
       the laying of the straws,
      the beauty of design with variance
       expressing the wonder of a sentinel,
      overlaid by the knowledge and ability to
       superimpose the confetti images:
       of a saucer in its boldness,
       of activation and completion,
      with the signing of a message,
       in the testing of the possibility of reply,
       of the likelihood of comprehension:
        in the language of consent.

Crop circles have no fear,
   have no jurisdiction,
   have no sense of existence,
    suffer the imposition of the feet with boots and shoes,
    suffer the tape measures as drawn tightly and examined,
    suffer the chatter of the ignorant but curious at heart—
     those without the knowledge to progress the findings of the few.

Crop circles are not capable of movement,
   sit and make a statement of that which has come and gone,
   are not heard in the time of creativity,
   are not seen in the presence of a full moon,
   have the ability to be generated while the cloaking of the saucer,
     projects a matching image which merges in the sky,
     or in the presence of a field with the attraction of a crop,

as readied to accept by the ripening and the moisture content for acceptance,
of a message which did not originate upon The Earth.

Crop circles of man are accepted and transmitted to the analysing laboratory,
via an active relay station far above the frequencies:
as encountered on The Earth,
as promoted on The Earth,
as generated on The Earth,
as sparked upon The Earth.

Crop circles of delight can leave a fragrance inherent in the laying of the crop,
can trigger a recollection of,
a recognition of,
the scent from aeons prior when The DNA recorded the favourite,
of the day and of the night,
so marking it as available for recall within the modern memory bank of man.

Crop circles with a lack of scent acknowledged from those present,
unmasks the historically absent and the useless from the gathered seen,
as they contribute the time-wasters and inane.

Crop circles can be discerned for authenticity by the security established,
by the presence of intelligent investigation,
of the application of thought as to the method of construction,
as the laying means of flattening the upright and the sturdy,
as the building of the pattern,
of the impregnating the odour:
the scent favoured by the ancients and still recognizable
today by some as the original Balm of Gilead,
as it again stands tall and straight in the limelight of the unexpected,
in it haunting of the memory cells embedded in The DNA of the
ancients and the crossbreeds,
who led unto The Neandertals through interbreeding,
who both flourished and succeeded in their purpose filled existence.

Crop circles stem from a related previously purpose filled existence,
which was one of preparation and welcoming,
of the caring for the arrival of more strangers,
as the dinosaurs were hunted and extinguished,
as Peace became the setting for the new arrivals,
as freed from the fear of predators,
as they were made to feel at home.

Crop circles now play a part in synchronising the distant past,
with the concurrency of the present situations,
as found across the acceptable climes of The Earth,
in a relationship where such were known and used for the inaugural habitats,
as established in use upon The Earth,

as acceptable landing zones,
where embarrassments did not occur,
where difficulties were already plotted for attention,
where the supervision by The Neandertals ensured;
both protection from the weather and the providing of nourishment,
as both declared and required.

Crop circles were not the initiating points of invasion,
because of a lack of crops which would take an imprint,
were the substituted:
by the sandy deserts,
by the sandy foreshores,
where inhabitance bespoke activity beyond the high water marks—
as evidenced by the tidal sweeps along the foreshores,
which were the resetters of the time frames of sand availability,
as cleaned and swept,
by the outgoing tides.

Crop circles are a modern occurrence,
have been waiting for the explosion in technology,
for the interlinking of the households,
for the serge in social media,
for the importance of the on-line networks which often is
the means,
of far-reaching conversations and the setting of objectives with accuracy,
of meaning and the transference of
the resources;
with accounting which is finite,
with deception which is widespread,
with integrity so threatened,
with the building blocks of Truth and Righteousness,
under the attack of the demeaning and denying,
as the lies are built and stacked for dishonesty to prosper,
without accountability across the networking of man,
and within the sight of God."

My Content Study Aid

_____

_____

_____

_____

_____

Crop Circles Considered

And I hear The Lord Jesus saying,
"Crop circles considered are requiring of solutions,
$\qquad$ are requiring of an outlook fitted for reply,
$\qquad$ are requiring of the facts for when the stones were moved.

Crop circles considered are new phenomena upon The Earth:
$\qquad$ are new additions,
$\qquad\qquad$ with the scope wide open,
$\qquad\qquad$ to the likely flowing of the technology of man,
$\qquad$ are in need of cross-referencing across the nations of The Earth.

Crop circles considered need a complete compilation of an earth borne database,
$\qquad$ where comparisons can be made,
$\qquad$ where possibilities and their alternatives can be composed,
$\qquad\qquad$ to be thought through as to the likely outcomes,
$\qquad$ where meaning is not uncovered,
$\qquad\qquad$ so still remains in doubt.

Crop circles considered verify and disentangle the fraudulent from the real,
$\qquad\qquad$ the plaything from the entrusted,
$\qquad\qquad$ the misleading from the statements
$\qquad\qquad\qquad$ of position,
$\qquad\qquad$ within the overriding sight of man,
$\qquad\qquad$ as a mystery awaiting a solution
$\qquad\qquad\qquad$ of validity,
$\qquad\qquad$ within The End-time of Faith and Grace.

Crop circles considered seek the gathering of patterns from around the world,
$\qquad\qquad$ across the ups and downs of The Earth,
$\qquad\qquad$ across the highland and the lowlands,
$\qquad\qquad$ across the steppes and the plains for
$\qquad\qquad\qquad$ discerning the outreach of the prospects,
$\qquad\qquad\qquad$ who created them just so,
$\qquad\qquad\qquad$ to leave them open for inspection—
$\qquad\qquad\qquad$ which invites an answer to be sent,
$\qquad\qquad\qquad$ as a handshake to the stars.

Crop circles considered introduce a curriculum for the universities of man,
$\qquad$ introduce a posit for the stars,
$\qquad$ introduce the need for understanding of the
$\qquad\qquad\qquad$ facts uncontaminated,
$\qquad\qquad$ by those who interfere and think it is a joke.

Crop circles considered are a call to a study of all aspects of the crop circles,
$\qquad\qquad$ of an assessment outside the field of jokes

ANTHONY A EDDY (SCRIBE)

and infringements born of trespass,
whether the diameter of a crop circle is a measure of a flight
born diameter of the carrier of a pilot,
with others in need of attendance for completion to be assured.

Crop circles considered should not be ignored,
should not be placed in the too hard basket and relegated to
another day,
should not be seen to dwell in the land of make believe,
where history is ignored with the placement of the stones—
in locations around The Earth:
which overcome the disconnect of continents and islands,
whereon the stones were moved.

Crop circles considered are not a question of the lifting power,
but rather a question of the flattening power:
where a moveable object comes to rest,
while the pattern is inlaid on the crop underneath,
with an indication that such is not an accident,
but rather a deliberate attempt to leave an imprint on the crop,
for discovery by the locals—
who are known to dwell nearby.

Crop circles considered have no leeway for guesswork,
have no slack to play what ifs,
have no time to play ignores,
have no reason to look at suppositions not borne out by the facts,
when outside the realms of practicality and the calls to
common sense.

Crop circles considered need to sprout the grain of Truth,
need to escape the insidious and the dangerous,
need to bear in mind the peacefulness of activity,
as the circles are completed,
as witnesses of position and intent,
as the circles are installed without a hint of violence,
as Peace becomes the recurring message;
as exposed with repeating emphasis unto the light of day.

Crop circles considered may be constructed for the honest with integrity,
may be a testing of response,
may be a reviewing of the intellect in discerning the problem
base deployed.

Crop circles considered have a quite limited time frame for display,
for assimilation as to meaning,
for analysis of conceptual gradients,
for comparison between the years of presence in the crops—

for similarity where repetition summons the recording,
of what has previously come and gone.

Crop circles considered leave open plenty of room for speculation,
leave open doubt as to the composition of The Truth,
leave open the questions concerning motivation,
leave open the approaching of the promised rule of
Righteousness and Truth.

Crop circles considered have much to be resolved,
require earnest attention paid to the achieving of a solution in answering
the where the when the why with the what the who the how.

Crop circles considered are away out in left field,
are not an expected method for an initial contact,
leave much to be desired in the learning of identity,
in the ability to interrogate and overcome—
the possible missteps in approaching
and assisting,
in learning and acquiring,
in resolving and achieving,
the shared road to the future as technology leads past the present,
into the pandora's box where the future resides,
as if mixed with a slow release fertilizer to lead the way,
so it all comes together in the melting pot of DNA,
with the combinations lined up and making sense for the options and alternatives:
as postulated and studied for the overall success of the dreams and aspirations—
to lead into a future of achievement under the oversight of The Living God."

My Content Study Aid

_____
_____
_____
_____
_____
_____
_____
_____
_____
_____

Crop Circles Conforming

And I hear The Lord Jesus saying,
"Crop circles in conformity are recognized and tabulated,
        are synchronous and similar,
        are garnered in togetherness,
        are searched for repetitive fragments of design which can
                bring a breakthrough.

Crop circles in conformity are graded for diameter,
        are graded for distance apart and for the speed required,
        are graded for capacity to handle and as for a landing zone,
                where isolation is important.

Crop circles in conformity speak of a bonding in design,
        speak of a unity in understanding,
        speak of passiveness in application.

Crop circles in conformity share and share alike,
        do not break the rhythm of relationships,
        do hold true to the objectives of the night to impact in
                the daylight.

Crop circles in conformity do not encounter bickering,
        do not set the table with an argument,
        do not reach out in disclosure of the hidden and the buried.

Crop circles in conformity set the seal on habitations sought and occupied,
        set the seal of conveyancing at large,
        set the seal for the enlarging of the telescopes,
        set the seal for watching,
            for waiting,
            for attendance built on Trust and Faith.

Crop circles in conformity are the interest gatherers for the cameras,
        where the message awaits an opening of the coded
                factors of release.

Crop circles in conformity are not cries for help,
        are silent in their reclusiveness within the countrysides of
                wonder and amusement,
        are circumspect in the selecting of a crop,
            wherein the nest is both built and laid:
            to the present puzzlement of man.

Crop circles in conformity are not rationed in production,
        are not enlarged unnecessarily,
        are neither prohibited nor confiscated,

when there is a chance of earlier discovery,
before the paste is dry.

Crop circles in conformity are preened and polished in readiness for a viewing,
are neither rushed nor stamped on,
are neither squashed nor hurried to a messy completion,
where the timing is the enemy,
where the skillsets are not evident,
as doubt rests on the origins:
where the inspecting eyes can be read,
where the brows are furrowed in a
frown of non-acceptance:
of all that appears to be left on show.

Crop circles in conformity like to cling together,
like to surprise the neighbourhood,
like to appeal to reason and to intellect.

Crop circles in conformity are sometimes quite suspicious,
are sometimes quite unreasonable,
are sometime seemingly there as a distraction of what has
seen the amateur in action,
with a second-rate ring which was known for its
existence elsewhere.

Crop circles in conformity have credence when separated by great distances:
where one cannot bring influence to bear
upon another,
where one has detailing of a standard;
such that there is a matching of intent with originality:
as the message is conveyed and left open for both
inspection and consideration.

Crop circles in conformity beg the question of continuity,
beg the question of occasional similarity,
beg the question as to whether such are time dependent with
a warning or a greeting;
or a simple transposition of a modern drawing,
as if in a cave when there was time to spare.

Crop circles in conformity without due concentration may bring confusion to
the window,
may bring mistaken apprehension to what lies before the eyes,
may bring circuitous travelling when the end is but the start.

Crop circles in conformity can vie with excellence of presentation,
can vie for supremacy among the crops,
can vie for photographic zeal where the image is incredible

and the detail is minute but circumspect.

Crop circles in conformity are at the common end of the chain;
carry the what ifs,
shun the must be's;
describe a display to the casual and the common;
stretch out in consideration to the curious and
the exaggerators.

Crop circles in conformity are not growing as expected,
appear to be a fad now passing with the time of relevance,
to the season of the ripening:
where the fields are golden in readiness for the harvesting of
the crops,
but now mostly untainted with the graffiti as once inscribed
within the fields of grain.

Crop circles in conformity require tokens of precision:
for the etching of the design scopes implicit in the layouts;
requires aspects of design as found in the repertoires
of architects,
or apprentices at foot,
with foreknowledge and experience of the impressions to convey.

Crop circles in conformity yield unto the daylight,
yield unto reasoned consideration,
yield unto due consternation:
when understanding is not present,
as ignorance is heard to comment on the productions of the night.

Crop circles in conformity when executed for attention in the presence of
the competent and the experienced,
the skilled and the informed,
the knowing and the recorders:
when among the secrets and denials of the reports as made by
the qualified and trusted:
designed to hold The Multitudes at bay,
to keep the media bottled up and silenced,
with the claiming of alternative unlikelihoods,
to what is true and surfacing for the explanations which satisfy the facts."

My Content Study Aid

_____

_____

Crop Circles Analysed

And I hear The Lord Jesus saying,
"Crop circles in analysis is a declaring of The Truth as known,
                is a mystery worth sorting to completion,
                is an establishing of an end-time presence where knowledge
                bursts asunder for the encircling of The Earth.

Crop circles in analysis speak and leave the consortium of power,
                speak and return to silence with the workload of a guest,
                speak united in an obligation which is coming to the fore.

Crop circles in analysis are the agencies bearing signs and wonders to the home of man,
                are the agencies found where creation sang and witnessed,
                      the happenings on the homes of distant strangers:
            those established in accompanying distant star groups
                which have aged,
                which see the offshoots travelling to the guiding beacons,
                where they hope to find a welcome,
                which are expectant of The God of ages
                    who was and is expecting them,
                    who welcomes them on arrival,
                    who knows the mysteries enveloping in agapé care,
                      within surroundings of protection,
                      while establishment was and is achieved.

Crop circles in analysis are there to be deciphered,
                are there to be examined,
                are there to bring witness of the strangers
            as the travellers and the kinsman of The Neandertals:
            as their incumbent technology was used by all who asked and
                        sought assistance,
            with their visions involving displays of lifting and placing,
             with preparation,
             with the greatest of precision,
            as the monolithic stones were settled in obedience,
                to so create the demonstrations of the abilities of
                      paying homage,
                to the requesting tribes across the face of The Earth.

Crop circles in analysis speak of a way of doing things,
                have clues aplenty as to how the stones were placed,
            as to how the stones were locked in place through melding to
                      their neighbours,
            as to how they are impervious to the shaking of The Earth,
            as to how they withstood the cascading of defeat—

in the heating of the stones unto their melding temperatures;
for the flowing of the edges and the blending as the stones,
so cooled after their treatment from the beamed microwaves;
as driven by,
as supplied from,
the presence of the sunlight in conversion.

Crop circles in analysis are not the playthings of the idle,
the playthings of the children,
the playthings set for emulation in the confines
of security.

Crop circles in analysis are there for examination,
are there to disclose the intent of the installer,
are there to make sense of the activity deployed.

Crop circles in analysis on the face of it can be seen as neither friend nor foe,
can be seen as if introducing an armistice of Peace,
can be seen only as a finished product where the
means and the mode remain,
as part of the mystery for which the intellect needs to find
the solution,
of the puzzle with its parameters as it has been set and stamped.

Crop circles in analysis require the technology of the day for both closeup scrutiny,
and afar impressions of the individual componentry,
of the patterns as laid out.

Crop circles in analysis show no sign of danger,
show no sign of entrapment,
show no sign of impending peril,
show no sign of a relationship where threats hide behind their
ugly faces.

Crop circles in analysis can support fear within the unknown,
can support dismay within a loss of integrity of purpose,
can support the querying of the obvious which does not sustain
the progression of the mystery:
as to the endeavour inherent in the finished article
which appears to have neither rhyme nor reason for its existence in a field,
which seems to have no function but to manipulate the testing of the intellect of man,
where they seem to want to make comparisons with the intellect of The Neandertals,
in order to determine the intellectual progression of both in time,
and how this has may have affected their survival capability,
as problem solvers at large upon The Earth.

Crop circles in analysis appear to be a test of perception,
a test of functioning understanding,

a test of the ability to posture and to conclude.

Crop circles in analysis appear to be enigmas,
within the field of presentation,
appear to be a puzzle where the rules of determination
remain hidden,
as if a needle in a haystack,
appear to be awaiting a postering of position,
which leads to a golden search.

Crop circles in analysis can be put in the too-hard basket,
which never brings results into the daylight,
which never overcomes a shoulder with a shrug,
which never enhances an intellect in training:
where the expositor expresses no interest—
when the smoke is determined to stay within the smokestack.

Crop circles in analysis must not be seen as wasted effort by the unknown principals
who are guiding and directing,
who are formulating and generating the patterns for each circle of integrity,
who stay and hold fast to the concepts as gathered and decreed as ready;
to assail the gradients of man's intellect in the
absence of inferior or superior motivations,
which ultimately do not tender solutions to the puzzles of the day.

Crop circles in analysis appear to be well-bred conundrums where the box constrains,
the thoughts of likely relevance:
which may prove vital to considerations,
where the thinkers may find it necessary to think outside the box,
in permitting free reign of the spirit and the soul,
where the vocabulary of man may well be in need of additions,
to enable accurate and worthwhile constructions,
to attach to the concept gradients arising from
the considerations:
of why the crop circles of The Earth are seen and placed—
with the fields of existence and of the favour of God."

My Content Study Aid

_____
_____
_____
_____
_____

Crop Circles Disclosed

And I hear The Lord Jesus saying,
"Crop circles disclosed are the sign posting of the travellers.

Crop circles disclosed are the signing of their passage of fulfilment,
        are The Way Stations where they have stopped to mark their
            movements on The Earth.

Crop circles disclosed are the understandings falling into line,
        with the knowledge as received from the well of Living Water,
            when Wisdom is to the fore.

Crop circles disclosed are encountered without triggering:
        an upheaval of the planet,
        an upheaval from the seabed,
        an upheaval from the windswept,
        an upheaval from the firestorm with its hungry maw,
        an upheaval of the lava as it determinedly follows the
            pathway of least resistance,
             of acceptance,
             of certainty.

Crop circles disclosed do not readily succumb to fire,
        do not readily burn the recollections of the youth,
        do not readily consume those who know the three paths of
            certain victory—
        The Path of Righteousness in company with The Path of Truth,
           as merged into The Path of Faith with Grace.

Crop circles disclosed yearn for recognition,
        yearn for someone to whom to talk,
        yearn to be thought worth while in sharing the destinies compiled,
        yearn to have the readers concentrated and absorbing,
            that of the knowledgable and the competent,
        yearn to have the information shared,
        yearn to be considered to be worth the time and effort,
            with the password of the times—
      as set and primed for their revelation of the addresses,
      of the very distant envoys who live there and also know the way.

Crop circles disclosed do not speak in their sleep,
        do neither mutter nor murmur where they are likely to
            be overheard.

Crop circles disclosed can have their circles read from very far away,
        know the language that is best when issuing instructions to
            computers wide awake,

with no intentions of being made to go to sleep.

Crop circles disclosed can have their patterning changed upon request,
        can have their encodings cleaned and polished,
        can have their source files modified and transferred,
        can have the records competently overwritten or erased
                within simplicity.

Crop circles disclosed carry great responsibilities when newly fletched and honoured,
        are capable of reaching across divides,
        have the capability for the instance of existence to reach into the
                wayward past,
           or into the uncertain future,
           or to stay imprisoned in the present
      until time weathers and destroys the circle,
          which is at risk while the weather batters all,
      until such are tempted to succumb.

Crop circles disclosed know the intergalactic co-ordinates,
             for which they are responsible,
        neither know the earth-bound ones nor any others,
        which are specific to a stable platform out in space;
        which have the hint of interference and trouble for the interloper,
           who cannot leave well alone.

Crop circles disclosed are so blindingly fast that their transmission and reception rates
                jump over,
        to surpass the archaic speeds of the relay channels,
        as used by the sluggards borne by The Earth.

Crop circles disclosed still keep their secrets to themselves,
        are not read by residents,
        are not read by stragglers,
        are not read by the cyclists and the herders,
        are not read by the sequestered and the ignorant,
        are not read by the numerous and the retained.

Crop circles disclosed are threatened unto silence,
        are impacted by the shocks,
        are modified by excessive water,
          become unreliable when the water mounts the fences and
           spreads over onto the crops wherein the circles lie.

Crop circles disclosed seek the valuable and the guarded,
        seek the surplus and the finite,
        seek the infinite and the stockpile,
        seek the countable and the accruals,
        seek the non-bickerers and the perceivers,

seek the non-colourblind and the hearing,
seek the satisfied yet earnest,
seek the impulsive yet co-ordinated,
seek the imposers of the checkmates on the kings and queens.

Crop circles disclosed can be victims of the football scrum,
can be the dancers on hot coals,
can be the huddlers in the winds of change,
can be the runners with the batons who are desperate not to
drop one,
while in a test of speed.

Crop circles disclosed are high technologies at a pristine level on The Earth,
are futuristic technologies where no locals have familiarity,
are incumbent technologies where the sources are well guarded,
are remote technologies with a powerhouse of ability,
are circumspect technologies where it is sometimes best to sit
back and watch.

Crop circles disclosed are the alien mapping of The Earth,
which may be read and actioned at great heights,
can be read by alien computers to record and plot the pathways:
both home and to the stars with the counting metronomes of God,
with the friendship of the strangers and the wanderers,
with the guidance of The Neandertals as the operators of equipment,
which is both unique and challenging,
with a language which is hidden with the icons born of simulation,
where the meddlers have a life expectancy of close to zero.

Crop circles disclosed are linked closely to the ongoing interests of The Living God
of man."

My Content Study Aid

_____

_____

_____

_____

_____

_____

_____

_____

Crop Circles Revealed

And I hear The Lord Jesus saying,
"Crop circles revealed declares their safety as bound by their points of reference.

Crop circles revealed show their passive nature in the sunlight of the day,
          show their reflections in the eyes of the beholders,
          show their derivations in the immediacy of their creation.

Crop circles revealed carry a statement unto man,
          a statement ending the isolation of man,
          on an arm within the universe of these dimensions in particular.

Crop circles revealed are the epitome of projection,
          are the initiators of discovery,
          are the homing signals for the band waggons.

Crop circles revealed do not go on journeys,
          stay where they are planted for a time within a journey,
          as a beacon for the starships in their travels back and forth,
      with the interlocking of the data as scrambled but defined,
      with the recording of the status and the bearings of The Earth,
      with the finality of the beamed approval through the announcing
                and reception,
          which broke the bandwidths open.

Crop circles revealed are attractive,
          yet suspicious,
          when understanding fails and common sense has no grip,
          as an anchoring point to a standard of selection.

Crop circles revealed lose the curtaining of fear from their first encounter,
          lose the mystery which surrounds the unsolicited presence in
                a field,
          lose the worst case scenario in which the speculation is rife,
          as the functioning is unknown,
          but suspected,
          to have an ulterior motive hidden from both sight
          and application,
          which would not be to the benefit of man.

Crop circles revealed bring sighs of relief among the populace at large,
          bring smiles to the fore as introductions are expected,
          bring the children out in droves as curiosity awaits the sating,
          by a viewing in a welcome change of stance.

Crop circles revealed assert the pathways of existence to either superior intelligence,
          or to the residual effects of much longer term development.

ANTHONY A EDDY (SCRIBE)

Crop circles revealed carry The Promises of much information to be showered upon
The Earth,
as comprehension is gained,
as games involving the shooting of the 'monsters' are
rapidly withdrawn,
to be parcelled out of sight.

Crop circles revealed are the carriers of good news:
of Godly relationships already established,
of consideration and of friendship,
of companionship and interest,
of sharing and of showing the extent of
their discoveries.

Crop circles revealed have discoverers who are aware of the need to honour those whom
they encounter on their travels.

Crop circles revealed are the introducers of unknown alternatives,
are the evidence of life established elsewhere other than on
The Earth,
are as the waggons heading west two centuries ago—
with all that they encountered with dismay and warlike attitudes—
those which did not bring solutions to encroachment,
without a great loss of life and the onset of mourning,
which could have been avoided:
if The Truth were told from the beginning;
if The Truth with The Promises were upheld
by integrity of purpose,
where lying was unknown and of no longterm use—
as a solution to the woes encountered.

Crop circles revealed are a measure of advancement,
are a measure of accomplishment,
are not the instigators of conflict nor of violence,
in a struggle for a founding settlement.

Crop circles revealed can be seen as the initiators,
as the revealers,
of new truths already discovered with applications:
away beyond the imaginings of man,
away beyond the capabilities of man to produce what they are seeing—
for the very first time,
away beyond man's present ability to comprehend the manufacturing,
the operational use with the effects available,
upon livelihoods within the stars of God.

Crop circles revealed are ultimately for the benefit of man,
will save man from the re-inventing of the wheel,

from the designing and the testing from a base of ignorance,
of that which can already fly and transport faster—
from what was believed to be the limiter of mass,
to where transformation will now be possible prior to eternity,
as to then be experienced hand-in-hand with God.

Crop circles revealed opens up the parent pathways to a new stage of flight,
opens up the orchestrations of the soul of man,
opens up the opportunities for the voyages of dreams,
opens up a new reality among the maze of the 'what ifs',
opens up and begs the question of where does man go from here—
of how of why of when—
for he will no longer be the first arrival,
for being seated on an usurped throne.

Crop circles revealed have brought likely alliances,
with agreements to the fore and centre,
where man is no longer the equal partner
in which he finds himself negotiating,
from weakness rather than the strength,
which superior knowledge brings to the table,
in the seeking of affirmation in agreement,
where the future remains unclouded as God upholds The
Faith and Miracles within His Temples on The Earth."

My Content Study Aid

_____

_____

_____

_____

_____

_____

_____

_____

_____

_____

_____

Crop Circles Resolved

And I hear The Lord Jesus saying,
"Crop circles resolved speak of matters borne and overcome,
>> conquered and settled down,
>> listed and recorded.

Crop circles resolved are enumerated according to the structures,
>> according to the navigational points,
>> according to the reference points intended for afar.

Crop circles resolved are bereft of mystery eventually,
> are bereft of mystery within a soliloquy of the heart,
> are bereft of mystery when function is determined and is
>>>> so announced.

Crop circles resolved establish a record of resistance,
> a record of a summary,
> a record of the nonsense spoken both before and after,
>> as the scene does ripen,
>> as the scene does bore into the intelligence,
> with all which has contaminated as it went before.

Crop circles resolved put an end to confrontation,
> put an end to useless slaughter,
> put an end to stupid sacrifices—
>> for where there is no pain–
>> for where there is no gathering,
>> to where there is no benefit accruing from the act.

Crop circles resolved can end up with the burdens heaped to cause a stumble,
>>> heaped to hide a step in-waiting,
>>> heaped to un-suspend with shattering:
>> as they strike the floor and do not bounce.

Crop circles resolved mend their ways of behaviour within the ways and means:
>> of each behavioural impulse.

Crop circles resolved do not stay long in the water which supports the ice.

Crop circles resolved raise the temperature of the covered,
> raise the temperature of the driven and the strained,
> lower the temperature when in relief when all would prefer
>>>> to return,
>> from whence they came without undue delay.

Crop circles resolved inspect both the impervious and the water-logged,
> inspect the automated record for a cloud burst from the skies,
> inspect the time frame since rain last appeared within the record to

so encourage growth.

Crop circles resolved become part of the landscape which is not questioned further,
become part of the landscape which is viewed from very distant
places within the sky of God,
become part of the landscape whereon the mountains continually
grow and develop intermittently as their tops fall off.

Crop circles resolved frequent the crops of bounty where conditions are ideal,
where the stems do ripen into stalks with rigidity,
which no longer flow and bend when bowing to
the wind.

Crop circles resolved see the tenure of their holding decreasing by the day,
extending by the night;
retreating by the day from the arrangements of the prim and proper,
extending by the night into the carelessness of the relaxed and carefree.

Crop circles resolved gradually become acquainted with the withered and the wilting,
the damaged and the decaying,
the waiting and the wistful of
what has been,
has gone,
is not expecting to return to function as before.

Crop circles resolved are only built from templates prepared for specific journeys,
are not prepared for weathering in stone,
are not prepared to send light into the darkness,
are not prepared to radiate a beacon beam into the shortwaves of
man's determining.

Crop circles resolved carry their own aesthetic beauty to wherever they are viewable,
to wherever they are set to be read without undue delay,
to wherever they are set to yield their classification languages to
the travellers as assigned—
those who do report and magnify all that they gather from the determined points,
on The Earth from where the navigational watchdogs mark and list and send:
the catch points for a journey in the safety of being viewable and understood,
from where the skies are clear,
while navigational bounds are surmounted and resolved,
at the receiving vessels which,
although they may be far from home,
are still confident that the stations will safely see,
the reaching of their target for the day.

Crop circles resolved are there to play lookout with the guidance,
for those who move and dwell inside the orbiting range
of Venus,

and all the relative moons included as desirable
monitoring locations.

Crop circles resolved are within the local conformity for the call for Peace,
are not supplied with creaking covers which would alert a need
for servicing,
or put doubt upon abilities.

Crop circles resolved fall and faint upon The Earth,
do not move when they are comfortable,
do not worry in the sustaining of their objectives tied to the
messages they carry,
with reliability and reliance on the host.

Crop circles resolved are the guests of summer and of autumn,
are the guests of sunny days and the health of stalks,
are not the chasteners of destruction for destruction's sake,
are the pop-up artists for the unexpected and the peculiar,
appearing where they were neither wanted nor expected,
but were welcome exponents of the beautiful together with the majesty,
of the layout as its message was extolled to all who stopped to look.

For such are the ways of God.

For such are the coverings of God.

For such are the links established for the benefit of His People on His Ark:
which travels once around His fiery mountain every year,
with everything in place and operational."

My Content Study Aid

_____

_____

_____

_____

_____

_____

_____

_____

_____

_____

Appendix

Journaling & Notes (1)

Journaling & Notes (2)

Journaling & Notes (3)

20 Questions As Posed by God, As Answered by God

1. "Where are some of the bases of The Neandertals?"

Answer: *And I hear The Lord Jesus saying,*
"The Neandertals have many bases staffed from less than twenty to many hundreds. They stretch across the areas of under-population by human habitation. Specifically they are where it is unlikely they will be interrupted in their life styles. Places where there is a lack of water, where The Earth is not at its surface best for growing or for feeding, where the temperature makes it an unwelcome environment for man, where the mountains are tall and craggy and without appeal to man, where the rock is hard and solid and can be drilled and tunnelled without fear of collapse, where the shoreline waters have sharp drop-offs to the deep and fishing is not popular. They are best located by a temperature survey from the sky which is searching for anomalies at variance from the mean - where the hot is unexpectedly cool, where the cold is unexpectedly warm. Where they are well established over the centuries on both The Moon and Mars - where they have burrowed underground, where entry points are hidden from cameras of remoteness, and where children are not encouraged to attempt to play."

2. "What are the prime objectives of The Neandertals?"

Answer: *And I hear The Lord Jesus saying,*
"The Strangers came to install themselves in the time of Dinosaurs, prior to the habitation of man, when The Earth was still in its time of preparation for man. They have long ago already succeeded in colonising The Earth, of eliminating The Dinosaurs as apex predators at large, of interbreeding and cross-breeding with man where the future was seen to lie with assimilation based on interbreeding. The blood line of The Neandertals is still alive and well - carries resentment for the need for secrecy, often has vengeance running wild. The Neandertals on the bases mostly do not honour their own descendants, often do not recognise the lines of descent, regard all humans to ultimately be rejected from participation with the species of intellectual dominance, which is so designed to rule wherever it is found with its technology intact."

3. "What food sources do The Neandertals require?"

Answer: *And I hear The Lord Jesus saying,*
"Some Neandertals, who have been well interbred, are reflected by The Strangers' larger craniums which are now also widely attained by the huge majority of Humans with a Neandertal Base DNA. These Neandertals are scarcely discernible from The Human race and can now mix freely with them as their body parts and organs are identical with those of man, as is their diet and their biological functioning. The strangers still have the uniqueness of their own metabolism which uses Carbon Dioxide and Nitrogen absorbed through their skins. They enjoy a Carbon Dioxide rich atmosphere around them which is why the mining is taking place in seeking carbonates and nitrates. They have no stomach, no lungs, no kidneys, no urine and no

excreta of any significant quantity, and generally tend to be somewhat cold-blooded when compared with Humans."

4. "If Neandertals have superior technology why have they sought to remain hidden in secrecy?"

Answer: *And I hear The Lord Jesus saying,*
"The Neandertals seek to keep their presence a secret because they are very much aware that they are completely overwhelmed by the numbers of Humans; that if it came to a pitched battle everywhere they could not kill massed attackers quickly enough. Their weapons can handle items of importance on the battlefield or in the air but not separate humans running here and there with fire."

5. "Why are the world-wide leaderships kept in ignorance?"

Answer: *And I hear The Lord Jesus saying,*
"They are kept in ignorance because The Majestic Twelve have an agreement with The Neandertal Leadership that this be so. If it were not so The Majestic Twelve would have no reason for existence. For when The Majestic Twelve have sufficient authority over The Neandertal then The Majestic Twelve can mount an attack to take over any or all nations on The Earth. The Majestic Twelve are of a religious persuasion which only favours one, and puts the rest at risk."

6. "What is to be the outcome of this disclosure deemed to be so secret?"

Answer: *And I hear The Lord Jesus saying,*
"This disclosure is to protect The Truth, is to ensure The Truth has a voice which can be trusted, is to ensure that there is no splitting of the secret— as war cabinets are prepared for joint discussion in the seeking of advantage: in the attempts to commandeer the weaponry of technology— for use in isolation of a surprise attack. This simultaneous disclosure is to have an outcome similar to the stand-off arising from the nuclear age, where MAD has its meaning in ensuring none were foolish enough to go a step too far."

7. "Is this a part of the on-going Divine plan for man?"

Answer: *And I hear The Lord Jesus saying,*
"Yes, it is a part, a very important part, which has bred its packs of lies, of guesstimates, of false reports, of rumours, of denials of first-hand reports, and of deliberate denigrations of The Truth and witnesses as to what their eyes beheld."

8. "What is the concept behind The Majestic Twelve?"

Answer: *And I hear The Lord Jesus saying,*
"On an approach from The Neandertals in 673 BC, The Majestic Twelve was originally formed with a representative of influence from each of the tribes of Israel. They each served during the balance of their lifetime, and on death were replaced by the survivors extending a call to an individual, who is acceptable to all the remaining voices. That person was sworn to secrecy prior to being given— the information on The Neandertals and their ability and the scale of their technology. The Majestic

Twelve's function was to act as a negotiating arm in unison with the best interests of Israel at heart. The current Majestic Twelve still individually carry The Tribal Name which they have sworn to represent. Over the intervening years their wealth has continually increased, especially in times of war, with its doubling every nine years or so on average. As could be expected, they had an interest in The Knights Templar and in the crusades: which rewarded them handsomely for the effort expended."

9. "Will the friction between the two sides finally be resolved?"

Answer: *And I hear The Lord Jesus saying,*
"Yes, it will be resolved by fighting among themselves, by their self-fragmenting of their ability to come to unity of purpose, where dissent is seen as endemic, and conceptual traits are ingrained and almost impossible to modulate— either one way or another. This is most unlikely to impact on the human side unless greed and avarice swing the scales to interference, and lies do steal the accord of Peace."

10. "Is extremely high velocity space travel faster than the speed of light presently in existence from a station on The Earth or one of its close neighbours?"

Answer: *And I hear The Lord Jesus saying,*
"Yes, it is, and it is marked by the effect known as The Absence of Entity. It is available under ground: from Antarctica; from The blind side of The Moon; and from Mars— the three interstellar supply bases where journeys are on demand for shipping the digital data as required, which can then be transferred and reconstructed into the reality as needed and applied."

11. "Are there any human defence mechanisms necessary for which man is able to prepare?"

Answer: *And I hear The Lord Jesus saying,*
"Yes, fire is man's greatest weapon against The Neandertals— whether manipulated by man, or manipulated by God. While mirror-clad tanks will combat Lasers, sending the beams back to their origins just slightly out of a perfect alignment. Fire is best applied as personal flame throwers where numbers will win the day, or enshrouded in the mobile mirror-clad tanks."

12. "Is this a part of The End-time of Faith and Grace with a God-fearing result resulting in a quartering of The Earth?"

Answer: *And I hear The Lord Jesus saying,*
" No, it is not a part. Enactment of Scripture is not influenced by such matters."

13. "Have pilots of crashed Flying Saucers been taken alive and survived with their origin discovered later?"

Answer: *And I hear The Lord Jesus saying,*
"Yes, they have in several different areas of the world — in America, in South America, and in Europe in its widest sense. Their origin is outside the reach of Earth's cosmic sensors, has co-ordinates without any significant meaning to man, may well

be within another universe where dimensions are important."

14. "Are Crop Circles of significance - in carrying messages indicating unknown truths?"

Answer: *And I hear The Lord Jesus saying,*
"Genuine Crop Circles are now becoming quite rare, some are thought by man to have carried acknowledgments of both Space and Time; failed man in lacking the means of interpretation. Unknown truths, if any, would have failed for the non-existence of a common language: able to carry the technicality of the concepts in need of a description."

15. "How is the human population of The Earth expected to react to this news from eons past and their being carriers of the base loading of Neandertal DNA?"

Answer: *And I hear The Lord Jesus saying,*
"Firstly, they will need to understand what is being declared. Secondly, they will need to not be frightened. Thirdly, they will need to overcome the feeling to shut themselves away while the non-existent threat is spoken into a magnified existence by the media at large; and with neither responsibility nor accountability for the flouting of the flagrant lies straight into the face of Truth. Fourthly, they should rightly be amazed that they carry The DNA line arising from The Neandertals and all which that implies. Fifthly, they should celebrate and rejoice in that they all have the intelligence and brainpower as an inheritance from The Neandertals of History— who knew how to move and place the rocks and stones at the will of man."

16. "Do the strangers have a fast shuttle service in action for a replenishment of supplies from a local or near-by supply base?"

Answer: *And I hear The Lord Jesus saying,*
"Yes, they have an infrequent ferry service on demand which can mend or ship supplies— as called forth for despatch to service a damaged item. Again their means of travel makes them invisible because no mass is moving but only digital data enabling items to be repaired, replaced, or renewed. They are rarer in numbers than The Neandertals, but they have a much extended lifetime, and go out of their way to avoid a human contact, by ensuring their nests are very well hidden. They are likely to be much more violent if molested or dislodged— from their sanctuary established and secreted away. They should not be approached, but if so, no weapons should be carried so there can be no misinterpretation of intent."

17. "How long ago did these strangers first arrive upon The Earth?"

Answer: *And I hear The Lord Jesus saying,*
"The Strangers first set foot upon The Earth prior to Time being put to use: by any living thing that dwelt thereon. In the count by God, The Strangers arrived just before The Dinosaurs became suddenly extinct close to thirty-one thousand years ago. To then wage war on The Dinosaurs for nine hundred years: as The Strangers, taking time to colonise the whole of The Earth, moved with sun-powered lasers, until The Dinosaurs became extinct world-wide: signalling the removal of the predation threat."

18. "Where is the site where The Strangers took any kidnapped Humans for a laboratory examination?"

Answer: *And I hear The Lord Jesus saying,*

"Kidnapped Humans were, and may still be, taken to the under-ground staging base: on the rear side of The Moon. The Strangers multiplied upon The Earth in the absence of the dinosaurs, but were far outstripped by the reproductive speed of The Human race. Hence their interest in The Humans' reproductive abilities via the modifying of their DNA for breeding compatibility— achieved sixteen hundred years after the creation of man."

19. "What is the overall relationship of God to these strangers' initial arrival from an origin in space?"

Answer: *And I hear The Lord Jesus saying,*

"The relationship to God varies with The Freewill traits of the various splinter groups of Neandertals. Several groups are quite close to God with Faith and commitment both valid and sustained. These groups are treated in a similar way to The Gentile Flock. These groups, at the end of their mortality, are also welcomed into His presence.

Refer: The Settlers in My Garden, in the prelude and as being a part of the overall subject matter of This Book."

20. "What is the intent of God for the coexistence of the races and the species which inter- and cross-breading have produced and sustained from the disobedient Sons of God?"

Answer: *And I hear The Lord Jesus saying,*

"The intent of God is that all have access to God; He who will never forsake those within His care and attention. So these first immigrants to The Earth, who have now made it their home, and have accepted The God of The Earth, have the same rites of passage as The Gentile believers.

Refer: **Scribal Notes:** At the bottom of The Settlers in My Garden where Genesis 6:1-3 (NKJV) records My visit to the spirits in prison, plus additional details about their disobedience in 1 Peter 3:18-20 (NKJV), The Bible. Used by permission."

My Content Study Aid

_____

_____

_____

_____

_____

32 Questions As Posed by Man and Answered by God

1a. What groups have bases underground, ...? undersea, Antarctica, and the moon?

"Underground bases are attached to the miners.

Undersea to the pilot group both versatile and transportable within The Unidentified Flying Objects which can penetrate the seas, to laser out the caves as patterned and decreed by the past centuries, of experimenting with the rocks and relative hardnesses involved.

Antarctica is inhabited by those upset by heat, by those who would be recluses from the world of enquiries and of investigations. They present as the violent, without any sanctity of life, are nicknamed the providers of the carrion. They are not, and should well not be, the flavour of the month among the humans who are now careful not to misjudge a step or two or three when approaching the edge of a crevasse with what possibly lies beneath.

The moon is currently the breeding grounds where there is ample warning of the potential interruptions from the paddlers to the moon."

1b. Did they build The Moon as an observation satellite?

"No, it was already there. They slowed it down, by changing its orbit slightly, so it would be synchronised with The Earth when one side would remain hidden from observation until a much later contact could be deferred until established safely."

1c. Why did they ask us not to build bases on The Moon?

"They did not believe they would retain their independence, with the secrecy they sought, as their knowledge base on man was built. Initially they were about even in numbers with man but now have seen the explosion of numbers by man and they are struggling with which is the best way to contain it."

2a. Are they related and work cooperatively? The Neandertals (1a Clan, Trait: Leaders) with The Neandertals (2a Clan Trait: Trustworthy)

"They are related from differing home bases, gravity fields, climates, and temperatures - which has enabled them to develop with superficial differences of skin colour, features, belief systems and abilities within the physical."

2b. Which group is antagonistic or destructive either against us or other Neandertals?

"The Antarctic tribe which spend their time in plotting the death of humans or of their total dominance."

2c. Who are our enemies and who are our friends?

"There are no friends - only those with a pretence - such as The Neandertals (1a Clan, Trait: Leaders)."

2d. What are their functions besides observations?

"Learning the ways of man - his strengths and his weaknesses - his ability to defend himself with the how and when and why."

3a. Was there a nuclear war on Mars ...? which destroyed its civilisation?

"No, it was a Laser war between their own people which evaporated targets (Not oxidised them) and left no target residues."

3b. Are there still living hominids living on Mars?

"Yes, underground, with much decreased numbers."

3c. What are they mining?

"Common carbonates for generating Carbon Dioxide for their enclosed areas where it is their source of food;"

3d. and why are so many in our solar system?

"On discovery of The Earth, it became an immigration centre of renown where other celestial bodies were within a day trip of their new base and had the moon provided as a companion of note— with the possibility of being synced to the rotation of The Earth."

3e. Was there a nuclear war on Earth that wiped out earlier civilizations?

"No, again it was a Laser war between competing bids for supremacy by like with like."

3f. How come we can find 200 thousand year old archaeological evidence of tools and intelligence present?

"This is The Neandertals own infancy where the new born, prior to reaching maturity, were left to their own devices as a test of their ability to succeed. It should be particularly considered that the time stamp here is seriously overstated, where the technology needs refining, or a different benchmark established with greater accuracy."

4a. Why is the big secrecy from world leaders?

"The secret is now too big to have the responsibility transferred. Would create an immediate and discordant outcry, where nothing is a solution, where suggested alternatives fail the test of Truth and of practicality, where the future too quickly becomes the past with violence mixed with bloodshed: already waiting in the wings to capture the stage of life."

4bi. Why did our government (or whoever) make agreements for cooperation, like hightec help and transfer

"The whoever made agreements with The Neandertals (1a Clan, Trait: Leaders) The Greys because they were seen as the leaders in intelligence, the thought operators, with several other factors."

4bii. and with which group in exchange for further kidnaping and examining human individuals without further genetic or reproductive experiences on them?

"Again the whoever dealt with The Neandertals (1a Clan, Trait: Leaders): The Greys because of ease of access and the urgency attached to the agreement: as womenfolk began to recount their experiences. The Greys re-allocated the restriction to The Blues who could be relied upon to hold to their agreements and to enforce such if necessary upon The Neandertals (4a Clan Trait: Terrorists) Browns who carried the ultimate responsibility for both this and for the data feeds."

5. Which Neandertal groups live among us ...? and how do we identify them?

"The semi-passive groups live among us and if suspicious of identity look to the burka, the hoodie, the helmet with the motor cycle as mastered by The Neandertals (4a Clan Trait: Terrorists) Brownish hued skin. Look to The UV Radiation generator— best carried as a portable— which will make fluorescence visible on all their skins in a greenish hue. The Neandertals (3a Clan Trait: U.V., Shyness)"

6a. How can they exceed the speed of light ...? traveling through and across the universes?

"With ability to move only digital information which has no mass and is moved by thought patterning which can be recreated into a presence on reception. "

6b. How many Universe are there?

"49; Seven sevens, and more can be created."

7a. Many of them live around 500 years ...? of earth time and what happens with them when they die?

"They lie down and quickly become transparent without any trace residues."

7b. Why do they mostly appear around nuclear and military bases?

"The military interest discloses the intent - to seek and understand the current capability of the defence systems as created and active within the present ability of man."

7c. They claim to belong to The Sapiens, but not homo-sapiens so we cannot cross or interbreed. Why?

"They are Sapiens only when gauged by the measuring of intelligence, otherwise they are related somewhat closely to the cold-blooded creatures on The Earth. And so the species are utterly different and without the common genes."

8. Why some of them don't believe in God ...? or have any religion or spiritual awareness?

"Their differing home bases over the millennia brought differing belief structures as to their origins with the reasons for their initial immigrations."

9a. What is our agreement with The Neandertals ...? in Antarctica and why are we afraid of them?

"The parties to agreement have both been sworn to the utmost secrecy. For this is a secret in a secret in a secret in a secret - the penalty for disclosure has no greater penalty than the actioning of sacrificial lives - calling for of all those who are signatories to the contract of the dishonoured party— to be sacrificed to the sun god as in the days of The Aztecs and their predecessors: where the body is incised and drained as life farewells its being before non-blinking eyes. With the mutual contract broken, the offended party has the right to plunder and to storm— the habitations as represented by the offending party: where no quarter is the call, where death is the harbinger of the onset of decay, where vital stores and munitions are opened to attack with superior technology, resulting in a slaughter of unimaginable proportions. The human signatories known as The Majestic Twelve are frightened, in the extreme, if one of them, on his deathbed or shortly before it, resolves to speak, so to release the secret into a maelstrom of unpremeditated violence: as the streets of The World run red with the blood of man without an end in sight. The Majestic Twelve have emissaries standing watch at each deathbed to ensure such does not happen as a mistaken tribute to the finality of death. The killing power of a single Neandertals with a laser will far outweigh a hundred men with automatic weapons— even if such could be assembled at extremely short notice into a world of secrets: where disbelief is un-contained and defence is at a loss."

9b. Can we have their language and writing decoded and when?

"They really have no need to write, transfer thoughts by mastery of the brain. Consider the writers are using an archaic system well beneath what would be expected from such seeking equivalence with postering. Have long lost the mouth and tongue via non-use with degeneration."

9c. How can we or as individuals communicate with them?

"Via lasers weakly attuned to the frequencies of burst and directed at blank UV coated panels within their viewing scope, which will fluoresce as a measure of intent. English can be used, or, indeed any language native to The Earth. For they know them well. They attempt to deceive if they pretend not to understand or to ignore the approach entirely."

9d. What is God's plan for them?

"To see to our protection from those portraying a false belief in God."

9e. What is their plan for us?

"Dominance, or death, on all counts of freedom or existence."

10a. Like to know their diet? And ...

"Carbon Dioxide and Nitrogen for production of complex Carbonates and Nitrates, Magnesium Carbonate as Magnesite or Calcium Carbonate such as Limestone are mined, so Carbon Dioxide can be captured for and by the diffusion process of their skin."

10b. understand their messages to mankind contained in the crop circles,

"There are no messages within the crop circles, are distractions mixed with false alarms. Those caught making crop circles should be treated with great suspicion and at the very least be submitted to UV radiation for the presence of green fluorescence."

10c. and how to decode them.

"A distraction with a waste of effort in searching for the non-existent. Their testing to determine to what extent humans will attempt to make sense of the non-sensical at large."

11. Can we meet them and learn from them?

'They are not here to teach their latest technology. They are here to drip feed us with the mediocre and the obsolete in terms of their technology so we are less a threat to their eventual mastery."

My Content Study Aid

_____
_____
_____
_____
_____
_____
_____
_____
_____
_____
_____
_____
_____
_____
_____
_____
_____
_____
_____
_____

The End-time Psalms of God

The Parts of The End-time Psalms of God are—

	Pages	Total Words
1. GOD Speaks of Return and Bannered	418	87,061
2. GOD Speaks to Man on The Internet	498	122,349
3. GOD Speaks as His Spirit Empowers	272	65,494
4. GOD Speaks to Man in The End-time	Being Completed	
5. GOD Speaks in Letters of Eternity	202	48,174
6. GOD Speaks to His Bridal Presence	326	78,183
7. GOD Speaks to His Edifice	512	122,516
8. GOD Speaks of Loving His Creation	280	67,234
9. GOD Speaks Now of a Seal Revealed	124	25,174

Companion Books—

10. GOD End-time Updates Ancient Alien History	310	86,461
11. GOD End-time Updates The Multitudes	166	47,454

My Content Study Aid

_____

_____

_____

_____

_____

_____

_____

_____

_____

_____

_____

_____

_____

ANTHONY A EDDY (SCRIBE)

Book Reviews (9)

Part 1 'GOD Speaks of Return and Bannered' Reviewer: AJE

This is where it all began: The very first collection in Anthony Eddy's "God Speaks" series of poetry. This is the very beginning of fictional prophet Anthony Eddy's communion with The Lord and transmission of His missives from above. In this book, God announces His return to the world of man and reiterates the messages present in The Biblical scriptures: Man's fall, damnation, and salvation at His hands.

Although a bit more fire-and-brimstone oriented than later works in the series, "GOD SPEAKS of Return and Bannered" is still a must-have for any believer's ebook library. The messages of salvation and inspiration presented herein are spectacularly written. They absolutely should not go to waste. My one nitpick is that the nature of Eddy's prophethood is never explicitly stated to be a fictional trapping for the poems presented; however, I don't really think that's a big deal, since it's clear from a close reading of the text. A+, I highly recommend.

Part 2 'GOD Speaks to Man on The Internet' Reviewer: AJE

Anthony Eddy does it again! In this masterful collection of more than one hundred fifty poems, Eddy, speaking in his fictional role as a prophet of The Lord, presents a clever commentary on the synthesis of traditional Christian religion with modern-day technology. In this smartly-written collection, Eddy speaks extensively on God's love for His People, His willingness to save us from damnation, and the quirky "Website of The Lord", run by Eddy as a tie-in to this book series.

The Website of The Lord is also written in the same in-character format as the "God Speaks..." series, lending an extra air of verisimilitude to the entire affair. It gives the entire series the feeling of an Alternate Reality Game, and with ARGs being highly popular these days I applaud Eddy's forward thinking in combining Christian tradition with the ever-evolving modern world. I wonder if he has considered the possibility of a television series centered around his fictional prophet avatar? I'm sure it would be a big hit. But in the meantime, we'll have to make do with these books.

Part 3 'GOD Speaks as His Spirit Empowers' Reviewer: JF

This is my second book that I have read by author Anthony Eddy. As with his first book this current book focuses on poems that are meant as conversations for the entire earth to hear. The book speaks on the coming storm for all of mankind. When I read the section on blessings of the faithful I felt these poems do relate to the theory of what I believe the world feels in regards to blessings and their effects upon us. From further reading this section I do understand a little more why we should be thankful for blessings. I feel author Eddy leaves no stone unturned in this recent book about God and his purpose for mankind in his message of the coming storm.

As in the first book I read from Mr. Eddy there are tons of repetition of poems and the words are constantly repeated. I believe the repetition is used to relate and focus on a clearer meaning of the poems and their messages. Since we all don't grasp the meaning of things at the same level I feel repetition is a good way for a person to keep reading until they can grasp the meaning of the message. I found the section on the soul interesting.

The book outlines in great detail what the author feels the coming storm is meant and how it relates to God and all of mankind.

There's a section dedicated to both men and women, how they relate to God and his purposes for and about them. There's even mention on subjects such as: The innocent, righteousness, grace and mercy, speaking in tongues, Satan, and a whole lot of other subjects. Basically, something for everyone. The last chapter of the book is dedicated to the prophet Ezekiel. I found the coming storm poems very interesting and informative.

Part 4 'GOD Speaks to Man in The End-time' Reviewer: RM

This is quite an intriguing book. It is not like the traditional stories with characters and a story line. It is different. In terms of contents, it is great, full of warnings about many different subjects, all related to how God expect us to behave in different contexts. The format is different of what you would expect from a traditional writing. It remind me poetry style, but with some special particularities. This is a book that you do not read in one sit, but read a topic per day, savoring its message. And although the format might be difficult to read, the message is crystal clear. We should stay away from sin and be prepared for the return of Christ at the end of times, keeping our faith strong.

At the introduction he claims that the calls he describe in the book are not of his own writing, but should have the words "And I hear The Lord Jesus saying..." denoting that part of the text is of a Divine origin. The author divides the topics (or calls) he addresses mostly in two pages sections for a total of 56 calls, like "Surroundings of Man", "Purity of My Bride", "Lack of Faith", "My People", etc.

I recommend this book to all Christians that wants a boost of confidence that they are in the correct path for their salvation. The author shares his views and his solid faith and we should praise him for that!

Inkspand.com was kind enough to provide this book for me for reviewing and I was not requested to provide a positive review. Opinions expressed here are my own.

Part 5 'GOD Speaks in Letters of Eternity' Reviewer: AJE

Anthony Eddy has done it again; "GOD Speaks in Letters of Eternity", the fifth in the preacher's "God Speaks" series of poetry, is a masterpiece worthy of the centuries. It definitely deserves a place in any believer's ebook library.

Once again presented as a series of missives presented by The Lord to his fictional prophet, sharing the name of the author, this book focuses on the relationship of Jesus Christ to His People. I was particularly inspired by "The Inside of The Eyelids", the fifth of eighty-one poems, which shed light on God's plan through the use of a rarely-employed metaphor. Kudos, Eddy, for thinking outside the box.

A common feature of Eddy's writing is word repetition. For example, most of his poems begin with the same repeated word or phrase which is generally also the title of the poem, and I find that this works very well in a lyrical sense. This isn't always the case, of course, and those breaks from the pattern only serve to illuminate Eddy's unique and pleasing writing style.

In conclusion, I would gladly purchase "GOD Speaks in Letters of Eternity", and recommend it to anyone.

Part 6 'GOD Speaks to His Bridal Presence' Reviewer: AJE

Yet another masterpiece in Anthony Eddy's *God Speaks* series, *GOD Speaks to His Bridal Presence* is a collection of 115 religious poems that speak directly to the soul of a true believer. Like his other works, this book is presented in the format of Eddy's fictional avatar, a prophet, receiving missives from The Lord and recording them to spread to the world. My one complaint is that this fictional wrapping must be intuited from the text and is not explicitly shown, but any savvy reader will have no trouble deducing it.

In the vein of his other works, *GOD Speaks to His Bridal Presence* carries a theme of fallen humanity's redemption from its sins via its trust in The Lord, and God's reciprocal love for and protection of His flock, us, His children. Frequently Eddy speaks of how Satan and his minions will be vanquished, bringing God's children into the light. Truly a must-have for any religious lover of lyrical prose.

Part 7 'GOD Speaks to His Edifice' Reviewer: AJE

GOD Speaks to All of His Edifices is a remarkable collection of poetry centered around the theme of religion, reverence, and redemption. Presented under the pretense of God's revelations to a prophet, the fictional avatar of the author Anthony Eddy, this collection of fifty poems is the seventh in a series of inspirational spiritual literature.

This book is a must have for any dedicated believer who needs a bit of uplift to their day. Through rhymeless stanza, Eddy brings to life the kingdom of The Lord in an easy-to-read, accessible format for the everyday Christian.

The primary problem with the narrative, however, is the lack of clarification that this book is a work of fiction. The poetry itself is solid from a Christian viewpoint, but the brief interludes explaining that Eddy himself received a divine message from The Lord are not properly explained to be fiction. However, that much is easily deduced by the clever reader, and as a whole the work stands up on its own. I would gladly purchase it if given the chance, and would recommend it to any believing friend or family member.

Part 8 'GOD Speaks of Loving His Creation' Reviewer: SH

This is the eighth book in a series of End-time psalms dictated by God through The Scribe, Anthony A Eddy. While the psalms contain counselling and commentary on the current state of humanity, a major theme running through this book is man's freewill to choose or not, his eternal destiny within The Garden of God.

While there is truth for the intellectual in Eddy's recommendation not to read these psalms as stand-alone psalms, as they build sequentially, others will be thought-provoked enough by the first attention-grabbing sentence of each: The days of embitterment filled with dissatisfaction are about to come as thunderstorms within the sky.

The arrowheads of God are the means of sending messages to the hearts of man.

In the sights of God is a dangerous place to be, is a blessed place to be.— reminding me of what Mr Beaver says about Aslan in C.S. Lewis' The Lion, The Witch and The Wardrobe: Course he isn't safe. But he is good. He is The King.

Again, others will be thought-provoked enough, encouraged and uplifted by a particular stanza:

The beauty of My Garden has the fragrance of delight,
> has the fragrance of the morning dew,

has the fragrance of the evening dusk.
The glory of My garden showcases the beautiful and the lovely,
the wonderful and marvellous,
the glorified and stately.

Some of the psalms reflect the current first world state. My first thought was that The Tableting of Man' would relate to our electronic devices but it doesn't. It speaks about the climate of fear induced by advertising which impels us to take supplements for every perceived dietary deficiency and every perceived health benefit.

Some of the psalms reflect the world opinion that dismissing the intellect is a prerequisite of faith. The meetings of the minds verifies and supports the edifice of God.

The scholar in me found it was sometimes necessary to resort to the dictionary: the difference between salutations and greetings, crevasse and crevice, variance and variability.

The theologian in me was challenged: The welcome to my garden has catch-up schools for those who were taught that the tongues of God did not exist,
were of no avail,
were to be ignored,
were not relevant,
were a demonic babbling of the day.

I conclude that these psalms could be used as a daily devotional, study topics for home-groups, sermon titles and for those who just love the language of poetry. It was almost impossible to write a review of this book as each first line, stanza or psalm really requires a review of its own! I recommend that you take the time to savour and reflect on each of these beautiful offerings.

Part 9 'GOD Speaks Now of a Seal Revealed' Reviewer: SH

This book, the first dictated by God through The Scribe, Anthony A. Eddy, was hidden for 26 years. In 1990 after rejection by his church leadership, the manuscript was placed for safekeeping with a bank. When the family shifted towns it was retrieved and placed in a desk. In due course, when the desk was sold it was placed in a bookcase until rediscovery by Eddy in 2016! The first introductory Psalms received in 2017 and 2016 explain this hiding.

My Little Book: It is My Alpha and Omega,
My First and My Last,
The Beginning and The End.

About My Little Book:

My little book has been waiting a long time in the calendar of man,
has been ready for release in the calendar of God,
has been awaiting the end-time networking of man.

The psalms of Book 9 were originally written in story form with chapters differentiating the topics. The chapters are retained in publishing but the psalms were revised to a rhythmic presentation in keeping with the other eight books, reminding me of the sermons of the late Peter Marshall which were also published in this form to enable the reader to engage easily in the flow of the messages.

Book 9 is full of instruction, explanations and Truth statements intermixed with counselling. I found Chapter 5 Languages of Heaven and Hell particularly interesting. These psalms cover: The Languages of Heaven, The Fire of The Lord, The Tongues of The Spirit, The Tongues of Angels, The Tongues of Demons, The Tongue of Lucifer, The Functioning of Tongues, The Actions of The Spirit, The Tongue of Praise, The Tongue of Worship, The Tongue of Prayer and The Song of The Lord. This list may seem daunting but each psalm is eminently readable and thought provoking.

The tongues of the spirit of man converse with The Spirit on high;
converse via The Spirit with man;
converse in the spirit with man;
converse in The Spirit with God.

The use of the word converse, implies a free flowing dialogue with God, personal and intimate which I am sure is how it is meant to be. Then I ask myself how often I participate in the tongue of Lucifer.

The tongue of Lucifer rejoices at The Lost;
rejoices at the lie believed;
rejoices at the deception planned;
rejoices at the lie confirmed;
rejoices at creating doubt;
rejoices at the destruction of the saints.

To conclude: I found this book to be less of an intellectual commitment than Book 8 while still being informative and thought provoking. One of my favourites is The Prayers of The Indwelt. I love the word and the concept of being indwelt.

The prayers of the indwelt reverberate in Heaven,
echo in the halls,
carry through the courts.

My Content Study Aid

_____

_____

_____

_____

_____

_____

_____

_____

_____

About The Scribe

Updated 18 February 2019

Anthony is 78, having been married to his wife, Adrienne, for 55 years. They have five married children: Carolyn, Alan, Marie, Emma and Sarah and fourteen grandchildren: Matthew & Ella; Phillipa & Jonathan; Jeremy, Ngaire & Trevor; Jake, Finn, Crystal & Caleb; Bjorn, Greta & Minka.

Anthony was raised on a dairy farm in Springston, Canterbury, NZ in the 1940s. He graduated from Canterbury University, Christchurch, NZ with a B.Sc. in chemistry and mathematics in 1962. He was initially employed as an industrial chemist in flour milling and linear programming applications.

These used the first IBM 360 at the university for determining least cost stock food formulations and production parameters. Later he was involved in similar applications on the refining side of the oil industry in Britain, Australia and New Zealand. This was followed by sales and managerial experience in the chemical industry.

The family moved to a Bay of Plenty, NZ, town in 1976 when Anthony took up funeral directing, as a principal, expanding an initial sibling partnership until the close of the century. Anthony acquired practical experience in accounting, business management, and computer usage (early Apples— including The Lisa).

Upon retiring from active funeral directing in 2000 and selling his interests, he then commenced the promotion and the writing of funeral management software for The NZ funeral environment. Rewarded with national success, he has now retired, in 2007, from the active management of that interest, living near some of his family in Hamilton NZ.

Anthony was brought up in The Methodism of his father until his mid-teens, his mother's side was Open Brethren. He is Christian in belief within an Apostolic Pentecostal Charismatic framework of choice (since the 1990s) having been earlier in The Mormon church for several years. Thereafter he was in The Baptist denomination followed by finding a home within The Acts (Apostolic) church movement for some years, and now in Glory Release Ministries, one where all have made him welcome.

He and his wife, who has visited a number of Asian countries, have been to India in 2011, 12, 13, 16 and 18 on The Lord's tasks and have witnessed and participated in many miracles which befall His People and The Multitudes.

His forbears William Henry Eddy and Margaret Jane Eddy, née Oats, emigrated to New Zealand from Gulval, Cornwall, England in 1878 on a sailing ship, with a very slow passage time of 79 days, and with their three month old infant child, Margaret Anne, dying 21 October 1878 from Congestion of the brain on board The Marlborough while en route to NZ. The Marlborough sailed London 19 September 1878, via Plymouth 26 September 1878, and arrived Lyttelton 14 December 1878 with 336 assisted immigrants. His grandfather, Alfred Charles Eddy, then but three years old, together with an older brother aged four, obviously survived the trials of the sea voyage to become a part of a family with a further eleven New Zealand born siblings all living to maturity.

ANTHONY A EDDY (SCRIBE)

CPSIA information can be obtained
at www.ICGtesting.com
Printed in the USA
BVHW041100200619
551533BV00011B/388/P